4-06-05

5/05

W9-AHB-387

Bloom's Modern Critical Views

Bloom's Modern Critical Views

Bloom's Modern Critical Views

Tony Kushner

Edited and with an introduction by
Harold Bloom
Sterling Professor of the Humanities
Yale University

CHELSEA HOUSE
P U B L I S H E R S
A Haights Cross Communications Company ®

Philadelphia

810.9
KUSHNER,T/
BLO

Printed and bound in the United States of America.
10 9 8 7 6 5 4 3 2 1

Library of Congress Cataloging-in-Publication Data

Tony Kushner / [edited and with an introduction by] Harold Bloom.
    p. cm. — (Bloom's modern critical views)
  Includes bibliographical references.
  ISBN 0-7910-8139-7 (alk. paper)
  1. Kushner, Tony—Criticism and interpretation. 2. Kushner, Tony. Angels in America.
3. AIDS (Disease) in literature. 4. Gay men in literature. I. Bloom, Harold. II. Series.
  PS3561.U778Z89 2005
  812'.54—dc22
                          2005003910

Contributing Editor: Pamela Loos

Cover designed by Keith Trego

Cover photo: Associated Press, AP/Gino Domenic ©

Layout by EJB Publishing Services

All links and web addresses were checked and verified to be correct at the time of
publication. Because of the dynamic nature of the web, some addresses and links may
have changed since publication and may no longer be valid.

Every effort has been made to trace the owners of copyrighted material and secure
copyright permission. Articles appearing in this volume generally appear much as they
did in their original publication with little to no editorial changes. Those interested in
locating the original source will find bibliographic information on the first page of each
article as well as in the bibliography and acknowledgments sections of this volume.

Contents

Editor's Note

My Introduction centers upon the interplay of the spiritual and the political in Kushner, and states an aesthetic preference for the fantasia element in his art.

Mark Steyn reviews *Slavs!* and finds it "nervous and ambiguous," and comparable to the musical *Oklahoma!*, in that they share a common form, the revue.

Examining the ambivalences of *Angels in America*, David Savran finds one of its authentic sources in Walter Benjamin's allegorical angel of history, and another in early Mormonism.

Charles McNulty also cites Walter Benjamin as a Kushnerian source, but finds Kushner a wistful idealist in contrast to Benjamin.

To Janelle Reinelt, *Angels in America* is not Brechtian enough to qualify as American "epic theater," while Allen J. Frantzen takes us back to Chaucer, the Venerable Bede, and Bale before coming forward to Kushner's Prior Walter and his rather diffuse relation to Anglo-Saxon tradition.

Jonathan Freedman directly confronts Jewish identity in *Angels*, tracing the parallel history of homoerotic and Jewish otherness, and goes on to see the plays as losing much of the Jewish element in the "collapse" of its conclusion, judged by Freedman to be essentially Christian.

Medieval mystery plays are invoked as *Angels*' genre by Benilde Montgomery, though she rightly saw little of this form in George C. Wolfe's direction of the New York City presentation of the epic extravaganza.

An erudite reading of Kushner's little-known epic farce, *Hydriotaphia, or the Death of Dr. Browne* is provided by James Fisher, who seems to me the most deeply informed of Kushner scholars.

Homebody/Kabul is celebrated by James Reston Jr. as apt prophecy, after which Framji Minwalla assimilates the play, all too accurately, to our current "post-colonial" shibboleths.

Introduction

As an American dramatist, Tony Kushner represents (amidst much else) the confluence of several literary traditions that, to me, seem antithetical to one another: Bertolt Brecht's Marxist stage epics; the lyrical phantasmagorias of Tennessee Williams; Yiddish theater in its long history from the earliest *purimshpil* (Leipzig, 1697) to the exuberant flourishing that was still prevalent in my own youth. A fierce admirer of Kushner's work, I confess an increasing aesthetic aversion to Brecht as I age. Politically I have no differences with Kushner, but for more than a decade now, I have experienced a purely literary anxiety that this dramatist's genius might be so deformed by public concerns that he could dwindle into another Clifford Odets, rather than fulfill his extraordinary gifts by transcending even Tennessee Williams and Thornton Wilder among his American precursors.

Kushner passionately insists that he is a political dramatist, but reading his plays and attending their performance persuade me otherwise. His largest American ancestors are Walt Whitman and Herman Melville, and while *Song of Myself* and *Moby-Dick* are the epics of democracy, their spiritual and metaphysical elements are far more vital than their politics. Brecht's dramas (if they *are* his, rather than Elizabeth Hauptmann's, Margarete Steffin's, and Ruth Berlau's) increasingly threaten to become Period Pieces, just as Clifford Odets's *Waiting for Lefty* is now nothing but a Period Piece. Kushner's *A Bright Room Called Day* (1985) is a Ronald Reagan Period Piece which depresses me, two decades later, because Reagan now appears virtually harmless in comparison to our astonishing current President, who defies any ironic representation whatsoever. Shakespeare himself could not render George W. Bush dramatically plausible. Nathanael West's Shagpoke Whipple, in *A Cool Million*, cannot match Bush II in blatancy, patriotic

1

religiosity, and bland righteousness. Reality in America has beggared fantasy and one wants to implore Kushner to turn inward, rather than dramatically confront a continuous outrageousness that no stage representation can hope to rival. I need only turn on Fox TV to witness parodistic excess accepted as reality by a majority of my fellow citizens who cared enough to vote. Oscar Wilde, wisely urging art to be perfectly useless, would at this moment be the best of mentors for Tony Kushner.

II

Roy Cohn, to date, is Kushner's best creation, an all but Shakespearean hero-villain. The three versions I have seen of the Kushnerian Cohn were performed by Ron Leibman, F. Murray Abraham, and Al Pacino. All were effective, but Leibman was the best, because he played it with a Yiddish aura of outrageousness and of having been outraged. The only time I recall being moved by Arthur Miller's *Death of a Salesman* was when I saw it in Yiddish translation in 1952, with Joseph Buloff as Loman. I wish that Joseph Wiseman had been young enough to play Roy Cohn. Wiseman was a magnificent Edmund in a terrible *King Lear* I recall seeing in 1950, and later he performed an unforgettable mad Duke in John Webster's *The Duchess of Malfi*. Watching and listening to Leibman flooded me with memories of Wiseman, presumably because both actors played with excess and *sprezzatura*, in a mode I had worshipped in Maurice Schwartz, who perhaps had learned it from Jacob Adler. Kushner, whose superb *A Dybbuk* is undervalued, is a natural throwback to the hyperbolical Yiddish theater where I first saw Shylock, played by Schwartz as hero, not as hero-villain or the farcical bogyman that Shakespeare designed to go Marlowe's Barabas, Jew of Malta, one better.

Kushner is a whirligig of change, unpredictable and unprecedented, except for Tennessee Williams at his strongest. The one time I met Williams (was it in the late Seventies?) he proudly handed me his treasured copy of *The Collected Poems of Hart Crane*, so that I could see he had liberated it from the Washington University of St. Louis Library. We talked about Crane, our mutually favorite poet. I have met Kushner at length primarily in front of a large audience, and so have not been able to ascertain his favorite poet, but surely it must be Walt Whitman, still (in my judgment) the greatest writer brought forth by our Evening Land, the Americas. I delight that *Perestroika* boldly plagiarizes Whitman, just as it is audacious enough to send up Blance DuBois's: "I have always depended upon the kindness of strangers." But that is High Camp, whereas the employment of the sublime Walt seems to me crucial; since he *is* the Angel Principality of America, despite her inconvenient gender, and her negativity:

> Hiding from Me one place you will find me in another.
> I I I I stop down the road, waiting for you.

That is an Angelic variation upon the very close of *Song of Myself*, substituting "hiding" for "seeking." Just before, this negative version of Whitman has proclaimed: "Forsake the Open Road." What Hart Crane was to Tennessee Williams, a fusion of Whitman and Melville is for Kushner, except that the overwhelmingly personal investment of Williams in Crane is not present in Kushner's veneration of his American fathers, Melville and Whitman. Williams's other prime precursor was D.H. Lawrence, like Melville an evader of homoeroticism.

III

Angels in America, indisputably Kushner's masterwork to date, is accurately described by him as "fantasia." A careful rereading of it demonstrates that Kushner's mastery of controlled phantasmagoria is his highest dramatic gift. Except for Roy Cohn, the double-play has no characters wholly memorable as personalities, fully endowed with individuated voices. The black, gay male nurse Belize has been much praised, but I fear that is mere political correctness. Louie Ironson seems a self-parody on Kushner's part, and the prophet Prior Walter is poignant but scarcely persuasive. The Mormon closet gay and right-wing lawyer, Joe Pitt, is a caricature. Except for Cohn, Kushner's women are stronger, Harper in particular, but then she is at home in fantasy. What carries *Angels in America*, the daemonic Cohn aside, is its extraordinary inventiveness in regard to what might as well be termed the spirit world.

Having been defeated by a stubborn Kushner in a public debate on theatre and religion (March 22, 2004), in New York City, I am only too aware he will continue to insist he is a political dramatist, rather than a theological one, long after I have departed for whatever spirit-world there may be. Not being exactly a devoted Brechtian, I am unable to see how "a relationship of complaint and struggle and pursuit between the human and divine"— Kushner's eloquent characterization of his own Judaism—involves politics. When Kushner declares that "drama without politics is inconceivable," I wonder just how he reads Shakespeare. Those who endeavor to interpret *Hamlet* or *King Lear* or *Macbeth* as political theater lose my interest rather quickly. Is Reagan or Bush II really Kushner's motive for metaphor? No. Kushner has more in common with Kafka than with Brecht, though he does not want to see this. Like his angels, Kushner has filed a suit against God for desertion. God shrewdly has taken on Roy Cohn as his defense attorney and so the angels (and Kushner) are going to lose their case.

IV

I have read *Caroline, or Change* in manuscript, but have not seen it performed, and doubtless by now Kushner has revised it anyway. I do not know how much intrinsic relevance it will retain a decade hence, an apprehension I experience also in regard to *Homebody/Kabul*. Kushner hardly is going to agree with me on this, but I think *A Dybbuk* will outlast them both. Social ironies, like political concerns, drive Kushner into the composition of Period Pieces. The dramatic impulse towards phantasmagoria always will be his aesthetic redemption.

Roy Cohn is a hero-villain and a strong individuality. To Kushner, that individuality is one with Cohn's evil. Yet that seems to me Kushner's incessant error. To invoke what ultimately is an Hegelian distinction, singularity *cares* about itself *and others*, while individuality is indifferent, whether to the self or to otherness. Rosalind, in *As You Like It*, is a singularity, as is Falstaff in his plays. Hamlet is an individuality, who loves neither himself nor others, but I can locate nothing political in Hamlet, or in Iago.

Kushner's Roy Cohn is a fascinating blend of singularity and individuality, neither of them a source of his murderous malice. Coleridge mistakenly spoke of Iago's "motiveless malignancy", but Iago, like his disciple, Satan in Milton's *Paradise Lost*, suffers from a Sense of Injured Merit. So, as I read him, does Tony Kushner's Roy Cohn. He wants to have been a major demon like Joe McCarthy, but God has passed him over for promotion. Iago, passed over for Cassio, determines to bring his war-god Othello down to the abyss, to uncreate Othello. Cohn, outraged and outrageous, finds his proper employment only in the afterlife, in the superb (and invariably unperformed) Scene 7 of Act V of *Perestroika*:

> *As Prior journeys to earth he sees Roy, at a great distance, in Heaven, or Hell or Purgatory—standing waist-deep in a smoldering pit, facing a volcanic, pulsating red light. Underneath, a basso-profundo roar, like a thousand Bessemer furnaces going at once, deep underground.*

ROY: Paternity suit? Abandonment? Family court is my particular metier, I'm an absolute fucking demon with Family Law. Just tell me who the judge is, and what kind of jewelry does he like? If it's a jury, it's harder, juries take more talk but sometimes it's worth it, going jury, for what it saves you in bribes. Yes I will represent you, King of the Universe, yes I will sing and eviscerate, I will bully and seduce, I will win for you and make the plaintiffs, those traitors, wish they had never heard the name of ...

(*Huge thunderclap.*)

ROY: Is it a done deal, are we on? Good, then I gotta start by telling you you ain't got a case here, you're guilty as hell, no question, you have nothing to plead but not to worry, darling, I will make something up.

Is it possible to read this without delighting in Roy Cohn? He *will* win God's case, thus vindicating his entire career, and severely putting into question all Kushnerian dramatic politics. The Messenger, who is the Angel of *A Dybbuk*, at the play's close receives Rabbi Azriel's eloquent charge:

(*Softly*) It doesn't matter. Tell Him that. The more cause He gives to doubt Him. Tell Him that. The deeper delves faith. Though His love becomes only abrasion, derision, excoriation, tell Him, I cling. We cling. He made us, He can never shake us off. We will always find Him out. Promise Him that. We will always find Him, no matter how few there are, tell Him we will find Him. To deliver our complaint.

Kushner, like Azriel, always will deliver his complaint. Pathos, eloquence, fantasia: these never will forsake him. If, as I firmly believe, he yet will surpass Tennessee Williams, it will not be because of his Brechtian faith in the political possibilities of theater.

MARK STEYN

Communism Is Dead; Long Live the King!

Tony Kushner's *Angels in America* began with an image: a man in bed dying of AIDS. Well, big deal. Been there, done that, seen it off-Broadway and on TV. But Kushner enlarged the image—an angel comes crashing through the bedroom ceiling—and, in that one act, set himself on the path to a Pulitzer, a Tony, and bus-poster fame as a Gap model. According to one of the Pulitzer jurors, *Variety*'s Jeremy Gerard, "*Angels* was in a category by itself in terms of the scope and theatrical imagination it represented." The key word there is "scope": Kushner has always resented the way that most playwrights, unlike novelists, are restricted to two hours of staged traffic management, so, in *Angels*, whenever he found himself in a bind dramatically, he simply raised the stakes. As he sees it, "You fuck up when you chicken out"—and, although he's out, he's no chicken. In your ordinary run-of-the-bathhouse gay play, "divine intervention" means the arrival of a Judy Garland impersonator; with Kushner, you start off with yet another enfeebled husk on his sickbed, and, before you know it, you're pitched into a world where God has gone and the angels are incompetent bureaucrats with dark plans to kill off humanity. At one level, *Angels* works in the same way as *Cats*: hey, bud, when have you ever seen anything like *this*?

But, of course, it has higher ambitions. As Kushner said at the time, "If your politics are good enough, your playwriting will be good enough." He

From *The New Criterion 13*, no. 6 (February 1995). ©1995 by The Foundation for Cultural Review, Inc.

meant, one assumes, that the courage of your convictions will carry you through. But the line lends itself to another interpretation: as far as your peers and the arts establishment and fashionable opinion are concerned, if your politics are good enough, let's not be too picky about the playwriting. Half a century from now, the success of *Angels* will seem as bizarre and unfathomable as that of *Abie's Irish Rose* does today. Indeed, if it comes to preposterously well-meaning, moralizing sentimentalists, Kushner probably has the edge over Anne Nichols: her coupling of Jewish Abie and his Irish Catholic Rose is marginally more convincing than Kushner's uncoupling of the closeted gay Mormon husband and his wife.

The difference is that, in 1922, everyone ridiculed Miss Nichols and scorned her success. Back then, if your heart was in the right place, it didn't necessarily excuse your play-writing. By 1992, though, the AIDS play had stalled: we'd had *As Is* and *The Normal Heart*, when both sheer rage and the mere adumbration of symptoms were still novelties; and ho-hum Main Stem dramas like Richard Greenberg's *Eastern Standard* had settled down to augmenting the role of the token gay with the role of the token HIV-positive gay. It took Kushner to give the disease the dramatic size and significance the campaigners had long claimed for it—"the age of AIDS" and all that—to make it the central theme of an epic national meditation and then, by enlarging his canvas to encompass not only the country but the heavens too, to sanctify the condition.

To find the proper theatrical precedent for *Angels*, you have to go back to 1863, and the sensation caused by the arrival of the latest theatrical illusion, the Pepper's Ghost. Every play instantly jumped on the hearse and transformed itself into a spectral melodrama, prompting one Broadway columnist to offer his own spoof theatrical listings guide:

> Wallack's Theatre: *Ghost*;
> New Bowery Theatre: *Ghost*;
> Old Bowery Theatre: *Ghost*;
> Bryant's Minstrels: *Colored Ghost*.

None of these ghost shows has survived, but that's not the point. At the time, America was in the midst of the Civil War and, for the first time, the young Republic had to come to terms with a mortality rate it had never contemplated, as the best and brightest of its youth were wiped out. Today, the Pepper's Ghost effect—an actors reflection cast on a sheet of glass between stage and audience—would be laughable, but, preoccupied with mortality and the afterlife, theatergoers found the luminous figures parading on stage oddly reassuring. This is precisely the function *Angels in America* fulfills for its audience. It takes insignificant, individual death and makes it part of a Civil War; it translates the humiliating attrition of a young, healthy body by a behavioral disease contracted in the most banal way into a front-line sacrifice, part of the great cultural currents swirling across our age, part of a struggle for the nation's soul—against, inevitably, Presidents Reagan and Bush, or, as Kushner with his penetrating Pulitzer pen puts it, "those criminals." It's ridiculous, but it is effective; *ce n'est pas la guerre, mais c'est magnifique*.

With Kushner, size is everything: like a restless frog, he skims across the pond from lily pad to lily pad, clocking up the air miles. Everyone else is standing by the water's edge terrified of dipping their toes. As an example, look no further than *Angels'* successor at the Walter Kerr, *Love! Valour! Compassion!* In these pages in October, apropos *A Perfect Ganesh*, I bemoaned Terrence McNally's inability to set his sights above showtune chit-chat, but, in his latest play here we go again: the biggest laugh is when a musical-theater buff says he's had nightmares about a revival of *The King and I* starring Tommy Tune and Elaine Stritch—a divine intervention, to be sure, but also the sound of a theater feeding on itself. McNally's play is about eight gays weekending at a farmhouse in Dutchess County, and what's depressing is not that they're all gays, but that they're all showfolk: they are the kind of people you meet if you work in the theater; you're grateful that he's raised his horizons sufficiently to locate the play up the other end of the Taconic State Parkway. AIDS is in danger of becoming a metaphor for New York theater: shrunken, emaciated, unable to see beyond the window sill. We live in interesting times, but what do America's dramatists have to say about them?

For that reason, Kushner is worth treasuring and so even is his unsatisfactory play *Slavs!* (New York Theater Workshop). *C'est vraiment la guerre* this time, the big one: the collapse of the Soviet Union—which is what's been happening in the rest of the world while American playwrights have been writing AIDS dramas. With a recycling zeal environmentalists will applaud, Kushner has taken three-quarters of this ninety-minute one-acter from scenes cut from *Angels*: the result is a montage of sketches, babushkas and nomenclature and security guards discoursing on socialism in Moscow, Siberia, and—inevitably—heaven. Kushner has spoken of "a twinned destiny," a "sea change," a "revolution" that is sweeping through both Russia and America. He's never very specific about what he means, so we have to feel our own way. In Russia, though, "revolution" is actual, involving the civilian bombardment of Chechen cities; in America, presumably, "revolution" would be "cultural," involving, say, President Clinton enacting reciprocal-pensions legislation for same-sex couples. On the whole, then, its best to approach Kushner's "twinned destiny" as a post–Cold War update of the "moral equivalence" argument favored by British playwrights of the last thirty years: the most you could ever get Harold Pinter to say against the Soviet Union was that the West was just as bad. That's the trouble with political art: almost all of it turns out to be bunk. In the years after Mrs. Thatcher's election, "artists," who in bourgeois societies always complain that they're not listened to despite the special insight with which they're endowed, churned out one subsidized play after another about the British fascist tyranny but failed to spot anything that really happened—like the death of Communism, the resumption of ancient ethnic hatreds, even the bland homogenizing tide of Euro-federalism. For all the political and artistic legacy of these plays, the National and the RSC and the Royal Court might as well have been performing *42nd Street* eight shows a week: at least then they wouldn't have been wrong. For me, the hysterical impotence of political drama was best expressed by the finale of Adrian Mitchell's *Love Songs of World War III* at the National Theatre, at which the middle-class audience was led through "Fuck-Off Friday," a song about unemployment concluding triumphantly with:

> I can't wait for that great day when
> Fuck-Off Friday comes to Number Ten.

Slavs! reaches its equivalent ferocity in a Siberian hospital, when the mother of one of the dumb chromosome-damaged "yellow children" lashes out at the visiting Moscow apparatchik: "Fuck this century! Fuck your leader! Fuck the state! Fuck all governments! Fuck the motherland! Fuck your mother, your father and you!" The tone of "Fuck-Off Friday" and of almost all subsidized left-wing British drama is defiant certainty: this we know to be right, and Mrs. Thatcher's election and re-election and re-re-election cannot alter that. The tone of Barbara eda-Young's outburst is the opposite: the anger is empty and aimless; it flares and dies; by the end of it, everything is ... fucked.

In an earlier scene, deploring the Gorbachev reforms, "the world's oldest living Bolshevik" demands to know: "How are we to proceed without theory?" And you wonder if this isn't more of a dilemma for left-wing Western playwrights than it is for the Russian people. The mood of Lisa Peterson's production is oddly faltering, veering between a glib nihilism and a sort of melancholic ambivalence. It's a voice you don't often hear in the theater: that of the guy who doesn't know. The one production value is the lightly falling snow, a double-edged symbol: it's pure and cleansing but it's also blanking, a blizzard, a white-out. Ideology gave the battleground clear lines—and dramatists prefer a clean, simple structure. Take it away, and you're left with the Vance-Owen partition plan for Bosnia: you can just about figure it out, but you wouldn't want to make a two-act play out of it. When "the world's oldest living Bolshevik" drops dead—the final collapse of ideology, geddit?—a nervous comrade puts it down to excessive debate: "Now I'm calling security," he warns. "And no more metaphors!" Again, you wonder if this isn't the great fear of the dramatist—that, in a world made safe for Western consumerism, there are no symbols, no metaphors; everything just *is*. After all, even the most explicitly political art can be wrenched from its moorings. Think of that old fraud Bertolt Brecht and the best-known song from his blistering, savage text to *The Threepenny Opera*. In the late Eighties, even before the Wall fell, "Mack the Knife" completed its slow inexorable defection and signed up to push hamburgers on television:

> Its the great taste of McDonald's
> Come on, make it ...
> Mac tonight!

Brecht sells burgers! Well, there's a metaphor—and, like all the best ones, it's accidental. The commercial is artless—and, in the face of artlessness, art has a hard job holding its own. If the content of *Slavs!* is nervous and ambiguous, the form is revealing. *Angels in America*, billed as "A Gay Fantasia on National Themes," lasted seven hours, two nights, and gave its separate halves the dignified, portentous titles of *Millennium Approaches* and *Perestroika*; the collapse of the Soviet Union merits an hour and a half and gets labeled *Slavs!* At one time, it was the musicals which had the exclamation marks, the final stage in the adaptive process from *Green Grow the Lilacs* to *Oklahoma!*, *The Matchmaker* to *Hello, Dolly!*, or *The Man Who Came to Dinner* to *Sherry!* With the last one, incidentally, the titles tell you everything you need to know about the difference between the play and the musical, between a drama which grows organically and one which runs around expending a lot of phony energy. Eventually, the exclamation mark came to be seen as a premature ejaculation: if the show gets that excited in the title, chances are it's pooped by Act One, Scene Two.

Ah, but surely Kushner's exclamation point is pointedly ironic, an exclamation mark in quote marks? Up to a point. In 1943, off the back of *Pal*

Joey, you could probably find Richard Rodgers fans willing to argue that *Oklahoma!*'s exclamation was ironic—as, come to think of it, in those days, *any* exclamation mark after Oklahoma must have been. As it happens, *Slavs!* and *Oklahoma!* have more than their punctuation in common: they're both set among fractious, feuding communities trying to find enough common ground on which to build a new state. This may seem a frivolous comparison, but it's prompted by Kushner's form. The play opens with two roly-poly, whiskery, headscarfed babushkas discussing the present state of affairs as they sweep the still-falling snow outside the Hall of the Soviets: "However reluctant one may be to grant it," growls one, "history and the experience of this century presses upon us the inescapable conclusion that there is a direct continuum from dictatorship of the proletariat and the embrace of violence as a means of effecting change that one finds in later Marx and Engels to dictatorship plain and simple—you missed a spot—and state terror."

This is a good joke, but it's a revue joke: thirty years ago in London and New York, it would have been the province of shows like *Beyond the Fringe*. So the question follows: in what way is Kushner's joke more than revue? There is a ratchet effect in our culture: revue has gone; and "Saturday Night Live" satirizes not the news but merely its forms of transmission—the press conferences and network anchors; and so we go to new plays by Pulitzer Prize-winning authors to hear harmless little university jests. It's a comfortable joke, easy to laugh at, like the old comrades called Antedilluvianovich and other funny names leaping round the samovar in the next scene. Much of what Kushner has to say is thoughtful and unsettling, but his play doesn't unsettle because of its form. When John Weidman and Stephen Sondheim used a revue structure for *Assassins*, it had a kind of logic. Here, it feels inappropriate and parochial—and, opening as Yeltsin bombs Grozny, an inadequate response. The playwriting is still not good enough.

You can't entirely blame Kushner. The final stage of the Cold War was fought in pop-culture slogans. Gennadi Gerasimov announced the replacement of the Brezhnev Doctrine by the Sinatra Doctrine: you do it your way; a State Department official, struggling to keep tabs on the collapsing dominoes, said, "If it's Tuesday, it must be Czechoslovakia." This is nothing new in America, where we're happy to define the national tragedy of a terminated Presidency in terms of a Lerner and Loewe title song. But, if anything represented the final capitulation of stolid, non-vernacular Marxist-Leninism, it was not what the Sinatra Doctrine meant but how it was expressed.

For much of this century, there was a uniquely American tension between popular culture and high art. That's gone now: pop culture is all, and the highbrow fellows are left with nothing to do but beam it back to us through a distorting lens. For my own part, I have a simple philosophy: eliminate the middle man. I'd rather have a Campbell's Soup can than a Warhol rendering of one, and I'd rather dance to old Beach Boys records than go watch a contemporary dance ensemble doing technique-free movement to old Beach Boys records. There's something snide and joyless about the way the higher forms drape their ironic inverted commas around harmless schlock: a happy gamboling lamb dressed as mutton.

Down at the Public Theater, they've finally cottoned on to Elvis and given him a play of his own, by the actor Christopher Walken—one act, ninety minutes, just like the fall of the Soviet Union. The title is *Him*, which is appropriately Godly: if the play's about anything, it's about Elvis as religion. The King is in Limbo, but a Limbo populated by Elvis look-alikes and apparently accessible to *Vanity Fair* interviewers (no doubt the Limbo press agent insists on picture approval). Already, it's all beginning to sound a bit forced. The night I attended, the audience had been expecting to have a better time—a play about Elvis: hey, it's the great taste of legitimate theater now in new easy-to-swallow capsule form! Oh, there were a few real laughs on "Would you like a donut?" and "Give me five orders of double cheeseburgers with onion rings"—the usual stuff—but for the rest of the time there were just those nervous titters you usually get at the start of a play when the audience is waiting for it to find its rhythm. This one never does, mainly because Walken and his director, Jim Simpson, seem to take a perverse delight in just shambling around the stage and grinding the evening to a halt. There's a set-piece where he walks out of the auditorium to show an audience plant the gun he was given by Nixon; after a while, he and the stooge return, and Elvis/Walken declares, "He broke the fourth wall!" But a lot of the rest of the time he just halts at the end of a line as if he can't believe he said something that clever: "*Je regrette ri-en*. In the end, the love you take is equal to the love you make." By this stage, Walken is dressed as a waitress: Elvis has faked his death, been taken to Morocco and turned into a woman.

The trouble is, when you fight on this turf, the real Elvis will always win. To many of his fans, he is a religion, a Presleyterian Church with its own sacred relics—toenail clippings retrieved from the shagpile of the Jungle Room at Graceland and a huge wart removed when he entered the army but preserved by the doctor, though there are those who doubt its provenance. Any cult whose adherents sell toenails to each other is bound to prove difficult to satirize. But there are other aspects of Elvis worth considering. Traditionally, the pop celebrity gets rich, buys a house in Beverly Hills and a penthouse on Central Park West, starts collecting fine art and eating haute cuisine. When Elvis got rich, he just did all the things poor people do but on a grand scale: instead of eating one cheeseburger, he'd eat ten; instead of watching one TV set, he'd watch five; instead of living in a trailer, he bought an old plantation home but turned it into a virtual shrine to trailer taste; save for the army, he never went abroad and never had any desire to. Even his records: if you listen to the later ones, the backing arrangements sound like karaoke night at a sports bar. Smart people—the sort who go to the Public Theater—mock him because he never broke faith with his fans, he never crossed the tracks. By comparison, Madonna—for all that she's photographed writhing naked on top of her Doberman—is a far more conventional celebrity.

You might just conceivably get a play out of this, but it certainly isn't Walken's series of disconnected, whimsical verbal guitar licks, which manage, like many arty takes on pop culture, to seem both pretentious and parasitic. Elvis's connection to his audience is so direct, there's no room for art to intercede. When you ask his fans why they like him, they'll say, "Oh, well, I'll never forget the first time I heard 'Rock-A-Hula Baby.'" And that's it. Honestly. It's only a problem for playwrights, who, like that old Bolshevik, can't conceive of a world without theory, without metaphor, without symbols: there must be more to it than that. But sometimes there isn't. Elvis is mainly a symbol of Elvis.

DAVID SAVRAN

Ambivalence, Utopia, and a Queer Sort of Materialism: How Angels in America *Reconstructs the Nation*

C ritics, pundits, and producers have placed Tony Kushner's *Angels in America: A Gay Fantasia on National Themes* in the unenviable position of having to rescue the American theatre. The latter, by all accounts, is in a sorry state. It has attempted to maintain its elite cultural status despite the fact that the differences between "high" and "low" have become precarious. On Broadway, increasingly expensive productions survive more and more by mimicking mass culture, either in the form of mind-numbing spectacles featuring singing cats, falling chandeliers, and dancing dinnerware, or plays, like *The Heidi Chronicles* or *Prelude to a Kiss*, whose style and themes aspire to "quality" television. In regional theatres, meanwhile, subscriptions continue to decline, and with them the adventurousness of artistic directors. Given this dismal situation, *Angels in America* has almost singlehandedly resuscitated a category of play that has become almost extinct: the serious Broadway drama that is neither a British import nor a revival.

Not within memory has a new American play been canonized by the press as rapidly as *Angels in America*.[1] Indeed, critics have been stumbling over each other in an adulatory stupor. John Lahr hails *Perestroika* as a "masterpiece" and notes that "[n]ot since Williams has a playwright announced his poetic vision with such authority on the Broadway stage."[2] Jack Kroll judges both parts "the broadest, deepest, most searching American

From *Theatre Journal* 47, no. 2 (May 1995). © 1995 by The Johns Hopkins University Press.

play of our time," while Robert Brustein deems *Millennium Approaches* "the authoritative achievement of a radical dramatic artist with a fresh, clear voice."[3] In the gay press, meanwhile, the play is viewed as testifying to the fact that "Broadway now leads the way in the industry with its unapologetic portrayals of gay characters."[4] For both Frank Rich and John Clum, *Angels* is far more than just a successful play; it is the marker of a decisive historical shift in American theatre. According to Rich, the play's success is in part the result of its ability to conduct "a searching and radical rethinking of the whole aesthetic of American political drama."[5] For Clum, the play's appearance on Broadway "marks a turning point in the history of gay drama, the history of American drama, and of American literary culture."[6] In its reception, *Angels*—so deeply preoccupied with teleological process—is itself positioned as both the culmination of history and as that which rewrites the past.

Despite the enormity of the claims cited above, I am less interested in disputing them than in trying to understand why they are being made—and why now. Why is a play featuring five gay male characters being universalized as a "turning point" in the American theatre, and minoritized as the preeminent gay male artifact of the 1990s? Why is it both popular and "radical?" What is the linkage between the two primary sources for the play's theory of history and utopia—Walter Benjamin and Mormonism? And what does this linkage suggest about the constitution of the nation? Finally, why has queer drama become the theatrical sensation of the 1990s? I hope it's not too perverse of me to attempt to answer these questions by focusing less on the construction of queer subjectivities per se than on the field of cultural production in which *Angels in America* is situated. After all, how else would one practice a queer materialism?

THE ANGEL OF HISTORY

The opposite of nearly everything you say about *Angels in America* will also hold true: *Angels* valorizes identity politics; it offers an anti-foundationalist critique of identity politics. *Angels* mounts an attack against ideologies of individualism; it problematizes the idea of community. *Angels* submits liberalism to a trenchant examination; it finally opts for yet another version of American liberal pluralism. *Angels* launches a critique of the very mechanisms that produce pathologized and acquiescent female bodies; it represents yet another pathologization and silencing of women. A conscientious reader or spectator might well rebuke the play, as Belize does Louis: "you're ambivalent about everything."[7] And so it is. The play's ambivalence, however, is not simply the result of Kushner hedging his bets on the most controversial issues. Rather, it functions, I believe—quite independently of the intent of its author—as the play's political unconscious, playing itself out on many different levels: formal, ideological, characterological, and rhetorical. (Frank Rich refers to this as Kushner's "refusal to adhere to any theatrical or political theory."[8]) Yet the fact that ambivalence—or undecidability—is the watchword of this text (which is, after all, *two* plays) does not mean that all the questions it raises remain unresolved. On the contrary, I will argue that the play's undecidability is, in fact, always already resolved because the questions that appear to be ambivalent in fact already have been decided consciously or unconsciously by the text itself. Moreover, the relentless operation of normalizing reading practices works to reinforce these decisions. If I am correct, the play turns out (*pace* Frank Rich) to adhere all too well to a particular political theory.

Formally, *Angels* is a promiscuously complicated play that is very difficult to categorize generically. Clum's characterization of it as being "like a Shakespearean romance" is doubtlessly motivated by the play's rambling and episodic form, its interweaving of multiple plotlines, its mixture of realism and fantasy, its invocation of various theological and mythological narratives, as well as by its success in evoking those characteristics that are usually associated with both comedy and tragedy.[9] Moreover, *Perestroika's* luminous finale is remarkably suggestive of the beatific scenes that end Shakespeare's romances. There is no question, moreover, but that the play deliberately evokes the long history of Western dramatic literature and positions itself as heir to the traditions of Sophocles, Shakespeare, Brecht, and others. Consider, for example, its use of the blindness/insight opposition and the way that Prior Walter is carefully constructed (like the blind Prelapsarianov) as a kind of Teiresias, "going blind, as prophets do."[10] This binarism, the paradigmatic emblem of the tragic subject (and mark of Teiresias, Oedipus, and Gloucester), deftly links cause and effect—because one is blind to truth, one loses one's sight—and is used to claim Prior's priority, his epistemologically privileged position in the text. Or consider the parallels often drawn in the press between Kushner's Roy Cohn and Shakespeare's Richard III.[11] Or Kushner's use of a fate motif, reminiscent of *Macbeth*, whereby Prior insists that Louis not return until the seemingly impossible comes to pass, until he sees Louis "black and blue" (2:89). Or Kushner's rewriting of those momentous moral and political debates that riddle not just classical tragedy (*Antigone, Richard II*) but also the work of Brecht and his (mainly British) successors (Howard Brenton, David Hare,

Caryl Churchill). Or the focus on the presence/absence of God that one finds not just in early modern tragedy but also in so-called Absurdism (Beckett, Ionesco, Stoppard). Moreover, these characteristics tend to be balanced, on the one hand, by the play's insistent tendency to ironize and, on the other, by the familiar ingredients of romantic comedies (ill-matched paramours, repentant lovers, characters suddenly finding themselves in unfamiliar places, plus a lot of good jokes). Despite the ironic/comic tone, however, none of the interlaced couples survives the onslaught of chaos, disease, and revelation. Prior and Louis, Louis and Joe, Joe and Harper have all parted by the end of the play and the romantic dyad (as primary social unit) is replaced in the final scene of *Perestroika* by a utopian concept of (erotic) affiliation and a new definition of family.

Angels in America's title, its idea of utopia, and its model for a particular kind of ambivalence are derived in part from Benjamin's extraordinary meditation, "Theses on the Philosophy of History," written shortly before his death in 1940. Composed during the first months of World War II, with fascism on its march across Europe, the darkness (and simultaneous luminosity) of Benjamin's "Theses" attest not only to the seeming invincibility of Hitler, but also to the impossible position of the European left, "[s]tranded," as Terry Eagleton notes, "between social democracy and Stalinism."[12] In this essay, Benjamin sketches a discontinuous theory of history in which "the services of theology" are enlisted in the aid of reconceiving "historical materialism."[13] Opposing the universalizing strategies of bourgeois historicism with historical materialism's project of brushing "history against the grain" (257), he attempts a radical revision of Marxist historiography. Suturing the Jewish notion of Messianic time (in which all history is given meaning retrospectively by the sudden and unexpected coming of the Messiah) to the Marxist concept of revolution, Benjamin reimagines proletariat revolution not as the culmination of a conflict between classes, or between traditional institutions and new forms of production, but as a "blast[ing] open" of "the continuum of history" (262). Unlike traditional Marxist (or idealist) historiographers, he rejects the idea of the present as a moment of "transition" and instead conceives it as *Jetztzeit*: "time filled by the presence of the now" (261), a moment in which "time stands still and has come to a stop" (262). Facing *Jetztzeit*, and opposing all forms of gradualism, Benjamin's historical materialist is given the task not of imagining and inciting progressive change (or a movement toward socialism), but of "blast[ing] a specific era out of the homogeneous course of history" (263).

The centerpiece of Benjamin's essay is his explication of a painting by

Paul Klee, which becomes a parable of history, of the time of the Now, in the face of catastrophe (which for him means all of human history):

> A Klee painting named "Angelus Novus" shows an angel looking as though he is about to move away from something he is fixedly contemplating. His eyes are staring, his mouth is open, his wings are spread. This is how one pictures the angel of history. His face is turned toward the past. Where we perceive a chain of events, he sees one single catastrophe which keeps piling wreckage upon wreckage and hurls it in front of his feet. The angel would like to stay, awaken the dead, and make whole what has been smashed. But a storm is blowing from Paradise; it has got caught in his wings with such violence that the angel can no longer close them. This storm irresistibly propels him into the future to which his back is turned, while the pile of debris before him grows skyward. This storm is what we call progress.
> [257–58]

In Benjamin's allegory, with its irresolvable play of contradictions, the doggedly well-intentioned angel of history embodies both the inconceivability of progress and the excruciating condition of the Now. Poised (not unlike Benjamin himself in Europe in 1940) between the past, which is to say "catastrophe," and an unknown and terrifying future, he is less a heavenly actor than a passive observer, "fixedly contemplating" that disaster which is the history of the world. His "Paradise," meanwhile, is not the site of a benign utopianism but a "storm" whose "violence" gets caught under his wings and propels him helplessly into an inconceivable future that stymies his gaze.

Benjamin's allegory of history is, in many respects, the primary generative fiction for *Angels in America*. Not only is its Angel clearly derived from Benjamin's text (although with gender reassignment surgery along the way—Kushner's Angel is "Hermaphroditically Equipped"), but so is its vision of Heaven, which has "*a deserted, derelict feel to it*," with "*rubble ... strewn everywhere*" (2:48; 121). And the play's conceptualizations of the past, of catastrophe, and of utopia are clearly inflected by Benjamin's "Theses," as is its linkage between historical materialism and theology. Moreover, rather than attempt to suppress the contradictions that inform Benjamin's materialist theology, Kushner expands them. As a result, the ideas of history, progress, and paradise that *Angels in America* invokes are irreducibly contradictory (often without appearing to be so). Just as Benjamin's notion of revolution is related dialectically to catastrophe, so are *Angels*'s concepts of deliverance and abjection, ecstasy and pain, utopia and dystopia, necessarily linked. Kushner's Angel (and her/his heaven) serve as a constant reminder both of catastrophe (AIDS, racism, homophobia, and the pathologization of queer and female bodies, to name only the play's most obvious examples) and of the perpetual possibility of millennium's approach, or in the words of Ethel Rosenberg (unmistakably echoing Benjamin), that "[h]istory is about to crack wide open" (1:112). And the concept of utopia/dystopia to which s/he is linked guarantees that the vehicle of hope and redemption in *Angels*—the prophet who foresees a new age—will be the character who must endure the most agony: Prior Walter, suffering from AIDS and Louis's desertion.

Within the economy of utopia/dystopia that *Angels* installs, the greatest promise of the millennium is the possibility of life freed from the shackles of hatred, oppression, and disease. It is hardly surprising, therefore, that Roy Cohn is constructed as the embodiment and guarantor of dystopia. Not only is he the paradigm of bourgeois individualism—and Reaganism—at its most murderous, hypocritical, and malignant, but he is the one with the most terrifying vision of the "universe," which he apprehends "as a kind of sandstorm in outer space with winds of mega-hurricane velocity, but instead of grains of sand it's shards and splinters of glass" (1:13). It is, however, a sign of the play's obsessively dialectical structure that Roy's vision of what sounds like hell should provide an uncanny echo of Benjamin's "storm blowing from Paradise." Yet even this dialectic, much like the play's ambivalences, is deceptive insofar as its habit of turning one pole of a binarism relentlessly into its opposite (rather than into a synthesis) describes a false dialectic. Prior, on the other hand, refusing the role of victim, becomes the sign of the unimaginable, of "[t]he Great Work" (2:148). Yet, as with Roy, so Prior's privileged position is a figure of contradiction, coupling not just blindness with prophecy, but also history with an impossible future, an ancient lineage (embodied by Prior 1 and Prior 2) with the millennium yet to come, and AIDS with a "most inner part, entirely free of disease" (1:34). Moreover, Prior's very name designates his temporal dislocation, the fact that he is at once too soon and belated, both that which anticipates and that which provides an epilogue (to the Walter family, if nothing else, since he seems to mark the end of the line). Prior Walter also serves as the queer commemoration of the Walter that came before—Walter Benjamin—whose revolutionary principles he both embodies and displaces insofar as he marks both the presence and absence of Walter Benjamin in this text.[14]

Throughout *Angels in America*, the utopia/dystopia coupling (wherein disaster becomes simultaneously the marker for and incitement to think

Paradise) plays itself out through a host of binary oppositions: heaven/hell, forgiveness/retribution, communitarianism/individualism, spirit/flesh, pleasure/pain, beauty/decay, future/past, homosexuality/heterosexuality, rationalism/indeterminacy, migration/staying put, progress/stasis, life/death. Each of these functions not just as a set of conceptual poles in relation to which characters and themes are worked out and interpreted, but also as an oxymoron, a figure of undecidability whose contradictory being becomes an incitement to think the impossible—revolution. For it is precisely the conjunction of opposites that allows what Benjamin calls "the flow of thoughts" to be given a "shock" and so turned into "the sign of a Messianic cessation of happening" (262–63). The oxymoron, in other words, becomes the privileged figure by which the unimaginable allows itself to be imagined.

In Kushner's reading of Benjamin, the hermaphroditic Angel becomes the most crucial site for the elaboration of contradiction. Because her/his body is the one on which an impossible—and utopian—sexual conjunction is played out, s/he decisively undermines the distinction between the heterosexual and the homosexual. With her/his "eight vaginas" and "Bouquet of Phalli" (2:48), s/he represents an absolute otherness, the impossible Other that fulfills the longing for both the maternal and paternal (or in Lacanian terms, both demand and the Law). On the one hand, as the maternal "Other," s/he is constituted by "[d]emand ... as already possessing the 'privilege' of satisfying needs, that is to say, the power of depriving them of that alone by which they are satisfied."[15] On the other hand, "[a]s the law of symbolic functioning," s/he simultaneously represents the "Other embodied in the figure of the symbolic father," "not a person but a place, the locus of law, language and the symbolic."[16] The impossible conjunction of the maternal and the paternal, s/he provides Prior with sexual pleasure of celestial quality—and gives a new meaning to safe sex. At the same time, s/he also fills and completes subjectivity, being the embodiment of and receptacle for Prior's "Released Female Essence" (2:48).

Although all of these characteristics suggest that the Angel is constructed as an extratemporal being, untouched by the ravages of passing time, s/he comes (quite literally for Prior) already culturally mediated. When s/he first appears at the end of *Millennium*, he exclaims, "*Very* Steven Spielberg" (1:118). Although his campy ejaculation is clearly calculated as a laugh line, defusing and undercutting (with typical postmodern cynicism) the deadly earnestness of the scene, it also betrays the fact that this miraculous apparition is in part the product of a culture industry and that any reading of her/him will be mediated by the success of Steven Spielberg and his ilk (in films like *Close Encounters of the Third Kind* and *E.T.*) in producing a particular vision of the miraculous—with lots of bright white light and music by John Williams. To that extent, the appearance of the Angel signals the degree to which utopia—and revolution!—have now become the product of commodity culture. Unlike earlier periods, when utopia tended to be imagined in terms of production (rather than consumption) and was sited in a preceding phase of capitalism (for example, in a preindustrial or agrarian society), late capitalism envisions utopia through the lens of the commodity and—not unlike Walter Benjamin at his most populist—projects it into a future and an elsewhere lit by that *"unearthly white light"* (1:118) which represents, among other things, the illimitable allure of the commodity form.[17]

Although the construction of the Angel represses her/his historicity, the heaven s/he calls home is explicitly the product (and victim) of temporality. Heaven is a simulacrum of San Francisco on 18 April 1906, the day of the Great Earthquake. For it is on this day that God *"[a]bandoned"* his angels and their heaven *"[a]nd did not return"* (2:51). Heaven thus appears frozen in time, *"deserted and derelict,"* with *"rubble strewn everywhere"* (2:121). The Council Room in Heaven, meanwhile, *"dimly lit by candles and a single great bulb"* (which periodically fails) is a monument to the past, specifically to the New Science of the seventeenth century and the Enlightenment project to which it is inextricably linked. The table in the Council Room is *"covered with antique and broken astronomical, astrological, mathematical and nautical objects of measurement and calculation...."* At its center sits a *"bulky radio, a 1940s model in very poor repair"* (2:128) on which the Angels are listening to the first reports of the Chernobyl disaster. Conflating different moments of the past and distinct (Western) histories, Heaven is a kind of museum, not the insignia of the Now, but of *before*, of an antique past, of the obsolete. Its decrepitude is also symptomatic of the Angels' fear that God will never return. More nightmare than utopia, marooned in history, Heaven commemorates disaster, despair, and stasis.

Because of its embeddedness in the past, the geography of Heaven is a key to the complex notion of temporality that governs *Angels in America*. Although the scheme does not become clear until *Perestroika*, there are two opposing concepts of time and history running through the play. First, there is the time of the Angels (and of Heaven), the time of dystopian "STASIS" (2:54) as decreed by the absence of a God who, Prior insists, "isn't coming back" (2:133). According to the Angel, this temporal paralysis is the direct result of the hyperactivity of human beings: *"YOU HAVE DRIVEN HIM AWAY!,"* the Angel enjoins Prior, *"YOU MUST STOP MOVING!"* (2:52), in the hope that immobility will once again prompt the return of God and the forward movement of time. Yet this concept of time as stasis is also linked to decay. In the Angel's threnody that ends the Council scene, s/he envisions the dissolution of "the Great Design, / The spiraling apart of the Work of Eternity" (2:134). Directly opposed to this concept is human temporality, of which Prior, in contradistinction to the Angel, becomes the spokesperson. This time—which is also apparently the time of God—is the temporality connected with Enlightenment epistemologies; it is the time of "Progress," "Science," and "Forward Motion" (2:132; 50). It is the time of "Change" (2:13) so fervently desired by Comrade Prelapsarianov and the "neo-Hegelian positivist sense of constant historical progress towards happiness or perfection" so precious to Louis (1:25). It is the promise fulfilled at the end of *Perestroika* when Louis, apprehending "the end of the Cold War," announces, "[t]he whole world is changing!" (2:145). Most important, the time of "progress, migration, motion" and "modernity" is also, in Prior's formulation, the time of "desire," because it is this last all-too-human characteristic that produces modernity (2:132). Without desire (for change, utopia, the Other), there could be no history.

Despite the fact that this binary opposition generates so much of the play's ideological framework, and that its two poles are at times indistinguishable, it seems to me that this is one question on which *Angels in America* is not ambivalent at all. Unlike the Benjamin of the "Theses on the Philosophy of History" for whom any concept of progress seems quite inconceivable, Kushner is devoted to rescuing Enlightenment epistemologies at a time when they are, to say the least, extremely unfashionable. On the one hand, *Angels in America* counters attacks from the pundits of the right, wallowing in their post–Cold War triumphalism, for whom socialism, or "the coordination of men's activities through central direction," is the road to "serfdom."[18] For these neoconservatives, "[w]e already live in the millennial new age," we already stand at "the end of history" and, as a result, in Francis Fukuyama's words, "we cannot picture to ourselves a world that is essentially different from the present one, and at the same time better."[19] Obsessed with "free markets and private property," and trying desperately to maintain the imperialist status quo, they can only imagine progress as regression.[20] On the other hand, *Angels* also challenges the orthodoxies of those poststructuralists on the left by whom the Marxian concept of history is often dismissed as hopelessly idealist, as "a contemptible attempt" to construct "grand narratives" and "totalizing (totalitarian?) knowledges."[21] In the face of these profound cynicisms, *Angels* unabashedly champions rationalism and progress. In the last words of *Perestroika*'s last act, Harper suggests that "[i]n this world, there is a kind of painful progress.

Longing for what we've left behind, and dreaming ahead" (2:144). The last words of the epilogue, meanwhile, are given to Prior who envisions a future in which "[w]e" (presumably gay men, lesbians, and persons with AIDS) "will be citizens." "*More Life*" (2:148), he demands.

Kushner's differences with Benjamin—and the poststructuralists—over the possibility of progress and his championing of modernity (and the desire that produces it) suggest that the string of binary oppositions that are foundational to the play are perhaps less undecidable than I originally suggested. Meaning is produced, in part, because these oppositions are constructed as interlocking homologies, each an analogy for all the others. And despite the fact that each term of each opposition is strictly dependent on the other and, indeed, is produced by its other, these relations are by no means symmetrical. Binary oppositions are always hierarchical, especially when the fact of hierarchy is repressed. *Angels* is carefully constructed so that communitarianism, rationalism, progress, and so forth, will be read as being preferable to their alternatives: individualism, indeterminacy, stasis, and so forth ("the playwright has been able to find hope in his chronicle of the poisonous 1980s"[22]). So at least as far as this string of interlocked binary oppositions is concerned, ambivalence turns out to be not especially ambivalent after all.

At the same time, what is one to make of other binarisms—most notably, the opposition between masculine and feminine—toward which the play seems to cultivate a certain studied ambivalence? On the one hand, it is clear that Kushner is making some effort to counter the long history of the marginalization and silencing of women in American culture generally and in American theatre, in particular. Harper's hallucinations are crucial to the play's articulation of its central themes, including questions of exile and of the utopia/dystopia binarism. They also give her a privileged relationship to Prior, in whose fantasies she sometimes partakes and with whom she visits Heaven. Her unequivocal rejection of Joe and expropriation of his credit card at the end of the play, moreover, signal her repossession of her life and her progress from imaginary to real travel. Hannah, meanwhile, is constructed as an extremely independent and strong-willed woman who becomes part of the new extended family that is consolidated at the end of the play. Most intriguingly, the play's deliberate foregrounding of the silencing of the Mormon Mother and Daughter in the diorama is symptomatic of Kushner's desire to let women speak. On the other hand, *Angels* seems to replicate many of the structures that historically have produced female subjectivity as Other. Harper may be crucial to the play's structure but she is still pathologized, like so many of her antecedents on the

American stage (from Mary Tyrone to Blanche DuBois to Honey in *Who's Afraid of Virginia Woolf?*). With her hallucinations and "emotional problems" (1:27), she functions as a scapegoat for Joe, the displacement of his sexual problems. Moreover, her false confession that she's "going to have a baby" (1:41) not only reinforces the link in the play between femininity and maternity but also literally hystericizes her. And Hannah, despite her strength, is defined almost entirely by her relationship to her real son and to Prior, her surrogate son. Like Belize, she is given the role of caretaker.

Most important, the celestial "sexual politics" (2:49) of the play guarantees that the feminine remains Other. After his visitation by the Angel, Prior explains that "God ... is a man. Well, not a man, he's a flaming Hebrew letter, but a male flaming Hebrew letter" (2:49). In comparison with this masculinized, Old Testament-style, "flaming"(!) patriarch, the Angels are decidedly hermaphroditic. Nonetheless, the play's stage directions use the feminine pronoun when designating the Angel and s/he has been played by a woman in all of the play's various American premieres. As a result of this clearly delineated gendered difference, femininity is associated (in Heaven at least) with "STASIS" and collapse, while a divine masculinity is coded as being simultaneously deterministic and absent. In the play's pseudo-Platonic—and heterosexualized—metaphysics, the "orgasm" of the *Angels* produces (a feminized) "protomatter, which fuels the [masculinized] Engine of Creation" (2:49).

Moreover, the play's use of doubling reinforces this sense of the centrality of masculinity. Unlike Caryl Churchill's *Cloud 9* (surely the locus classicus of genderfuck), *Angels* uses cross-gender casting only for minor characters. And the crossing of gender works in one direction only. The actresses playing Hannah, Harper, and the Angel take on a number of male heterosexual characters while the male actors double only in masculine roles. As a result, it seems to me that *Angels*, unlike the work of Churchill, does not denaturalize gender. Rather, masculinity—which, intriguingly, is always already queered in this text—is produced as a remarkably stable, if contradictory, essence that others can mime but which only a real (i.e., biological) male can embody. Thus, yet another ambivalence turns out to be always already decided.

THE AMERICAN RELIGION

The nation that *Angels in America* fantasizes has its roots in the early nineteenth century, the period during which the United States became constituted, to borrow Benedict Anderson's celebrated formulation, as "an imagined political community, ... imagined as both inherently limited and sovereign."[23] For not until the 1830s and 1840s, with the success of Jacksonian democracy and the development of the ideology of Manifest Destiny, did a sense of an imagined community of Americans begin to solidify, due to a number of factors: the consolidation of industrialization in the Northeast; the proliferation of large newspapers and state banks; and a transportation revolution that linked the urban centers with both agricultural producers and markets abroad.[24]

It is far more than coincidence that the birth of the modern idea of America coincided with what is often called the Second Great Awakening (the First had culminated in the Revolutionary War). During these years, as Klaus Hansen relates, "the old paternalistic reform impulse directed toward social control yielded to a romantic reform movement impelled by millennialism, immediatism, and individualism." This movement, in turn, "made possible the creation of the modern American capitalist empire with its fundamental belief in religious, political, and economic pluralism."[25] For those made uneasy (for a variety of reasons) by the new Jacksonian individualism, this pluralism authorized the emergence of alternative social and religious sects, both millennialist evangelical revivals and new communities like the Shakers, the Oneida Perfectionists, and, most prominently and successfully, the Mormons.[26] As Hansen emphasizes, "Mormonism was not merely one more variant of American Protestant pluralism but an articulate and sophisticated counterideology that attempted to establish a 'new heaven and a new earth....'" Moreover, "both in its origins and doctrines," Mormonism "insisted on the peculiarly American nature of its fundamental values" and on the identity of America as the promised land.[27]

Given the number and prominence of Mormon characters in the play, it should come as little surprise that Mormonism, at least as it was originally articulated in the 1820s and 1830s, maintains a very close relationship to the epistemology of *Angels in America*. Many of the explicitly hieratic qualities of the play—the notion of prophecy, the sacred book, as well as the Angel her/himself—owe as much to Mormonism as to Walter Benjamin. Even more important, the play's conceptualization of history, its millennialism, and its idea of America bring it startlingly close to the tenets of early Mormonism. Indeed, it is impossible to understand the concept of the nation with which *Angels* is obsessed (and even the idea of queering the nation!) without understanding the constitution of early Mormonism. Providing Calvinism with its most radical challenge during the National Period, it was deeply utopian in its thrust (and it remains so today). Indeed, its concept of time is identical to the temporality for which *Angels in America* polemicizes. Like *Angels*, Mormonism understands time as evolution and progress (in that sense, it is more closely linked to Enlightenment epistemologies than Romantic ones) and holds out the possibility of unlimited human growth: "As man is God once was: as God is man may become."[28] Part of a tremendous resurgence of interest in the millennium between 1828 and 1832, Mormonism went far beyond the ideology of progress implicit in Jacksonian democracy (just as *Angels*'s millennialism goes far beyond most contemporary ideologies of progress).[29] Understood historically, this utopianism was in part the result of the relatively marginal economic status of Joseph Smith and his followers, subsistence farmers and struggling petits bourgeois. Tending "to be 'agin the government,'" these early Mormons were a persecuted minority and, in their westward journey to Zion, became the subjects of widespread violence, beginning in 1832 when Smith was tarred and feathered in Ohio.[30] Much like twentieth-century lesbians and gay men—although most contemporary Mormons would be appalled by the comparison—Mormons were, throughout the 1830s and 1840s, attacked by mobs, arrested on false charges, imprisoned, and murdered. In 1838, the Governor of Missouri decreed that they must be "exterminated" or expelled from the state. In 1844, Smith and his brother were assassinated by an angry mob.[31]

The violent antipathy towards early Mormonism was in part the result of the fact that it presented a significant challenge to the principles of individualist social and economic organization. From the beginning, Mormonism was communitarian in nature and proposed a kind of ecclesiastical socialism in which "those entering the order were asked to 'consecrate' their property and belongings to the church...." To each male would then be returned enough to sustain him and his family, while the remainder would be apportioned to "'every man who has need....'" As Hansen emphasizes, this organization represents a repudiation of the principles of laissez-faire and an attempt "to restore a more traditional society in which the economy was regulated in behalf of the larger interests of the group...."[32] This nostalgia for an earlier period of capitalism (the agrarianism of the early colonies) is echoed by Mormonism's conceptualization of the continent as the promised land. Believing the Garden of Eden to have been sited in America and assigning all antediluvian history to the western hemisphere, early Mormonism believed that the term "'New World' was in fact a misnomer because America was really the cradle of man and civilization."[33] So the privileged character of the nation is linked to its sacred past and—as with Benjamin—history is tied to theology. At the same time, this essentially theological conceptualization of the nation bears witness to the "strong affinity," noted by Anderson, between "the nationalist imagining" and "religious imaginings."[34] As Timothy Brennan explains it, "nationalism largely extend[s] and modernize[s] (although [does] not replace) 'religious imaginings,' taking on religion's concern with death, continuity, and the desire for origins."[35] Like religion, the nation authorizes a reconfiguration of time and mortality, a "secular transformation of fatality into continuity, contingency into meaning."[36] Mormonism's spiritual geography was perfectly suited to this process, constructing America as both origin and meaning of history. Moreover, as Hans Kohn has pointed out, modern nationalism has expropriated three crucial concepts from those same Old Testament mythologies that provide the basis for Mormonism: "the idea of a chosen people, the emphasis on a common stock of memory of the past and of hopes for the future, and finally national messianism."[37]

This conceptualization of America as the site of a blessed past and a millennial future represents—simultaneously—the fulfillment of early nineteenth-century ideas of the nation and a repudiation of the ideologies of individualism and acquisitiveness that underwrite the Jacksonian marketplace. Yet, as Sacvan Bercovitch points out, this contradiction was at the heart of the nationalist project. As the economy was being transformed "from agrarian to industrial capitalism," the primary "source of dissent was an indigenous residual culture," which, like Mormonism, was "variously identified with agrarianism, libertarian thought, and the tradition of civic humanism." These ideologies, "by conserving the myths of a bygone age" and dreaming "of human wholeness and social regeneration," then produced "the notion of an ideal America with a politically transformative potential." Like the writers of the American Renaissance, Mormonism "adopted the culture's controlling metaphor—'America' as synonym for human possibility," and then turned it against the dominant class. Both producing and fulfilling the nationalist dream, it "portray[ed] the American ideology, as all ideology yearns to be portrayed, in the transcendent colors of utopia."[38] A form of dissent that ultimately (and contradictorily) reinforced hegemonic values, Mormonism reconceived America as the promised land, the land of an already achieved utopia, and simultaneously as the land of promise, the site of the millennium yet to come.

I recapitulate the early history of Mormonism because I believe it is crucial for understanding how *Angels in America* has been culturally positioned. It seems to me that the play replicates both the situation and project of early Mormonism with an uncanny accuracy and thereby documents the continued validity of both a particular regressive fantasy of

America and a particular understanding of oppositional cultural practices. Like the projects of Joseph Smith and his followers, *Angels* has, from the beginning, on the levels of authorial intention and reception, been constructed as an oppositional, and even "radical" work. Structurally and ideologically, the play challenges the conventions of American realism and the tenets of Reaganism. Indeed, it offers by far the most explicit and trenchant critique of neoconservativism to have been produced on Broadway. It also provides the most thoroughgoing—and unambivalent— deconstruction in memory of a binarism absolutely crucial to liberalism, the opposition between public and private. *Angels* demonstrates conclusively not only the constructedness of the difference between the political and the sexual, but also the murderous power of this distinction. Yet, at the same time, *not despite but because of these endeavors*, the play has been accommodated with stunning ease to the hegemonic ideology not just of the theatre-going public, but of the democratic majority—an ideology that has become the new American religion—liberal pluralism.[39]

The old-style American liberalisms, variously associated (reading from left to right) with trade unionism, reformism, and competitive individualism, tend to value freedom above all other qualities (the root word for liberalism is, after all, the Latin *liber*, meaning "free"). Taking the "free" individual subject as the fundamental social unit, liberalism has long been associated with the principle of laissez-faire and the "free" market, and is reformist rather than revolutionary in its politics. At the same time, however, because liberalism, particularly in its American versions, has always paid at least lip service to equality, certain irreducible contradictions have been bred in what did, after all, emerge during the seventeenth century as the ideological complement to (and justification for) mercantile capitalism. Historically, American liberalism has permitted dissent and fostered tolerance—within certain limits—and guaranteed that all men in principle are created equal (women were long excluded from the compact, as well as African American slaves). In fact, given the structure of American capitalism, the incommensurability of its commitment both to freedom and equality has proven a disabling contradiction, one that liberalism has tried continually, and with little success, to negotiate. Like the bourgeois subject that is its production and raison d'être, liberalism is hopelessly schizoid.

The new liberalism that has been consolidated in the United States since the decline of the New Left in the mid-1970s (but whose antecedents date back to the first stirrings of the nation) marks the adaptation of traditional liberalism to a post–welfare state economy. Pursuing a policy of regressive taxation, its major constituent is the corporate sector—all others it labels "special interest groups" (despite certain superficial changes, there is no fundamental difference between the economic and foreign policies of Reagan/Bush and Clinton). In spite of its corporatism, however, and its efficiency in redistributing the wealth upward, liberalism speaks the language of tolerance. Unable to support substantive changes in economic policy that might in fact produce a more equitable and less segregated society, it instead promotes a rhetoric of pluralism and moderation. Reformist in method, it endeavors to fine tune the status quo while at the same time acknowledging (and even celebrating) the diversity of American culture. For the liberal pluralist, America is less a melting pot than a smorgasbord. He or she takes pride in the ability to *consume* cultural difference—now understood as a commodity, a source of boundless pleasure, an expression of an exoticized Other. And yet, for him or her, access to and participation in so-called minority cultures is entirely consumerist. Like the new, passive racist characterized by Hazel Carby, the liberal pluralist uses "texts"—whether literary, musical, theatrical or cinematic—as "a way of gaining knowledge of the 'other,' a knowledge that appears to replace the desire to challenge existing frameworks of segregation."[40]

Liberal pluralism thus does far more than tolerate dissent. It actively enlists its aid in reaffirming a fundamentally conservative hegemony. In doing so, it reconsolidates a fantasy of America that dates back to the early nineteenth century. Liberal pluralism demonstrates the dogged persistence of a *consensus politic that masquerades as dissensus*. It proves once again, in Bercovitch's words, that

> [t]he American way is to turn potential conflict into a quarrel about fusion or fragmentation. It is a fixed match, a debate with a foregone conclusion: you must have your fusion and feed on fragmentation too. And the formula for doing so has become virtually a cultural reflex: you just alternate between harmony-in-diversity and diversity-in-harmony. It amounts to a hermeneutics of laissez-faire: all problems are obviated by the continual flow of the one into the many, and the many into the one.[41]

According to Bercovitch, a kind of dissensus (of which liberal pluralism is the contemporary avatar) has been the hallmark of the very idea of America— and American literature from the very beginning. In this most American of ideologies, an almost incomparably wide range of opinions, beliefs, and cultural positions are finally absorbed into a fantasy of a utopian nation in which anything and everything is possible, in which the millennium is simultaneously at hand and indefinitely deferred. Moreover, the nation is imagined as the geographical representation of that utopia which is both everywhere and nowhere. For as Lauren Berlant explains, "the contradiction between the 'nowhere' of utopia and the 'everywhere' of the nation [is] dissolved by the American recasting of the 'political' into the terms of providential ideality, 'one nation under God.'"[42] Under the sign of the "one," all contradictions are subsumed, all races and religions united, all politics theologized.

DISSENSUS AND THE FIELD OF CULTURAL PRODUCTION

It is my contention that *Angels*'s mobilization of a consensual politic (masquerading as dissensual) is precisely the source not only of the play's ambivalence, but also of its ability to be instantly recognized as part of the canon of American literature. Regardless of Kushner's intentions, *Angels* sets forth a project wherein the theological is constructed as a transcendent category into which politics and history finally disappear. For all its commitment to a historical materialist method, for all its attention to political struggle and the dynamics of oppression, *Angels* finally sets forth a liberal pluralist vision of America in which all, not in spite but because of their diversity, will be welcomed into the new Jerusalem (to this extent, it differs sharply from the more exclusionist character of early Mormonism and other, more recent millennialisms). Like other apocalyptic discourses, from Joseph Smith to Jerry Falwell, the millennialism of *Angels* reassures an "audience that knows it has lost control over events" not by enabling it to "regain ... control," but by letting it know "that history *is* nevertheless controlled by an underlying order and that it has a purpose that is nearing fulfillment." It thereby demonstrates that "*personal* pain," whether Prior's, or that of the reader or spectator, "is subsumed within the pattern of history."[43] Like Joseph Smith, Tony Kushner has resuscitated a vision of America as both promised land and land of infinite promise. Simultaneously, he has inspired virtually every theatre critic in the U.S. to a host of salvational fantasies about theatre, art, and politics. And he has done all this at a crucial juncture in history, at the end of the Cold War, as the geopolitical order of forty-five years has collapsed.

Despite the success of the 1991 Gulf War in signaling international "terrorism" as the successor to the Soviet empire and justification for the expansion of the national security state, the idea of the nation remains, I believe, in crisis (it seems to me that "terrorism," being less of a threat to individualism than communism, does not harness paranoia quite as effectively as the idea of an evil empire). If nothing else, *Angels in America* attests both to the continuing anxiety over national definition and mission and to the importance of an ideological means of assuaging that anxiety. In *Angels*, a series of political dialectics (which are, yet again, false dialectics) remains the primary means for producing this ideological fix, for producing dissensus, a sense of alternation between "harmony-in-diversity and diversity-in-harmony." The play is filled with political disputation—all of it between men since women, unless in drag, are excluded from the political realm. Most is centered around Louis, the unmistakably ambivalent, ironic Jew, who invariably sets the level of discussion and determines the tenor of the argument. If with Belize he takes a comparatively rightist (and racist) stance, with Joe he takes an explicitly leftist (and antihomophobic) one. And while the play unquestionably problematizes his several positions, he ends up, with all his contradictions, becoming by default the spokesperson for liberal pluralism, with all *its* contradictions. Belize, intriguingly, functions unlike the white gay men as an ideological point of reference, a kind of "moral bellwether," in the words of one critic.[44] Because his is the one point of view that is never submitted to a critique, he becomes, as David Román points out, "the political and ethical center of the plays." The purveyor of truth, "he carries the burden of race" and so seems to issue from what is unmistakably a "white imaginary" ("[t]his fetishization," Román notes, "of lesbian and gay people of color as a type of political catalyst is ubiquitous among the left").[45] He is also cast in the role of caretaker, a position long reserved for African Americans in "the white imaginary." Even Belize's name commemorates not the Name of the Father, but his status as a "*former drag queen*" (1:3), giving him an identity that is both performative and exoticized. He is the play's guarantee of diversity.

The pivotal scene for the enunciation of Louis's politics, meanwhile, is his long discussion with Belize in *Millennium* which begins with his question, "Why has democracy succeeded in America?" (1:89), a question whose assumption is belied by the unparalleled political and economic power of American corporatism to buy elections and from which Louis, as is his wont, almost immediately backs down. (His rhetorical strategy throughout this scene is to stake out a position from which he immediately draws a guilty retreat, thereby making Belize look like the aggressor.) Invoking "radical democracy" and "freedom" in one breath, and crying "[f]uck assimilation" (1:89–90) in the next, he careens wildly between a liberal discourse of rights and a rhetoric of identity politics. Alternating between universalizing and minoritizing concepts of the subject, he manages at once to dismiss a politics of race (and insult Belize) and to assert its irreducibility. Yet the gist of Louis's argument (if constant vacillation could be said to have a gist) is his disquisition about the nation:

> this reaching out for a spiritual past in a country where no indigenous spirits exist—only the Indians, I mean Native American spirits and we killed them off so now, there are no gods here, no ghosts and spirits in America, there are no angels in America, no spiritual past, no racial past, there's only the political. [1:92]

For Louis, America hardly exists as a community (whether real or imagined). Rather, for this confused liberal, America is defined entirely by its relationship to the "political." With characteristic irony, Kushner chooses to present this crucial idea (which does, after all, echo the play's title) in the negative, in the form of a statement which the rest of the play aggressively refutes. For if nothing else, *Angels in America*—like *The Book of Mormon*—demonstrates that there are angels in America, that America is in essence a utopian and theological construction, a nation with a divine mission. Politics is by no means banished insofar as it provides a crucial way in which the nation is imagined. But it is subordinated to utopian fantasies of harmony in diversity, of one nation under a derelict God.

Moreover, this scene between Louis and Belize reproduces millennialism in miniature, in its very structure, in the pattern whereby the political is finally subsumed by utopian fantasies. After the spirited argument between Louis and Belize (if one can call a discussion in which one person refuses to stake out a coherent position an argument), their conflict is suddenly overrun by an outbreak of lyricism, by the intrusion, after so much talk about culture, of what passes for the natural world:

> BELIZE: All day today it's felt like Thanksgiving. Soon, this
>   ... ruination will be blanketed white. You can smell
>   it—can you smell it?
> LOUIS: Smell what?
> BELIZE: Softness, compliance, forgiveness, grace.
>
> [1:100]

Argumentation gives way not to a resolution (nothing has been settled) but to the ostensible forces of nature: snow and smell. According to Belize, snow (an insignia of coldness and purity in the play) is linked to "[s]oftness, compliance, forgiveness, grace," in short, to the theological virtues. Like the ending of *Perestroika*, in which another dispute between Louis and Belize fades out behind Prior's benediction, this scene enacts a movement of transcendence whereby the political is not so much resolved as left trailing in the dust. In the American way, contradiction is less disentangled than immobilized. History gives way to a concept of cosmic evolution that is far closer to Joseph Smith than to Walter Benjamin.

In the person of Louis (who is, after all, constructed as the most empathic character in the play), with his unshakable faith in liberalism and the possibility of "radical democracy," *Angels in America* assures the (liberal) theatre-going public that a kind of liberal pluralism remains the best hope for change.[46] Revolution, in the Marxist sense, is rendered virtually unthinkable, oxymoronic. Amidst all the political disputation, there is no talk of social class. Oppression is understood not in relation to economics but to differences of race, gender and sexual orientation. In short: *an identity politic comes to substitute for Marxist analysis*. There is no clear sense that the political and social problems with which the characters wrestle might be connected to a particular economic system (comrade Prelapsarianov is, after all, a comic figure). And despite Kushner's avowed commitment to socialism, an alternative to capitalism, except in the form of an indefinitely deferred utopia, it remains absent from the play's dialectic.[47] Revolution, even in Benjamin's sense of the term, is evacuated of its political content, functioning less as a Marxist hermeneutic tool than a *trope*, a figure of speech (the oxymoron) that marks the place later to be occupied by a (liberal pluralist?) utopia. *Angels* thus falls into line behind the utopianisms of Joseph Smith and the American Renaissance and becomes less a subversion of hegemonic culture than its reaffirmation. As Berlant observes, "the temporal and spatial ambiguity of 'utopia' has the effect of obscuring the implications of political activity and power relations in American civil life."[48] Like "our classic texts" (as characterized by Bercovitch), *Angels* has a way of conceptualizing utopia so that it may be adopted by "the dominant culture ... for its purposes." "So molded, ritualized, and controlled," Bercovitch notes (and, I would like to add, stripped of its impulse for radical economic change), "utopianism has served ... to diffuse or deflect dissent, or actually to transmute it into a vehicle of socialization."[49]

The ambivalences that are so deeply inscribed in *Angels in America*, its conflicted relationship to various utopianisms, to the concept of America, to Marxism, Mormonism, and liberalism, function, I believe, to accommodate the play to what I see as a fundamentally conservative and paradigmatically American politic—dissensus, the "hermeneutics of laissez-faire." Yet it seems to me that the play's ambivalence (its way of being, in Eve Sedgwick's memorable phrase, "kinda subversive, kinda hegemonic"[50]) is finally, less a question of authorial intention than of the peculiar cultural and economic position of this play (and its writer) in relation to the theatre, theatre artists, and the theatre-going public in the United States. On the one hand, the Broadway and regional theatres remain in a uniquely marginal position in comparison with Hollywood. The subscribers to regional theatres continue to dwindle while more than half of Theatre Communications Group's sample theatres in their annual survey "played to smaller audiences in 1993 than they did five years ago." Moreover, in a move that bodes particularly ill for the future of new plays, "workshops, staged readings and other developmental activities decreased drastically over the five years studied."[51] On the other hand, serious Broadway drama does not have the same cultural capital as other forms of literature. Enmortgaged to a slew of others who must realize the playwright's text, it has long been regarded as a bastard art. Meanwhile, the relatively small public that today attends professional theatre in America is overwhelmingly middle-class and overwhelmingly liberal in its attitudes. Indeed, theatre audiences are in large part distinguished from the audiences for film and television on account of their tolerance for works that are more challenging both formally and thematically than the vast majority of major studio releases or prime-time miniseries.

Because of its marginal position, both economically and culturally, theatre is a privileged portion of what Pierre Bourdieu designates as the literary and artistic field. As he explains, this field is contained within a larger field of economic and political power, while, at the same time, "possessing a relative autonomy with respect to it...." It is this *relative autonomy* that gives the literary and artistic field—and theatre in particular—both its high level of symbolic forms of capital and its low level of economic capital. In other words, despite its artistic cachet, it "occupies a *dominated position*" with respect to the field of economic and political power as whole.[52] And the individual cultural producer (or theatre artist), insofar as he or she is a part of the bourgeoisie, represents a "dominated fraction of the dominant class."[53] The cultural producer is thus placed in an irreducibly contradictory position—and this has become particularly clear since the decline of patronage in the eighteenth century and the increasing dependence of the artist on the vicissitudes of the marketplace. On the one hand, he or she is licensed to challenge hegemonic values insofar as it is a particularly effective way of accruing cultural capital. On the other hand, the more effective his or her challenge, the less economic capital he or she is likely to amass. Because of theatre's marginality in American culture, it seems to be held hostage to this double bind in a particularly unnerving way: the very disposition of the field guarantees that Broadway and regional theatres (unlike mass culture) are constantly in the process of having to negotiate this impossible position.

What is perhaps most remarkable about *Angels in America* is that it has managed, against all odds, to amass significant levels of both cultural and economic capital. And while it by no means resolves the contradictions that are constitutive of theatre's cultural positioning, its production history has become a measure of the seemingly impossible juncture of these two forms of success. Just as the play's structure copes with argumentation by transcending it, so does the play as cultural phenomenon seemingly transcend the opposition between economic and cultural capital, between the hegemonic and the counterhegemonic. Moreover, it does so, I am arguing, by its skill in both reactivating a sense (derived from the early nineteenth century) of America as the utopian nation and mobilizing the principle of ambivalence—or more exactly, dissensus—to produce a vision of a once and future pluralist culture. And although the text's contradictory positioning is to a large extent defined by the marginal cultural position of Broadway, it is also related specifically to Tony Kushner's own class position. Like Joseph Smith, Kushner represents a dominated—and dissident—fraction of the dominant class. As a white gay man, he is able to amass considerable economic and cultural capital despite the fact that the class of which he is a part remains relatively disempowered politically (according to a 1993 survey, the average household income for gay men is 40% higher than that of the average American household).[54] As an avowed leftist and intellectual, he is committed (as *Angels* demonstrates) to mounting a critique of hegemonic ideology. Yet as a member of the bourgeoisie and as the recipient of two Tony awards, he is also committed—if only unconsciously—to the continuation of the system that has granted him no small measure of success.

A QUEER SORT OF NATION

Although I am tempted to see the celebrity of *Angels in America* as yet another measure of the power of liberal pluralism to neutralize oppositional practices, the play's success also suggests a willingness to recognize the contributions of gay men to American culture and to American literature, in particular. For as Eve Sedgwick and others have argued, both the American canon and the very principle of canonicity are centrally concerned with questions of male (homo)sexual definition and desire.[55] Thus, the issues of homoeroticism, of the anxiety generated by the instability of the homosocial/homosexual boundary, of coding, of secrecy and disclosure, and of the problems around securing a sexual identity, remain pivotal for so many of the writers who hold pride of place in the American canon, from Thoreau, Melville, Whitman, and James to Hart Crane, Tennessee Williams, and James Baldwin—in that sense, the American canon is always already queered. At the same time, however, unlike so much of the canon, and in particular, the canon of American drama, *Angels in America* foregrounds explicitly gay men. No more need the reader eager to queer the text read subversively between the lines, or transpose genders, as is so often done to the work of Williams, Inge, Albee, and others. Since the 1988 controversies over NEA funding for exhibitions of Mapplethorpe and Serrano and the subsequent attempt by the Endowment to revoke grants to the so-called NEA four (three of whom are queer), theatre, as a liberal form, has been distinguished from mass culture in large part by virtue of its queer content. In the 1990s, a play without a same-sex kiss may be entertainment, but it can hardly be considered a work of art. It appears that the representation of (usually male) homosexual desire has become the privileged emblem of that endangered species, the serious Broadway drama. But I wonder finally how subversive this queering of Broadway is when women, in this play at least, remain firmly in the background. What is one to make of the remarkable ease with which *Angels in America* has been accommodated to that lineage of American drama (and literature) that focuses on masculine experience and agency and produces women as the premise for history, as the ground on which it is constructed? Are not women sacrificed—yet again—to the male citizenry of a (queer) nation?

If Kushner, following Benjamin's prompting (and echoing his masculinism), attempts to "brush history against the grain" (257), he does so by demonstrating the crucial importance of (closeted) gay men in twentieth-century American politics—including, most prominently, Roy Cohn and two of his surrogate fathers, J. Edgar Hoover and Joseph McCarthy. By so highlighting the (homo)eroticization of patriarchy, the play demonstrates the always already queer status of American politics, and most provocatively, of those generals of the Cold War (and American imperialism) who were most assiduous in their denunciation of political and sexual dissidence. Moreover, unlike the work of most of Kushner's predecessors on the American stage, *Angels* does not pathologize gay men. Or more exactly, gay men as a class are not pathologized. Rather, they are revealed to be pathologized circumstantially: first, by their construction (through a singularly horrific stroke of ill luck) as one of the "risk groups" for HIV; and second, by the fact that some remain closeted and repressed (Joe's ulcer is unmistakably the price of disavowal). So, it turns out, it is not homosexuality that is pathological, but its *denial*. Flagrantly uncloseted, the play provides a devastating critique of the closeted gay man in two medicalized bodies: Roy Cohn and Joe Pitt.

If *Angels in America* queers historical materialism (at least as Benjamin understands it), it does so by exposing the process by which the political (which ostensibly drives history) intersects with the personal and sexual (which ostensibly are no more than footnotes to history). Reagan's presidency and the neoconservative hegemony of the 1980s provide not just the background to the play's exploration of ostensibly personal (i.e., sexual, marital, medical) problems, but the very ground on which desire is produced. For despite the trenchancy of its critique of neoconservativism, *Angels* also demonstrates the peculiar sexiness of Reagan's vision of America. Through Louis, it demonstrates the allure of a particular brand of machismo embodied by Joe Pitt: "The more appalling I find your politics the more I want to hump you" (2:36). And if the Angel is indeed "a cosmic reactionary" (2:55), it is in part because her/his position represents an analogue to the same utopian promises and hopes that Reagan so brilliantly and deceptively exploited. Moreover, in this history play, questions of male homosexual identity and desire are carefully juxtaposed against questions of equal protection for lesbians and gay men and debates about their military service. Louis attacks Joe for his participation in "an important bit of legal fag-bashing," a case that upholds the U.S. government's policy that it's not "unconstitutional to discriminate against homosexuals" (2:110). And while the case that Louis cites may be fictional, the continuing refusal of the courts in the wake of *Bowers v. Hardwick* to consider lesbians and gay men a suspect class, and thus eligible for protection under the provisions of the Fourteenth Amendment, is anything but.[56] Unilaterally constructing gay men as a suspect class (with sexual identity substituting for economic positionality), *Angels* realizes Benjamin's suggestion that it is not "man or men but the struggling, oppressed class itself [that] is the depository of historical knowledge" (260). More decisively than any other recent cultural text, *Angels* queers the America of Joseph Smith—and Ronald Reagan—by placing this oppressed class at the very center of American history, by showing it to be not just the depository of a special kind of knowledge, but by recognizing the central role that it has had in the construction of a national subject, polity, literature, and theatre. On this issue, the play is not ambivalent at all.

NOTES

1. Joseph Roach has suggested to me that the closest analogue to *Angels* on the

American stage is, in fact, *Uncle Tom's Cabin*, with its tremendous popularity before the Civil War, its epic length, and its skill in addressing the most controversial issues of the time in deeply equivocal ways.

2. John Lahr, "The Theatre: Earth Angels," *The New Yorker*, 13 December 1993, 133.

3. Jack Kroll, "Heaven and Earth on Broadway," *Newsweek*, 6 December 1993, 83; Robert Brustein, "Robert Brustein on Theatre: *Angels in America*," *The New Republic*, 24 May 1993, 29.

4. John E. Harris, "Miracle on 48th Street," *Christopher Street*, March 1994, 6.

5. Frank Rich, "Critic's Notebook: The Reaganite Ethos, With Roy Cohn As a Dark Metaphor," *New York Times*, 5 March 1992, C15.

6. John Clum, *Acting Gay: Male Homosexuality in Modern Drama* (New York: Columbia University Press, 1994), 324.

7. Tony Kushner, *Angels in America: A Gay Fantasia on National Themes. Part One: Millennium Approaches* (New York: Theatre Communications Group, 1993), 95. All further references will be noted in the text.

8. Frank Rich, "Following an Angel For a Healing Vision of Heaven and Earth," *New York Times*, 24 November 1993, C11.

9. Clum, 314.

10. Tony Kushner, *Angels in America: A Gay Fantasia on National Themes. Part Two: Perestroika* (New York: Theatre Communications Group, 1994), 56. All further references will be noted in the text.

11. See, for example, Andrea Stevens, "Finding a Devil Within to Portray Roy Cohn," *New York Times*, 18 April 1993, section 2, 1–28.

12. Terry Eagleton, *Walter Benjamin, or Towards a Revolutionary Criticism* (London: Verso, 1981), 177.

13. Walter Benjamin, "Theses on the Philosophy of History," in *Illuminations*, ed. Hannah Arendt, trans. Harry Zohn (New York: Schocken Books, 1969), 253. All further references will be noted in the text.

14. Tony Kushner explains: "I've written about my friend Kimberly [Flynn] who is a profound influence on me. And she and I were talking about this utopian thing that we share—she's the person who introduced me to that side of Walter Benjamin.... She said jokingly that at times she felt such an extraordinary kinship with him that she thought she was Walter Benjamin reincarnated. And so at one point in the conversation, when I was coming up with names for my characters, I said, 'I had to look up something in Benjamin—not you, but the prior Walter.' That's where the name came from. I had been looking for one of those WASP names that nobody gets called anymore." David Savran, "The Theatre of the Fabulous: An Interview with Tony Kushner," in *Speaking on Stage: Interviews with Contemporary American Playwrights*, ed. Philip C. Kolin and Colby H. Kullman (Tuscaloosa: University of Alabama Press), forthcoming.

15. Lacan, "The Signification of the Phallus," in *Ecrits: A Selection*, trans. Alan Sheridan (New York: Norton, 1977), 286.

16. Elizabeth A. Grosz, *Jacques Lacan: A Feminist Introduction* (London: Routledge, 1990), 74, 67.

17. Benjamin maintained a far less condemnatory attitude toward the increasing technologization of culture than many other Western Marxists. In "The Work of Art in the Age of Mechanical Reproduction," for example, he writes of his qualified approval of

the destruction of the aura associated with modern technologies. He explains that because "mechanical reproduction emancipates the work of art from its parasitical dependence on ritual, ... the total function of art" can "be based on another practice—politics," which for him is clearly preferable. Benjamin, "The Work of Art in the Age of Mechanical Reproduction," *Illuminations*, 224.

18. Although one could cite a myriad of sources, this quotation is extracted from Milton Friedman, "Once Again: Why Socialism Won't Work," *New York Times*, 13 August 1994, 21.

19. Krishan Kumar, "The End of Socialism? The End of Utopia? The End of History?," in *Utopias and the Millennium*, ed. Krishan Kumar and Stephen Bann (London: Reaktion Books, 1993), 61; Francis Fukuyama, *The End of History and the Last Man*, quoted in Kumar, 78.

20. Friedman, 21.

21. Aijaz Ahmad, *In Theory: Classes, Nations, Literatures* (London: Verso, 1992), 69. Ahmad is summarizing this position as part of his critique of poststructuralism.

22. David Richards, "'Angels' Finds a Poignant Note of Hope," *New York Times*, 28 November 1993, II, 1.

23. Benedict Anderson, *Imagined Communities: Reflections on the Origin and Spread of Nationalism* (London: Verso, 1991), 6.

24. See Lawrence Kohl, *The Politics of Individualism: Parties and the American Character in the Jacksonian Era* (New York: Oxford University Press, 1989).

25. Klaus J. Hansen, *Mormonism and the American Experience* (Chicago: University of Chicago Press, 1981), 49–50.

26. See Ernest R. Sandeen, *The Roots of Fundamentalism: British and American Millenarianism 1800–1930* (Chicago: University of Chicago Press, 1970), 42–58.

27. Hansen, 52.

28. Joseph Smith, quoted in Hansen, 72.

29. See Richard L. Bushman, *Joseph Smith and the Beginnings of Mormonism* (Urbana: University of Illinois Press, 1984), 170.

30. Hansen, 119.

31. For a catalogue of this violence, see Jan Shipps, *Mormonism: The Story of a New Religious Tradition* (Urbana: University of Illinois Press, 1985), 155–61.

32. Hansen, 124–26.

33. Hansen, 27, 66.

34. Anderson, 10–11.

35. Timothy Brennan, "The National Longing for Form," in *Nation and Narration*, ed. Homi K. Bhabha (London: Routledge, 1990), 50.

36. Anderson, 10–11.

37. Hans Kohn, *Nationalism: Its Meaning and History* (Princeton: Van Nostrand, 1965), 11.

38. Sacvan Bercovitch, "The Problem of Ideology in American Literary History," *Critical Inquiry* 12 (1986): 642–43; 645.

39. Despite the 1994 Republican House and Senate victories (in which the Republicans received the vote of only 20% of the electorate) and the grandstanding of Newt Gingrich, the country remains far less conservative on many social issues than the Republicans would like Americans to believe. See Thomas Ferguson, "G.O.P. $$$ Talked; Did Voters Listen?," *The Nation*, 26 December 1994, 792–98.

40. Hazel Carby, "The Multicultural Wan," in *Black Popular Culture, a project by Michele Wallace*, ed. Gina Dent (Seattle: Bay Press, 1992), 197.

41. Bercovitch, 649.

42. Lauren Berlant, *The Anatomy of National Fantasy: Hawthorne, Utopia, and Everyday Life* (Chicago: University of Chicago Press, 1991), 31.

43. Barry Brummett, *Contemporary Apocalyptic Rhetoric* (New York: Praeger, 1991), 37–38.

44. Lahr, "The Theatre: Earth Angels," 132.

45. David Román, "November 1, 1992: AIDS/*Angels in America*," from *Acts of Intervention: Gay Men, U.S. Performance, AIDS* (Bloomington: Indiana University Press, forthcoming).

46. This is corroborated by Kushner's own statements: "The strain in the American character that I feel the most affection for and that I feel has the most potential for growth is American liberalism, which is incredibly short of what it needs to be and incredibly limited and exclusionary and predicated on all sorts of racist, sexist, homophobic and classist prerogatives. And yet, as Louis asks, why has democracy succeeded in America? And why does it have this potential, as I believe it does? I really believe that there is the potential for radical democracy in this country, one of the few places on earth where I see it as a strong possibility. It doesn't seem to be happening in Russia. There is a tradition of liberalism, of a kind of social justice, fair play and tolerance—and each of these things is problematic and can certainly be played upon in the most horrid ways. Reagan kept the most hair-raising anarchist aspects of his agenda hidden and presented himself as a good old-fashioned liberal who kept invoking FDR. It may just be sentimentalism on my part because I am the child of liberal-pinko parents, but I do believe in it—as much as I often find it despicable. It's sort of like the Democratic National Convention every four years: it's horrendous and you can feel it sucking all the energy from progressive movements in this country, with everybody pinning their hopes on this sleazy bunch of guys. But you do have Jesse Jackson getting up and calling the Virgin Mary a single mother, and on an emotional level, and I hope also on a more practical level, I do believe that these are the people in whom to have hope." Savran, 24–25.

47. See Tony Kushner, "A Socialism of the Skin," *The Nation*, 4 July 1994, 9–14.

48. Berlant, 32.

49. Bercovitch, 644.

50. Sedgwick used this phrase during the question period that followed a lecture at Brown University, 1 October 1992.

51. Barbara Janowitz, "Theatre Facts 93," insert in *American Theatre*, April 1994, 4–5.

52. Pierre Bourdieu, "The Field of Cultural Production, or: The Economic World Reversed," in Bourdieu, *The Field of Cultural Production: Essays on Art and Literature*, ed. Randal Johnson (New York: Columbia University Press, 1993), 37–38.

53. Randal Johnson, Ed. Introd., Bourdieu, 15.

54. *Gay & Lesbian Stats: A Pocket Guide of Facts and Figures*, ed. Bennett L. Singer and David Deschamps (New York: The New Press, 1994), 32.

55. See Eve Kosofsky Sedgwick, *Epistemology of the Closet* (Berkeley: University of California Press, 1990), 48–59.

56. It is not the subjects who comprise a bona fide suspect class (like African Americans) that are suspect, but rather the forces of oppression that produce the class. For an analysis of the legal issues around equal protection, see Janet Halley, "The Politics of

the Closet: Towards Equal Protection for Gay, Lesbian, and Bisexual Identity," *UCLA Law Review* (June 1989): 915–76.

CHARLES McNULTY

Angels in America:
Tony Kushner's Theses on the Philosophy of History

AIDS plays have come to be thought of as a phenomenon of the 1980s, as Happenings were of the 1960s. Though the epidemic still rages, the bravely furious genre that began with William Hoffman's *As Is* and Larry Kramer's *The Normal Heart* has for the most part receded into the paragraphs of theater history textbooks. Nicholas de Jongh identifies the central mission of these plays as the fight against "an orthodoxy that regards AIDS as a mere local difficulty, principally affecting a reviled minority."[1] It is not entirely surprising, then, that the category has been said to have drawn to a close. The disease, after all, has been acknowledged, albeit belatedly, to be a widespread calamity; only the morally deaf, dumb, and blind have resisted this assessment, and they most certainly remain beyond the pale of agitprop, no matter how artfully conceived. To make things official, an obituary of the genre appeared in *American Theatre* in October of 1989:

> Recently, AIDS has fallen off as a central subject for new drama. It's no wonder. When, for instance, spectacle and public ritual are so movingly combined in the image and action of the Names Project Quilt, conventional theater seems redundant—at best a pale imitation of the formal, mass expressions that help give shape to real grief and anger. Time and again the spirited

From *Modern Drama* 39, no. 1 (Spring 1996). © 1996 by the University of Toronto.

protestors of ACT UP have demonstrated that the theater of AIDS is in the streets.[2]

The cult of Tony Kushner's *Angels in America*, by far the most celebrated play of the 1990s, would appear, however, to have rendered all this premature. Subtitled *A Gay Fantasia on National Themes*, Kushner's two-part epic features a deserted gay man with full-blown AIDS battling both heaven and earth. But *Angels* represents not so much a revival of the category as a radical rethinking of its boundaries. For the playwright, the question is no longer what is the place of AIDS in history, but what of history itself can be learned through the experience of gay men and AIDS.

Kushner's angels were inspired not from any Biblical ecstasy but from the great twentieth-century German-Jewish critic Walter Benjamin's "Theses on the Philosophy of History."[3] Benjamin, writing in the spring of 1940 in France only a few months before he was to kill himself trying to escape the German occupation, borrows Paul Klee's 1920 painting *Angelus Novus* to convey his rigorously anti-Hegelian understanding of the movement of history:

> This is how one pictures the angel of history. His face is turned toward the past. Where we perceive a chain of events, he sees one single catastrophe which keeps piling wreckage upon wreckage and hurls it in front of his feet. The angel would like to stay, awaken the dead, and make whole what has been smashed. But a storm is blowing from Paradise; it has got caught in his wings with such violence that the angel can no longer close them. This storm irresistibly propels him into the future to which his back is turned, while the pile of debris before him grows skyward. This storm is what we call progress.[4]

The movement of history is conceived not in terms of a dialectical narrative intent on progress, but as a steadfast path of destruction. All, however, is not lost. For Benjamin, the present represents a crisis point in which there is the opportunity to take cognizance of the homogeneous course of history, and thereby shift a specific era out of it.[5] For Kushner, a gay activist and dramatist enthralled by Benjamin's brooding analysis of history, the present crisis couldn't be more clear. Surveying five years of the first decade of the AIDS epidemic, the playwright casts a backward glance on America's domestic strife, and with it something unexpected flickers into view—the revolutionary chance to blast open the oppressive continuum of history and steer clear into the next millennium.

To realize this Benjamin-inspired vision, Kushner follows the lives of two couples and one political racketeer from the annals of the American closet—all in the throes of traumatic change. Louis, unable to deal with the fact his lover Prior has AIDS, abandons him; Joe, an ambitious Mormon lawyer, wants to abandon the homosexual part of himself, but ends, instead, abandoning his valium-popping wife Harper, and last, but not least, Roy Cohn, sick with AIDS, abandons nothing because he holds onto nothing. In an age in which shirkers of responsibility are encouraged to unite, Louis, the obstructed New York Jewish intellectual, and Joe, the shellacked all-American Mormon protégé of Cohn, spend a month together in bed, while their partners are forced to find ways of coping alone. "Children of the new morning, criminal minds. Selfish and greedy and loveless and blind. Reagan's children," is how Louis characterizes Joe and himself, in this most troubling trouble-free time. "You're scared. So am I. Everybody is in the land of the free. God help us all,"[6] he says to Joe, sincerely, though at the same time still groping for a way to move beyond guilt and self-consciousness into the intoxicating pleasures of sexual betrayal.

Kushner provides a quintessential American framework for the current historical dilemma in the play's opening scene, which features Rabbi Isidor Chemelwitz's eulogy for Louis's grandmother. Not knowing the departed too well, the Rabbi speaks of her as "not a person but a whole kind of person, the ones who crossed the ocean, who brought with us to America the villages of Russia and Lithuania—and how we struggled, and how we fought, for the family, for the Jewish home, so that you would not grow up here, in this strange place, in the melting pot where nothing melted" (1:10). Referring to the mourners as descendants, Rabbi Chemelwitz admits that great voyages from the old worlds are no longer possible, "[b]ut every day of your lives the miles that voyage between that place and this one you cross. Every day. You understand me? In you that journey is. [...] She was the last of the Mohicans, this one was. Pretty soon ... all the old will be dead" (1:10–11). For Kushner, the past's intersection with the present is inevitable, a fact of living; what disturbs him is the increasing failure of Americans to recognize this, the willful amnesia that threatens to blank out the nation's memory as it moves into the next millennium.

This fugitive wish to escape the clutches of the past is concentrated most intensely in Louis, who is faced with the heavy burden of having to care for his sick]over. An underemployed, hyper-rationalizing word processing clerk in the court system, he is unable to come to terms with his current life crisis. In a conversation with his Rabbi, he tries to explain why a person might be justified in abandoning a loved one at a time of great need:

Maybe because this person's sense of the world, that it will change for the better with struggle, maybe a person who has this neo-Hegelian positivist sense of constant historical progress towards happiness or perfection or something, who feels very powerful because he feels connected to these forces, moving uphill all the time ... maybe that person can't, um, incorporate sickness into his sense of how things are supposed to go. Maybe vomit ... and sores and disease ... really frighten him, maybe ... he isn't so good with death. (1:25)

Louis is determined to "maybe" himself out of his unfortunate present reality—and he's not beyond invoking the heaviest of nineteenth-century intellectual heavyweights to help him out. This peculiar trait is only magnified after he eventually leaves Prior for Joe. One of the more incendiary moments occurs at a coffee shop with Prior's ex-lover and closest friend, Belize. Wishing to ask about Prior's condition, Louis launches instead into a de Tocqueville-esque diatribe. "[T]here are no gods here, no ghosts and spirits in America, there are no angels in America, no spiritual past, no racial past, there's only the political, and the decoys and the ploys to maneuver around the inescapable battle of politics" (1:92), he explains breathlessly over coffee to Belize, who appears unimpressed by all the academic fireworks. In fact, Belize makes clear that he can see right through Louis's highbrow subterfuge. "[A]re you deliberately transforming yourself into an arrogant, sexual-political Stalinist-slash-racist flag-waving thug for my benefit" (1:94), he asks, knowing all too well from his experience as a gay African American drag queen that history is not simply some dry-as-dust abstraction, but an approximation of the way individuals lead both their public and private lives.

Though Kushner is critical of Louis, he in no way diminishes the gravity of what this character is forced to deal with. Louis has, after all, good reason for wanting to flee. When he confronts his lover on the floor of their bedroom, burning with fever and excreting blood, the full horror of this disease is conveyed in all its mercilessness and squalor. "Oh help. Oh help. Oh God oh God oh God help me I can't I can't I can't" (1:48), he says to himself, mantra-like, over his fainted lover—and who could be so heartless to argue with him? Louis's moral dilemma is compelling precisely because what he has to deal with is so overwhelming. Still, the playwright makes clear that all the talk of justice and politics will not free us from those terrifying yet fundamental responsibilities that accompany human sickness and death. All the Reaganite preaching of a survival-of-the-fittest creed will not exempt us from our most basic obligations to each other. Belize knows this, and he brings the discussion back to the matter at hand, Louis's desertion of his lover at a moment of profound need. "I've thought about it for a very long time, and I still don't understand what love is," he says before leaving Louis alone outside the coffee shop. "Justice is simple. Democracy is simple. Those things are unambivalent. But love is very hard. And it goes bad for you if you violate the hard law of love" (1:100).

Though stalwartly behind Belize's felt wisdom, Kushner observes an analogy between the ambivalence of love and the working out of democracy and justice, the bedroom and the courtroom not being as far apart as most would assume. Louis and Joe's ravenous infidelity, for example, is seen to be in keeping with the general dog-eat-dog direction of the country. During the warm-up to their affair, Joe tells Louis of a dream he had in which the whole Hall of Justice had gone out of business: "I just wondered what a thing it would be ... if overnight everything you owe anything to, justice, or love, had really gone away. Free" (1:72). Louis, whose motto has become "Land of the free. Home of the brave. Call me irresponsible" (1:72), has found the perfect soulless mate for a self-forgetting fling. "Want some company?" he asks. "For whatever?" (1:73). Later, in Part Two of *Angels*, when the two men get involved, they help each other get over the guilt of leaving their former lovers behind. First Joe:

> What you did when you walked out on him was hard to do. The world may not understand it or approve it but it was *your* choice, what you needed, not some fantasy Louis but *you*. You did what you needed to do. And I consider you very brave.

And then, somewhat more reluctantly, Louis:

> You seem to be able to live with what you've done, leaving your wife, you're not all torn up and guilty, you've ... blossomed, but you're not a terrible person, you're a decent, caring man. And I don't know how that's possible, but looking at you it seems to be. You do seem free.[7]

Joe, giving a new American spin to the phrase the "banality of evil," admits to being happy and sleeping peacefully. And so all would seem to be well in the couple's new-founded East Village love nest, except that Louis has bad dreams.

"In America, there's a great attempt to divest private life from political meaning," Kushner has said on the subject of his play's vision. "We have to recognize that our lives are fraught with politics. The oppression and suppression of homosexuality is part of a larger agenda."[8] In fact, nearly everything under the sun, from valium addiction to VD, is considered part of a larger agenda. For Kushner, politics is an intricate spiderweb of power relations. His most singular gift as a dramatist is in depicting this skein, in making visible the normally invisible cords that tether personal conscience to public policy. The playwright does this not by ideological pronouncement, but by tracking the moral and spiritual upheavals of his characters' lives. AIDS is the central fact of *Angels*, but it is one that implicates other facts, equally catastrophic. Racism, sexism, homophobia, moral erosion, and drug addiction come with the Kushnerian territory, and, as in life, characters are often forced to grapple with several of these at the same time.

Kushner uses split scenes to make more explicit the contrapuntal relationship between these seemingly disconnected narrative worlds. Roy's meeting with Joe, to discuss the junior attorney's future as a "Roy-Boy" in Washington, occurs alongside the scene in which Louis is sodomized in the Central Park Rambles by a leather-clad mama's boy. Louis's mini-symposium at the coffee shop is simultaneous with Prior's medical checkup at an outpatient clinic. Dreams, ghosts, and a flock of dithering, hermaphroditic angels are also used to break through the play's realistic structure, to conjoin seemingly disparate characters, and to reveal the poetic resonances and interconnectedness of everyday life. In a mutual dream, Harper, tranquilized and depressed, travels to Prior's boudoir, where she finds him applying the last touches of his Norma Desmond makeup. In a febrile state known portentously as the "[t]hreshold of revelation" (1:33), the two are endowed with clairvoyant insight, and it is here that Harper learns for sure that her husband is a "homo," and Prior understands that his illness hasn't touched his "most inner part," his heart (1:33–34). Even in his characters' most private, most alone moments, the "myth of the Individual," as Kushner calls it, is shot through with company.[9]

Nowhere is this merging of social realms more spectacularly revelatory, however, than in the presentation of Cohn. Though much is based on the historical record, Kushner publishes a disclaimer:

> Roy M. Cohn, the character, is based on the late Roy M. Cohn (1927–1986), who was all too real; for the most part the acts attributed to the character Roy [...] are to be found in the historical record. But this Roy is a work of dramatic fiction; his words are my invention, and liberties have been taken. (1:5)

Cohn, however, would have nothing to complain about: Kushner does the relentless overreacher proud. All Nietzschean grit and striving, Kushner's Cohn is forever trying to position himself beyond good and evil. "Transgress a little, Joseph," he tells his Mormon acolyte. "There are so many laws; find one you can break" (1:110). Power alone concerns him. Politics, the game of power, "the game of being alive," defines every atom of his being—even his sexuality, which refuses to be roped into traditional categories. Identity and other regulatory fictions are decidedly for other people, not for Cohn, who informs his doctor that labels like homosexuality

> tell you one thing and one thing only: where does an individual so identified fit in the food chain, in the pecking order? Not ideology, or sexual taste, but something much simpler: clout. Not who I fuck or who fucks me, but who will pick up the phone when I call, who owes me favours. This is what a label refers to. (1:45)

Cohn's own claim to transcendental fame is that he can get Nancy Reagan on the phone whenever he wants to. How different this is from Prior's relationship to his own sexuality; on his sickbed, he steels himself with the words: "I am a gay man and I am used to pressure, to trouble, I am tough and strong" (1:117).

But it is Louis, as Ross Posnock has noted, who is Cohn's true emotional antithesis.[10] Though the two share no scenes together, their approaches to the world represent the thematic struggle at the center of Kushner's play. Yes, Louis transforms himself into a Cohn wannabe, but in the end he proves too conscience-ridden to truly want to succeed. Early on, when he asks his Rabbi what the Holy Writ says about someone who abandons a loved one at a time of great need, it is clear that he will have trouble following Cohn's personal dictum: "Let nothing stand in your way" (1:58). "You want to confess, better you should find a priest," his Rabbi tells him. On being reminded that this isn't exactly religiously appropriate, his Rabbi adds, "Worse luck for you, bubbulah. Catholics believe in forgiveness. Jews believe in Guilt" (1:25). Louis is a would-be Machiavel hampered by the misgivings of his own inner-rabbi. "It's no fun picking on you Louis," Belize tell him, "you're so guilty, it's like throwing darts at a glob of jello, there's no satisfying hits, just quivering, the darts just blop in and vanish" (1:93). An exemplary neurotic, Louis internalizes the play's central conflict: the debt owed to the past vs. the desire for carte blanche in the future. Or as Louis himself puts it, "Nowadays. No connections. No responsibilities. All of us ... falling through the cracks that separate what we owe to ourselves and ... and what we owe to love" (1:71).

AIDS brings this dilemma to a rapid and painful reckoning. Grief has come into people's lives earlier in the late 1980s, occurring where it normally would have been postponed. Kushner believes this sad fact may very well force Americans to confront the consequences of their blind individualism. The trauma of AIDS holds for him the greatest potential source of social change. Early death, governmental back-turning, and whole populations of enraged mourning have created what Kushner would call a state of emergency. The conditions, in other words, are ripe for revolution. Communal consciousness, provoked by loss, has translated into militancy and activism. What's more, Kushner has convinced himself of Benjamin's prerequisite for radical change—the belief that "*even the dead* will not be safe from the enemy if he wins."[11] Haunting *Angels in America* is the restive ghost of Ethel Rosenberg, the woman Cohn famously prosecuted and had ruthlessly sentenced to death. "History is about to crack wide open" (1:112), she cries out with a vengeful laugh at her ailing enemy, who taunts her with the idea of his immortality. Indeed, "Millennium Approaches" has become the dead's battle-cry as well as that of the living.

To make clear that the forces of light are rallying against the forces of darkness, Kushner entitles the last act of *Millennium Approaches* "Not-Yet-Conscious, Forward Dawning." Even level-headed Belize shares this fervent sense that revolutionary change is coming. Outside the coffee shop, he assures Louis that "[s]oon, this ... ruination will be blanketed white. You can smell it—can you smell it? [...] Softness, compliance, forgiveness, grace" (1:100). It is on this hopeful note that the playwright ends the first part of his epic saga. An angel, crashing through Prior's bedroom ceiling, announces:

> Greetings, Prophet;
> The Great Work begins:
> The Messenger has arrived. (1:119)

The Great Work, however, begins with a nay-sayer. Aleksii Antedilluvianovich Prelapsarianov, the world's oldest living Bolshevik, begins *Part Two: Perestroika* declaring:

> The Great Question before us is: Are we doomed? The Great Question before us is: Will the Past release us? The Great Question before us is: Can we change? In Time? And we all desire that Change will come.
> (*Little pause*)
> (*With sudden, violent passion*) And *Theory?* How are we to proceed

without *Theory?* What System of Thought have these Reformers to present to this mad swirling planetary disorganization, to the Inevident Welter of fact, event, phenomenon, calamity? (2:13–14)

Kushner himself doesn't have a theory to offer before the lights come up on Prior cowering in bed with an Angel hovering over him. What the playwright has instead is an insight into the workings of history. "As Walter Benjamin wrote," the playwright reminds, "you have to be constantly looking back at the rubble of history. The most dangerous thing is to become set upon some notion of the future that isn't rooted in the bleakest, most terrifying idea of what's piled up behind you."[12] Kushner understands that the future needs to have its roots in the tragedies and calamities of the past in order for history not to repeat itself. The playwright's very difficult assignment, then, in *Perestroika* is to somehow move the narrative along into the future, while keeping history ever in sight; he must, in other words, find the dramatic equivalent of Klee's *Angelus Novus*, and bring us either to the threshold of a fresh catastrophe or to a utopia that throws into relief the suffering of the past.

Surprisingly, and in most un-Benjaminian fashion, Kushner rushes headlong into a fairy tale of progress. Torn between the reality of protracted calamity and the blind hope of a kinder, gentler millennium, the playwright opts for the latter, hands down. Kushner says of himself that he "would rather be spared and feel safer encircled protectively by a measure of obliviousness."[13] To that end, Prior not only survives his medical emergencies, but the playwright has him traipsing up a celestial scaffolding to heaven. Louis and Joe's torrid affair ends when Louis finds out the identity of Joe's boss. Calling Cohn "the most evil, twisted, vicious bastard ever to snort coke at Studio 54," Louis explodes at his month-long bedfellow, "He's got AIDS! Did you even *know* that? Stupid closeted bigots, you probably never figured out that each other was ..." (2:111). After Joe punches him in the nose, Louis goes back to Prior, who lovingly tells him it's too late to return. Cohn, at long last, kicks the bucket, only to have Louis and Belize (with help from the ghost of Rosenberg) say Kaddish over him. "Louis, I'd even pray for you," Belize admits, before explaining the reason for his unusual benevolence:

He was a terrible person. He died a hard death. So maybe.... A queen can forgive her vanquished foe. It isn't easy, it doesn't count if it's easy, it's the hardest thing. Forgiveness. Which is maybe where love and justice finally meet. Peace, at last. Isn't that what the Kaddish asks for? (2:124)

Though the two men end up ransacking the undearly departed's stockpile of AZT, it is Cohn who has the last laugh. In a fleeting moment of monstrous irony, Kushner grants Cohn his dream of immortality by letting him serve as God's defense attorney. Harper, tired of traveling through her own drug-and-loneliness-induced Antarctica, demands Joe's charge card and leaves for the airport to catch a night flight to San Francisco. "Nothing's lost forever," she says before making her final exit. "In this world, there is a kind of painful progress. Longing for what we've left behind, and dreaming ahead" (2:144).

The action concludes in a final pastoral scene in Central Park, in which Prior, Louis, Belize, and (somewhat implausibly) Hannah, Joe's Mormon mother and Prior's newest friend and sometimes caretaker, bask in the sun of a cold winter's day. "The Berlin Wall has fallen," Louis announces. "The Ceausescus are out. He's building democratic socialism. The New Internationalism. Gorbachev is the greatest political thinker since Lenin" (2:145). (Thus the title *Perestroika*.) The soothing story of the healing angel Bethesda is told, after which Prior sends us all contentedly home:

> This disease will be the end of many of us, but not nearly all, and the dead will be commemorated and will struggle on with the living and we are not going away. We won't die secret deaths anymore. The world only spins forward. We will be citizens.
> The time has come.
> Bye now.
> You are fabulous creatures, each and every one.
> And I bless you: *More Life*.
> The Great Work Begins. (2:148)

We won't die secret deaths anymore? The world only shins forward? Such uncritical faith in Progress would have been anathema to Benjamin, and to the Kushner of the first part, who so cogently applies the German's uncompromising historical materialism to America's current fin-de-siècle strife. The playwright has quite emphatically turned his attention away from the past and present turmoil, to a future that seems garishly optimistic in contrast. What happened?

There is a definite movement in *Perestroika* away from historical analysis towards a poetics of apocalypse. The pressure of reality seems to have induced an evangelical fervor in Kushner, in which social and political reality has become subordinate to religious fantasy. "The end of the world is at hand," Harper declares, while standing barefoot in the rain on the Brooklyn Heights Promenade. "Nothing like storm clouds over Manhattan to get you in the mood for Judgment Day" (2:101), she adds to the timely accompaniment of a peal of thunder. If that is not enough to convince us, Kushner whisks us around the heavens to hear the angels sing:

> We are failing, failing,
> The earth and the Angels.
> Look up, look up,
> It is Not-to-Be Time.
> Oh who asks of the Orders Blessing
> With Apocalypse Descending? (2:135)

As Frank Kermode points out in *The Sense of an Ending: Studies in the Theory of Fiction*, "[I]t seems to be a condition attaching to the exercise of thinking about the future that one should assume one's own time to stand in an extraordinary relation to it.... We think of our crisis as pre-eminent, more worrying, more interesting than other crises."[14] This is, of course, in large part a way to distract from the urgency of the present. Cultural anxiety is often transmuted into the myth of apocalypse; society, too, has its defense mechanisms for dealing with uncomfortable reality. On this point Savran agrees: "Regardless of Kushner's intentions, *Angels* sets forth a project wherein the theological is constructed as a transcendent category into which politics and history finally disappear."[15]

Ironically, though the play is set in a tragic time (a "murderous time" implies the Stanley Kunitz epigraph to *Millennium Approaches*), Kushner steers clear of tragic death, preferring instead to finish on a Broadway upnote. What makes this ending particularly hard to accept is that the playwright hasn't provided any convincing evidence to suggest that the state of emergency has let up in the least. Instead, he focuses on the gains in Prior's inner struggle, his will to live and general spiritual outlook. "Bless me anyway," Prior asks the angels before returning to a more earthbound reality. "I want more life. I can't help myself. I do. I've lived through such terrible times, and there are people who live through much much worse, but.... You see them living anyway. [...] If I can find hope anywhere, that's it, that's the best I can do" (2:135–36). New Age self-healing now takes precedence over politics, the spirit of individualism infects AIDS, and anger becomes merely an afterthought directed at God. "And if He returns, take Him to court," Prior says in a huff before leaving the cloudy heavens behind. "He walked out on us. He ought to pay" (2:136).

The situation parallels almost exactly the course of public response to AIDS in America. In the second decade of the epidemic little has changed, except for the fact that there is a diminishing sense of crisis. Activism has lulled, militancy has subsided into earnest concern, while conservatism, fundamentalism, and Jesse Helms-style homophobia are on the rise. AIDS, though still deadly, has been symbolically tamed. "Nothing has made gay men more visible than AIDS," Leo Bersani observes in *Homos*.[16] "But we may wonder if AIDS, in addition to transforming gay men into infinitely fascinating taboos, has made it less dangerous to look."[17] Troubled by the enormous success of *Angels*, Bersani argues that it is yet another sign of "how ready and anxious America is to see and hear about gays—provided we reassure America how familiar, how morally sincere, and particularly in the case of Kushner's work, how innocuously full of significance we can be."[18]

Bersani offers these comments as part of a larger critique on the Queer movement's spirited, if often hollow, rhetoric of community building, which has come in response to AIDS, and which he views as dangerously assimilationist. Sharing Louis's belief in "the prospect of some sort of radical democracy spreading outward and growing up" (1:80), Kushner insists on the possibility of this kind of Queer (i.e., communal) redemption. Indeed, the playwright has said (with no trace of self-irony) that he finds *Benjamin*'s sense of utopianism to be in the end profoundly apocalyptic.[19] Savran explains that, "[u]nlike the Benjamin of the 'Theses on the Philosophy of History,' for whom any concept of progress seems quite inconceivable, Kushner is devoted to rescuing Enlightenment epistemologies."[20] That is to say, "*Angels* unabashedly champions rationalism and progress."[21]

Benjamin's vision, however, seems ultimately far less bleak than either Kushner's or Savran's wishful idealism. Bertolt Brecht's remark on "Theses on the Philosophy of History" seems peculiarly apt: "[I]n short the little treatise is clear and presents complex issues simply (despite its metaphors and its judaisms) and it is frightening to think how few people there are who are prepared even to misunderstand such a piece."[22] Progress was for Benjamin a debased term primarily because it had become a dogmatic expectation, one that left the door open to very real destruction:

> One reason why Fascism has a chance is that in the name of progress its opponents treat it is as a historical norm. The current amazement that the things we are experiencing are "still" possible in the twentieth century is not philosophical. This amazement is not the beginning of knowledge—unless it is the knowledge that the view of history which gives rise to it is untenable.[23]

Kushner's brand of progress, in fact, seems dangerously close to that uncritical optimism on which Social Democratic theory, the antagonist of Benjamin's entire vision, relies:

> Progress as pictured in the minds of Social Democrats was, first of all, the progress of mankind itself (and not just advances in men's ability and knowledge). Secondly, it was something boundless, in keeping with the infinite perfectibility of mankind. Thirdly, progress was regarded as irresistible, something that automatically pursued a straight or spiral course.[24]

For Benjamin, history is essentially, the history of trauma. It is the sequence of violent breaks and sudden or catastrophic events that cannot be fully perceived as they occur, and which have an uncanny (in the rich Freudian sense of the word) tendency to repeat themselves. His essay is above all an inducement to consciousness, a clarion call to the mind to wake from its slumber and apprehend this persistent cycle of oppression and the mountain-high human wreckage left in its wake. Benjamin doesn't so much believe, as Savran suggests, that the present is doomed by the past, as that paradoxically in order for a society to free itself to move in a more utopian direction, the fundamental inescapability of the aggrieved past must be vigilantly acknowledged.

In her essay "Unclaimed Experience: Trauma and the Possibility of History," Cathy Caruth makes the crucial point that "the traumatic nature of history means that events are only historical to the extent that they implicate others ... that history is precisely the way we are implicated in each other's traumas."[25] This insight provides a way to understand not only the sweeping synthesis of Kushner's political vision in *Part One*, but also what may have gone awry in *Part Two*. From the vantage point of the traumatic experience of gay men and AIDS, Kushner taps into a much larger pool of American trauma, from the McCarthy witch hunt and Ethel Rosenberg to Reagan and neoconservatism. That Kushner is able to reveal from such an unabashedly gay, indeed flaming, position these indissoluble political bonds may be surprising to those who cannot conceive of sharing anything in common with men who imitate Tallulah Bankhead. But through the intimate concerns of Prior and Louis's relationship, Kushner opens up historical vistas onto generations of America's oppressed. The question is: were the almost unbearable scenes of Prior's illness, the pain of his and Harper's abandonment, and the punishing hypocrisy of Roy Cohn and his kind so overwhelming, so prolific of suffering, that they forced the playwright to seek the cover of angels?

By the end of *Perestroika*, Kushner stops asking those pinnacle questions of our time, in order to dispense "answers" and bromides—Belize's forgiveness of a rotten corpse; Harper's comforting "[n]othing's lost forever"; Louis's paean to Gorbachev and the fall of the Iron Curtain. By the final scene, Prior learns that "[t]o face loss. With Grace. Is Key ..." (2:122). This is no doubt sound knowledge. But to be truly convincing it must be passed through, dramatized, not eclipsed by celestial shenanigans peppered with *Wizard of Oz* insight. Surrounded by loved ones, Prior sends us off with hearty best wishes. AIDS has become an "issue" and all but vanished from sight. After convincing us brutally, graphically, of the centrality of AIDS in our history, and of the necessity of keeping the traumatic past ever in sight, the playwright abandons the house of his uncommon wisdom. *Millennium Approaches* may be the most persuasive and expansive AIDS play to date, but, as the silent backtracking of *Perestroika* suggests, the genre needs continuous reinforcing.

NOTES

1. Nicholas de Jongh, *Not in Front of the Audience: Homosexuality on Stage* (London, 1992), 179.

2. Alisa Solomon, "AIDS Crusaders Act Up a Storm," *American Theatre* (Oct. 1989), 39.

3. David Savran, "Tony Kushner Considers the Longstanding Problems of Virtue and Happiness," *American Theatre* (Oct. 1994), 22–23.

4. Walter Benjamin, "Theses on the Philosophy of History," in *Illuminations*, ed. Hannah Arendt, trans. Harry Zohn (New York, 1968), 257–58.

5. Benjamin, 265.

6. Tony Kushner, *Angels in America; A Gay Fantasia on National Themes. Part One: Millennium Approaches* (New York, 1993), 74. Subsequent references will be included in the text, preceded by the numeral 1.

7. Tony Kushner, *Angels in America: A Gay Fantasia on National Themes. Part Two: Perestroika* (New York, 1994), 38. Subsequent page references will be included in the text, preceded by the numeral 2.

8. John Lahr, "Beyond Nelly," *New Yorker* (23 Nov. 194), 127.

9. Kushner, "Afterword," *Perestroika*, 150.

10. Ross Posnock, "Roy Cohn in America," *Raritan*, 13:3 (Winter 1994), 69.

11. Benjamin, 257.

12. Savran, "Tony Kushner," 25.

13. Kushner, "Afterword," 155.

14. Frank Kermode, *The Sense of an Ending: Studies in the Theory of Fiction* (London, 1966), 94.

15. David Savran, "Ambivalence, Utopia, and a Queer Sort of Materialism: How *Angels in America* Reconstructs the Nation," *Theatre Journal*, 47:2 (1995), 221.

16. Leo Bersani, *Homos* (Cambridge, MA, 1995), 19.

17. Ibid., 21.

18. Ibid., 69.

19. Savran, "Tony Kushner," 26.

20. Savran, "Ambivalence," 214.

21. Ibid., 214.

22. Bertolt Brecht, *Journals 1934–1955*, trans. Hugh Rorrison (London, 1993), 159.

23. Benjamin, 259.

24. Ibid., 262.

25. Cathy Caruth, "Unclaimed Experience: Trauma and the Possibility of History," *Yale French Studies*, 79 (1991), 192.

JANELLE REINELT

Notes on Angels in America
as American Epic Theater

Many have the feeling that democracy is of such a nature that it could disappear from one hour to the next.

—Bertolt Brecht, "Letter to an Adult American"

I

Bert Brecht never really made it in America. We all know that. James Lyons finishes his portrait of Brecht in America by concluding, "Brecht was probably too far ahead of his time and too uncompromising in promoting his kind of theater in his own way to have succeeded in an alien environment like America."[1] Even suggesting that Brecht's day in the United States came in the 1960s and 1970s doesn't quite wash. Surveying the situation with fresh eyes for a special issue of *Theater*, Peter Ferrari commented that "the main force in this American avant-garde theater turned out to be Artaud, not Brecht."[2] In light of all the bad publicity surrounding Brecht's treatment of his women collaborators, combined with a new attack on his politics—mostly from John Fuegi's hatchet job biography *Brecht and Company*—there may be many who will wonder why I want to drag Brecht into a discussion of *Angels in America*.

Of course, he's already there, already present. Kushner himself evokes Brecht and all his contradictions in his own musings in the published text of

From *Approaching the Millennium: Essays on Angels in America*, Deborah R. Geis and Steven F. Kruger, ed. © 1997 by the University of Michigan.

Perestroika.[3] And then there are the names, scattered all through Kushner's acknowledgments, of the members of the Eureka Theatre Company: Oskar Eustis, Tony Taccone, Sigrid Wurschmidt. For ten years or so, in the mid-1970s to the mid-1980s, they were part of an epic theater in San Francisco that held the promise of a genuinely American appropriation and transformation of Brechtian dramaturgy. Kushner had his work produced there; in fact, the first production of *Millennium* and the first reading of what was to become *Perestroika* took place at the Eureka. There were other short-lived but vibrant experiments—the Brecht Company in Ann Arbor and Epic West in Berkeley come at once to mind. But Kushner was associated through the Eureka with a group of artists who, while not Brechtians themselves, particularly, were making a certain kind of politically engaged, left-wing theater on epic principles.[4]

These "epic principles" are summarized by familiar terms from the Brechtian lexicon: the historicization of the incidents, social gestus as mise-en-scène, and the odd *Verfremdungseffekt*. These parts of the epic critique still seem valid and necessary (even after the end of the Cold War has supposedly made socialism obsolete), although they might go by slightly different descriptions now that class society is passé and scientism has been shown to have its limits. Historicizing the incidents might become "A Gay Fantasia on National Themes," for instance. Social gestus means diverse and contradictory identity constructions within a cast not headed by a single hero-protagonist: certainly not Prior Walter nor even Roy Cohn but, rather, the group of characters, as they bump and collide throughout the play, ringing the changes on race, gender, age, religion, and, of course, sexuality. And *Verfremdungseffekt*? Lots to choose from there—cross-dressing, metatheatrical directions from Kushner that the magic has to be amazing but it's "OK if the wires show,"[5] or the scene at the Diorama Room of the Mormon Visitor's Center where, as Harper says, "They're having trouble with the machinery" (2:63).

Finally, I couldn't get Brecht out of my mind while I was watching the play—on either coast. In the East I faulted the production for not being Brechtian enough; in the West I praised the production because it finally achieved American epic style. It was actually *Caucasian Chalk Circle* I kept thinking about and *Good Person of Setzuan*, too. And how in recent decades, Brecht was criticized for his impossible "closed" dramaturgy and utopian play making. Suddenly Brecht seemed like a specter, like Ethel Rosenberg or Roy Cohn in the play: a specific historical presence conjured up, but as a dramatic fiction, to haunt the play through both limitation and aspiration.

II

Louis makes most of the political arguments in the script. He puts the discourse of democracy in play, although Roy Cohn also speaks a powerful political discourse. If considered abstractly, as a kind of "red thread" through the playtext, this democratic discourse emerges as a series of questions: how to reconcile difference, how to establish justice, how to effect social change, how to effect personal change, how to progress? This dimension of the social, of the body politic, is represented on the bodies of characters struggling for personal solutions to the contradictions of American life. They become sites for the traffic of history and the ideology of democracy: Mormon history, Red-baiting history, Jewish history, "family values history," sin and guilt through history, traditions of prophecy and transcendence. Incidents in the lives of the characters are typical of many contemporary Americans, and every character, from Hannah to Belize, Joe to Harper, represents one of these types. The social gestus of the playtexts seems to be disconnecting from identity, a kind of cutting loose from moorings, a not-very-Marxist letting go of fiercely held convictions or practices, or the refusal of great regressive temptations (most forcefully materialized in the person of the Angel) as the various characters "travel," or put themselves in motion away from the contexts and subject positions that have held them in place. By the end of *Perestroika*, and just barely, one sees the outline for a different society. And that is all there can really be—a glimmer. Otherwise, any firmer answer, any true solution, seems prescriptive and preachy, trite or sentimental, and ultimately false. Of course, *Angels* comes perilously close to that trap all through its text. In this regard, however, *Angels* is more closely related to *Good Person of Setzuan* than to the more sentimental parable, *Caucasian Chalk Circle*. Brecht posits a world in which Shui Ta is necessary and subjectivity is hopelessly split, throwing the dilemma back to the audience to "fix." In *Chalk Circle* Azdak, the mythical judge who made justice possible but then disappeared, and may never have been real in the first place (it's a "story"), offers more of a prescription: the land should be planted for the good of all, private property notwithstanding. No prescriptions end *Angels in America*. The last scene leaves Louis and Belize fighting about politics, their differences unresolved; it leaves Harper suspended on a "*jumbo-jet, airborne*" (2:144). Prior Walter remains alive, perhaps because of the AZT Belize commandeered from Roy Cohn, but has not been cured. The final gesture is toward a possibility of healing and progress, but the details have to be worked out in human space/time within the American national context. Not an easy task.

Epic theater needs to construct the experience of ideological contradiction as the mode of subjectivity it projects for spectators rather than the ideological totalization implied in *supporter*, *judgment*, *empathy*, or even *detachment*. This is an epic play, if the spectators engage the problems and understand the constraints operating on the nation and, on themselves as social subjects. It is an epic play *if* some sense of what might be done next is suggested but not spelled out. It is an epic play *if* it does not let spectators off the hook by allowing too much psychological investment in particular characters or too much good feeling of resolution at the end.

III

The subjunctive mode is always an essential part of epic theater. First, the provisional positing of a different way of organizing social life—what if the world were not like this? Second, the conditional—*if* the spectators and the actors and the play form a Brechtian triangle of speculation and critique, aesthetic pleasure, and political engagement, *then* the "epic" happens. Thus, even if Tony Kushner has written a perfectly crafted, totally brilliant epic playscript, whether or not it will result in an epic production is always an open question—that's always the gamble of political theater.

George C. Wolfe and Mark Wing-Davey, directors of the 1993 New York production and the 1994 San Francisco production, respectively, have different strengths as directors. Wolfe understands polish and theatrics and how to make a play succeed on Broadway. Wing-Davey has had success in New York, too, but he is a drier, starker, anti-illusionist and antisentimental director. His success with Caryl Churchill's *Mad Forest*, in New York and also in Berkeley, already marks him as an epic director. Then there are the audiences themselves. Seeing *Angels in America* toward the end of its successful New York run in April 1994, I was surrounded by comfortable upper-middle-class people who could easily afford the expensive tickets. Lots of gay couples, but lots of straight ones also, mixed with the crowd. Not too many people looked like students. It was a festive crowd, riding the crest of having one of the hottest tickets on Broadway. They reacted as if they were at an Alan Ayckbourn comedy—jolly, even boisterous, lots of laughter, and not much tension. In San Francisco some months later a quieter, more diverse crowd laughed while listening more intently. Class, age, race, and sexuality seemed more widely represented, and the mood of reception had clearly shifted.

Searching for these differences through reviews of the different productions, I find traces of production values and audience expectations that document both the latent epic qualities and the Broadway qualities of this play in performance. Clive Barnes finds "curious" what I find fundamental: "Curiously, when I first saw the play last year at Britain's National Theater—a far harsher, more political reading of a virtually identical text—its impact seemed greater."[6]

The reviews of the New York production praise Wolfe's directing for its technical acumen, the performances of Ron Leibman and Stephen Spinella for their richness and virtuosity, and the author for his inventiveness, literary capabilities, and theatrical savvy. Yet the comments that provide the traces I'm seeking are those that describe precisely what is valued by the reviewers. One of the most positive comments on the play is also the most damning from the point of view of the seeker after an American epic theater: "This heretofore almost unknown playwright is such a delightful, luscious, funny writer that, for all the political rage and the scathing unsanitized horror, the hours zip by with the breezy enjoyment of a great page-turner or a popcorn movie."[7] It is not the popular culture comparisons to popcorn movies that chill—after all, old Bert Brecht himself wanted a popular theater in that sense, theater to be like boxing not opera—it is the notion that a good night out in the theater dishes up politics and genuinely horrible insights in order to accommodate them to the culinary tastes of an audience for whom these things must be rendered palatable. Complaining about opera in the context of his discussion of the culinary, Brecht writes: "Values evolve which are based on the fodder principle. And this leads to a general habit of judging works of art by their suitability for the apparatus without ever judging the apparatus by its suitability for the work."[8] Thus poised between Barnes's suspicion that the British production, with its harsher politics, made a greater impact on its audience and Winer's assessment of the New York success based on its culinary pleasures, a trace of epic dramaturgy and its absence marks out a space of possibility. The shape of an American epic emerges.

It is too simple to say that the San Francisco production of *Angels in America* realized the promise of a great American epic dramaturgy. I do not even really believe that is the case. But both my own experience in the theater at the American Conservatory Theater (ACT) production and the San Francisco reviews do support the view that the play has epic capabilities that are sometimes reached in performance.

The San Francisco reception is clouded by the relationship between the play and the playwright and the San Francisco theater community. Almost every review begins with some claim on the play because of its San Francisco genesis. Perhaps because I also shared a commitment to the Eureka Theatre and identify closely with the Bay Area, my own view of the play is less than completely objective, but I prefer to stress that an emphasis on location, or rather on "the politics of location," may lead not only to local squabbles but also to a cultural and political investment in the production that activates spectatorial engagement. Headlines such as "'Angels' comes home to The City," "'Angels' Is Born Again," "Tony Kushner's epic returns home," all make a sentimental connection between the play and the city but also foreground it as something important to San Franciscans, something to be seen, responded to, and assessed from a position of relationship rather than distance. One could also argue that the play actually received extra critical scrutiny from the beginning, when director Mark Wing-Davey did not cast enough local actors to suit some portions of the San Francisco theater community. Comparisons to the Eureka production of *Millennium* and the memory of earlier performances also dot the journalism concerned with the play.

Most significant for the issues under discussion here are the aspects of the Wing-Davey production that mark it as deliberately epic. He provided abrupt and rapid transitions between scenes. In the New York production Wolfe staged the "split screen" scenes in *Millennium* as simultaneous but discretely separate scenes in stable space. Wing-Davey reframed these scenes as interconnected and uncontainable (actors "violated" one another's stage space to produce this effect of overflowing boundaries), staging the dissolution and blending of identities. As for the emotion/sentiment questions, Wing-Davey perhaps answered New York's Winer: "What I'm working toward is a sense of the fun but also the mess of the play—the circumstances, the disease, the visceral nature of the play. It should not be sanitized. It will not be polished in the sense that you can see your own reflection.... But maybe you can."[9] There is lots of blood on the stage; I wondered why I hadn't noticed that in New York.

The set design for the ACT production emerged as a key marker of the epic nature of the production because it was very controversial. Made up of industrial materials, large, almost oversized metal ramps and bridges, exposed light instruments, and aluminum rigging for the angel, Kate Edmunds's set either pleased people or raised their critical eyebrows. "'Angels': Wires and Pulleys" ran the headlines.[10] Steven Winn wrote that "the results range from striking scenic coups ... to distracting clutter"; Robert Hurwitt found the set "harshly anti-illusionist"; while Judith Green claimed that the "production goes out of its way to give visual offense."[11]

I found the set exactly the appropriate sort of Brechtian backdrop for a play intended to be about "national themes." New York reviewers often made reference to the domestic situation of the play or to its conventional depiction of three households. This kind of talk does not apply so easily to the San Francisco version, because the materials and scope of the set—industrial, urban, explicitly theatrical—continually place the domestic scenes within the context of the social, economic, and political structures of our nation at century's end. The detritus is real, and it is part and parcel of the emotional fallout facing the play's characters in their personal lives. In fact, the setting enhances or completes the play in this regard, strengthening the epic qualities and mitigating the tendency for the playscript to slip into bourgeois individualism but isolating personal, realistic spaces. In looking at Caspar Neher's drawings for Brecht's productions, the central tenet of epic staging is apparent: let the set contextualize or frame the action in such a way that it comments on the social world of the play. Let the props and the costumes also aspire to a functional realism that documents how people live and work in such a milieu.

The placement of the bedroom and hospital scenes on a kind of bridge/ramp that flew in undercut sentimentalism but raised the ire of one reviewer.[12] The many mechanized and working appliances in Harper's kitchen emphasized the mechanical, enforced domesticity of her life. Roy Cohn's plastic telephone and high-tech desk set functioned as both a toy and the key to his power in a telecom age. It followed him to his hospital bed as a portable switchboard. The Marines Memorial Theatre, where the plays were performed because ACT's regular venue, the Geary Theatre, had been damaged in the 1949 earthquake, became the focus of criticism for being too small for the set. The claustrophobia and clutter, however, seemed evocative of our current cultural life, with its bombardment of commodities, information, and garbage. Kate Edmunds's set for the San Francisco production of *Angels* was uncomfortable because it took these aesthetics as a starting point. She also, however, enabled the "fantasia on national themes" to evoke the nation and its contemporary structures.

This comparison of the New York and San Francisco productions merely establishes the different potentialities of the play in production under various circumstances for various audiences. Others will want to compare Los Angeles, London, or Chicago performances. That is, perhaps, exactly the point: that it is possible but not inevitable to see *Angels in America* as an American epic play and that it is also desirable and preferable to see it in this light.

IV

Howard Brenton, the contemporary British writer, remarked, "I sorted my mind out about Bert Brecht, the greatest playwright of our century, yes, the greatest, the best we have, alas."[13] He was trying to "sort out" both an homage to Brecht and a sense of failure that Brecht wasn't good enough and to say that it is a shame we don't have more and even better writers. I am persuaded of a similar attitude toward Tony Kushner in the context of this specific decade and nation. Hungrily seeking a left-wing voice in the American theater with the scope and ambition to work on a truly epic canvas, I am attracted to Kushner's themes, goals, theatrical accomplishments. Wanting the theater to become a site of national discourse about the future, I also wish for these plays to overreach themselves.

Like that of Bertolt Brecht, Kushner's work is based on the Enlightenment project of reason and progress; like Walter Benjamin's, it rests on a messianic desire. Because we are seemingly stuck in time, a leap or jump or break seems essential. While for Brecht socialism figured as a horizon of concrete possibility, for Kushner, in an age in which the grand narrative of Marxism is bankrupt, the leap catapults him into identity politics and a relative detachment from economic and social structural change. Backing off of Marx, however, produces a kind of liberal pluralism or benign tolerance, a promise but no program.

David Savran, in his brilliant analysis of *Angels in America*, has criticized the play for mobilizing a consensual politics that masquerades as dissensual in order to make an appeal to a possible utopian nation that rests on Enlightenment principles of rationalism, communitarianism, and progress.[14] Seeing this epistemology as part rational, part messianic, Savran also thinks it explains the play's great popular success: "*Angels* reassures an 'audience that knows it has lost control over events' not by enabling it to 'regain ... control' but by letting it know 'that history is nevertheless controlled by an underlying order and that it has a purpose that is nearing fulfillment.'"[15] Thus, the play promises too much and too little, finally signifying American liberal ideology as usual.

While I am generally persuaded by Savran's analysis, I wish to place the dilemmas of which he speaks within slightly different terms. Rather than focusing on the reiteration of liberal themes, I regret Kushner's drift away from socialist themes. The replacement of class analysis by other identity categories, while useful and strategic in terms of contemporary exigencies, leaves the play with no other foundation for social change than the individual subject, dependent on an atomized agency. Since this subjectivity is contradictory and collapsed, the only horizon of hope must be transcendent.

One key moment will illustrate how the playscript becomes entrapped in the ideology of individualism. It occurs when Belize takes the AZT from

Roy Cohn. In this scene the black man (who is, of course, tokenized and sentimentalized insofar as he is the great caretaker of the play, a fact many critics have realized) takes away the privileged man's private stash of medicine in order to share the wealth:

BELIZE:	If you live fifty more years you won't swallow all these pills. (*Pause*) I want some.
ROY:	That's illegal.
BELIZE:	Ten bottles.
ROY:	I'm gonna report you.
BELIZE:	There's a nursing shortage. I'm in a union. I'm real scared. I have friends who need there. Bad.

(2:60)

After a fierce argument Belize leaves with three bottles. Later, after Cohn's death, Belize gives a full bag to Prior.

What I am going to say next may seem completely unfair: that scene, those events, aren't good enough for an American epic play. But it is precisely the evocation of personal friends who need the medicine that undercuts a social critique by keeping the discourse personal. Nowhere in the play is there any indication of the community organizing, political agitation, liberal church and other networks involved in fighting AIDS. Prior and Louis and Joe are all left with their private consciousnesses to sort their doubts and fears out *on their own*. The play needs some gesture to the power of social and political organizing; that is, we need to see the social environment, ranges, background, mode of production. In this scene all the ingredients are there—Belize evokes his union to counter Roy's threat to his job. Why couldn't he also mention a network or organization in connection with the friends needing AZT? I do not presume to rewrite this scene; I do want to underscore the structural absence in the play of alternatives to bourgeois individualism.

On the other hand, perhaps any overt gesture to this kind of political solution would seem too programmatic, too Marxist, too *Caucasian Chalk Circle*. We do not, after all, live in a time when a rationalist epistemology convinces (even if a nostalgia for the unified subject still lingers). In the absence of programmatics, however, the kind of liberal pluralism tinged with despair that marks America at the end of the century goes unchallenged, in fact is reinscribed. The millennial hope of the last scene of the play must be founded on the transcendental *if* there is no basis for social change within the representation. The imperative to signal beyond its own terms marks *Angels in America*. But the play leaves us waiting at the fountain to discover an immanent means of making things better, of healing, of constructing democracy. The best we have, alas. For now.

NOTES

1. James K. Lyons, *Bertolt Brecht in America* (Princeton, N.J.: Princeton University Press, 1980), 347.

2. Peter W. Ferrari, "New Measures for Brecht in America," *Theater* 25:2 (1994) 9.

3. Tony Kushner, *Angels in America: A Gay Fantasia of National Themes. Part Two: Perestroika* (New York: Theatre Communications Group, 1994), 153. All further citations will be included in parentheses in the text.

4. Sigrid Wurschmidt, a brilliant actress whose life was tragically cut short by breast cancer, was the inspiration for the Angel. Kushner first met her in the Eureka's production of Kushner's play *A Bright Room Called Day*. For a profile of the company up to 1985, see my essay "New Beginnings/Second Wind: The Eureka Theatre," *Theater* 16:3 (Summer–Fall 1985): 17–21.

5. Tony Kushner, *Angels in America: A Gay Fantasia of National Themes. Part One: Millennium Approaches* (New York: Theatre Communications Group, 1993), 5. All further citations will be included in parentheses in the text.

6. Clive Barnes, "Angelically Gay about Our Decay," *New York Post*, 5 May 1993. (Also in *New York Theatre Critics' Reviews* 14:11 [1993]: 211.)

7. Linda Winer, "Pulitzer-Winning 'Angels' Emerges front the Wings," *New York Newsday*, 5 May 1993. (Also in *New York Theatre Critics' Reviews* 14:11 [1993]: 209.)

8. Bertolt Brecht, *Brecht On Theatre*, ed. and trans. John Willett (New York: Hill and Wang, 1964), 34.

9. Michael Fox, "Director Wing-Davey Does It His Way," *San Francisco Chronicle*, 5 September 1994, Datebook 33.

10. Laura Evenson, "'Angels' They Have Hoisted on High," *San Francisco Chronicle*, 10 October 1994. E1, 2.

11. Stephen Winn, "'Angels' Is Born Again," *San Francisco Chronicle*, 14 October 1994, C:1, 5, 18; Robert Hurwitt, "Return of the Millennium," *San Francisco Examiner*, 13 October 1994, C1, 12; Judith Green, "A Chorus of Angels," *San Jose Mercury News*, 21 October 1994, 41, 42.

12. Green, "Chorus of Angels."

13. Howard Brenton, "The Best We Have Alas: Bertolt Brecht," *Hot Irons* (London: Nick Herne Books, 1995), 64.

14. David Savran, "Ambivalence, Utopia, and a Queer Sort of Materialism: How *Angels in America* Reconstructs the Nation," *Theatre Journal* 47 (May 1995): 221ff. This essay is reprinted in the current volume.

15. Here Savran is glossing Barry Brummett, *Contemporary Apocalyptic Rhetoric* (New York: Praeger, 1991), 37–38.

ALLEN J. FRANTZEN

Alla, Angli, and Angels in America

Rome, not Northumbria, is the center of *The Man of Law's Tale*, and celibacy, not marital bliss, is the Man of Law's preferred mode for Christ's holy ministers. Chaucer's text looks neither to the vernacular tradition of married clergy that the Wycliffites sought nor to the celibate clerical world demanded by Roman canon law and espoused earlier by the Anglo-Saxon church of Ælfric and by Norman reformers. Instead, the Man of Law's heroine is a product of Chaucerian compromise. She practices what might be thought of as serial chastity. Custance marries Alla, but after she becomes pregnant she lives without his company for all but the last year of his life. Clerical ideals dominate *The Man of Law's Tale*, much of its domestic sentiment notoriously devalued not only by the narrator's self-dramatizing interruptions but by Chaucer's debt to the work of a great reforming cleric, Pope Innocent III, whose "De miseriis humane conditionis" (On the misery of the human condition) is quoted in the prologue to the tale and elsewhere in the text.[1]

Chaucer makes much of the dependence of the English church on Rome. His reform-minded contemporaries, the Lollards, regarded Rome as a dangerous influence; in the Reformation the city became a symbol used to attack Catholicism. But for the Anglo-Saxons and for orthodox Christians of Chaucer's time, Rome was the center of the Church on earth.

From *Before the Closet: Same-Sex Love from Beowulf to Angels in America*. © 1998 by the University of Chicago Press.

Correspondence with the pope and travel to and from Rome were means by
which the church of the frontier established its authenticity. In this chapter I
examine one small part of this traffic, an episode from Bede's *Ecclesiastical
History of the English People*, which describes the sale of angelic English boys
in Rome, a story subsequently retold by Wace, Laȝamon, and others,
including John Bale, a Reformation historian. I compare the juxtaposition of
angels and Angli, meaning "English," in these texts to angelic powers in
Tony Kushner's *Angels in America*, a play in which the Anglo-Saxons,
embodied in the stereotype of the WASP, play a small but significant role.
For a moment, however, I return to Chaucer's Alla and a scene in which he
too meets a boy in Rome.

ALLA AND ÆLLE

Alla registers a dim presence in *The Man of Law's Tale*. He is heard about after
Custance converts Hermengyld and her husband but otherwise, except for
letters to his mother, not heard from until a young boy (who proves to be his
son) is set before him at a feast. This act is part of Custance's plan. She too
has arrived in Rome but has refused to identify herself to the senator who
rescued her from the ship on which she was set adrift from Northumbria.
Now, in her husband's presence, she speaks through her son. "[A]t his
moodres heeste / Biforn Alla, durynge the metes space, / The child stood,
lookynge in the kynges face" (1013–15).[2] The child does not look like him,
however, but "as lyk unto Custance / As possible is a creature to be"
(1030–31). Because Alla has kept the faith (he is on a pilgrimage of
repentance for killing his wicked mother), he realizes that Christ might have
sent Custance to Rome just as he sent her to Northumbria. Shortly
thereafter Alla and Custance are reconciled. Only then does she reveal
herself to her father, the emperor, explaining for the first time who she is
(1105–13).

The story of Custance reminds many readers of a saint's life and recalls
some of the dynamics of stories about cross-dressed women saints
recounted in chapter 2.[3] Like Euphrosyne, Custance is betrothed, in
Custance's case to a sultan who becomes a Christian in order to marry her.
His mother, outraged, kills him and sends Custance out to sea, a scenario
repeated when Custance is expelled from Northumbria. Unlike
Euphrosyne, Custance marries and has a child. But in many ways her life as
a missionary is similar to the lives of the evangelizing saints commemorated
in Anglo-Saxon texts. The moment at which Custance reveals herself to her
father recalls the revelation made by both Euphrosyne and Eugenia to

theirs. And, like Eugenia, Custance preaches the word of God from within a same-sex community. It is, of course, a tiny one, just Custance and Hermengyld, but their same-sex love, symbolized by the bed they share, is genuine and more warmly demonstrated than such love is in the Anglo-Saxon texts.

Having been reunited in Rome, Custance and Alla return to Northumbria for a year of wedded bliss. After Alla's death, Custance goes back to Rome and takes up a life of virtue and good works, never again parting from her father (1156–57). Chaucer rejoined his roving heroine to patriarchal structures identical to those governing the lives of Eugenia and Euphrosyne. The difference is that Chaucer's holy woman is not just a daughter but also a wife and mother—a married evangelist. To a surprising degree *The Man of Law's Tale* conforms to what might have been a Lollard vision of evangelism in the true church. Custance's language, for example, recognized as "a maner Latyn corrupt" in Northumbria, is what the Lollards thought Italians spoke—that is, a vernacular, albeit not English. The tale discreetly hints of controversies building in the Church in Chaucer's time by effecting a radical redescription of the origins of the Church in the Anglo-Saxon period. According to the Man of Law, Northumbria was converted by a woman who arrives from Rome by way of Syria, directed only by God's will and the winds. But as Bede's *Ecclesiastical History* makes clear, the territory was converted by Irish missionaries and by holy men who came at the pope's behest from Rome—Augustine sent by Gregory the Great in 596, Theodore and Hadrian sent by Pope Vitalian over half a century later. Equally bold is the Man of Law's revised account of Alla, Chaucer's version of the Northumbrian king Ælle, the only English character in the text who is known to have been a historical person. Chaucer's Alla is converted to Christianity by Custance and with her has a son, Maurice, who was crowned emperor by the pope (1122). Bede's Ælle was not Christian but rather served as a symbol of pagan kingship awaiting redemption. Ælle's son, Edwin, converted to Christianity because he wished to marry Æthelburh, the daughter of the Christian king Æthelberht.[4] Thereafter Edwin "held under his sway the whole realm of Britain, not only English kingdoms but those ruled over by the Britons as well."[5]

Ælle's role in Bede is much smaller on the historical level but much greater on the symbolic level. He appears in Bede's text but once, in a description of some boys who, like Maurice, ended up in Rome through circumstances not of their own choosing. They too looked into the face of an important man, Pope Gregory. Or I should say, rather, that he looked into their faces, and what he saw there, depending on whose account we accept, was either the image of a chosen people waiting to be converted (the preferred explanation)—or love.[6]

> It is said that one day, soon after some merchants had arrived in Rome, a quantity of merchandise was exposed for sale in the market place. Crowds came to buy and Gregory too amongst them. As well as other merchandise he saw some boys put up for sale, with fair complexions, handsome faces, and lovely hair. On seeing them he asked, so it is said, from what region or land they had been brought. He was told that they came from the island of Britain, whose inhabitants were like that in appearance. He asked again whether those islanders were Christians or still entangled in the errors of heathenism. He was told that they were heathen. Then with a deep-drawn sigh he said, "Alas that the author of darkness should have men so bright of face in his grip, and that minds devoid of inward grace should bear so graceful an outward form." Again he asked for the name of the race. He was told that they were called Angli. "Good," he said, "they have the face of angels, and such men should be fellow-heirs of the angels in heaven." "What is the name," he asked, "of the kingdom from which they have been brought?" He was told that the men of the kingdom were called *Deiri*. "*Deiri*," he replied, "*De ira!* good! snatched from the wrath of Christ and called to his mercy. And what is the name of the king of the land?" He was told that it was Ælle; and playing on the name, he said, "Alleluia! the praise of God the Creator must be sung in those parts."[7]

The story of the Anglian boys in Rome is found at the start of book 2 of the *Ecclesiastical History*, where Bede encloses a summary of Gregory's life within a larger narrative of the origins of the English nation. Like Gildas, Bede portrayed the early British as a Chosen People who violated their covenant with God and were destroyed as a result.[8] Bede effected a complete break between the histories of the lapsed early Christian communities of the British—the community that Custance encounters when she lands in Northumbria and reads a "Britoun book"—and the heathen tribes, the Anglo-Saxons, whom Gregory's missionaries would convert. Bede located his own origins in the Anglo-Saxons, the new rather than the old chosen people.

The boys whom Gregory saw in the marketplace were descendants of Anglo-Saxons who, 150 years after coming to Britain, were still pagan. Gregory and Bede call the boys "Angli," a term that generally means

"English."[9] But Bede had a more particular understanding of the term, as his description of the settlements of Germanic tribes makes clear. Bede located the Jutes where the people of Kent live, and the Saxons where the West, East, and South Saxons live. He continued: "Besides this, from the country of the Angles, that is, the land between the kingdoms of the Jutes and the Saxons, which is called *Angulus*, came the East Angles, the Middle Angles, the Mercians, and all the Northumbrian race (that is those people who dwell north of the river Humber) as well as the other Anglian tribes. *Angulus* is said to have remained deserted from that day to this."[10] Bede seems to have meant "Anglian" in the more specific sense of "Northumbrian." He himself was born in the territory of Monkwearmouth-Jarrow, in Northumbria, and so was "Angli" in three senses—Northumbrian, Anglian, and English.[11] "Angli" also means "angels," of course, but Bede carefully understates this meaning, which in the anecdote is better left to Gregory. That the boys' beauty should make Gregory think of angels is significant, for it suggests a purely symbolic meaning for "angli" otherwise rare in Bede's *Ecclesiastical History*.

Bede affirms a natural affinity between Gregory and the Anglo-Saxons. It might seem curious that Gregory should find the boys attractive, since his admiration suggests that he prefers their unfamiliar appearance (light-complected and light-haired) to that of his own people. The discrepancy strongly suggests that the anecdote originates with an English author whose views Gregory is made to express. The episode is a pretext for witty verbal play that valorizes the boys' race, their nation, and their king. Young, innocent, and beautiful, the boys themselves represent a benign and neglected heathendom. When Gregory recognizes all the signs of a chosen people awaiting God's blessing, Bede is permitted to foresee the new Christian age of the English people that arrived in England with Gregory's missionaries.

For all its piety, the encounter between Gregory and the boys reflects earthly and political concerns. Bede shows us Gregory's interest in establishing the Church in England and in complementing the churches that Rome had already fostered so successfully elsewhere in western Europe. Bede's chief aim was to bolster the success of that Church especially in the land of his birth; he dedicated the work to the Northumbrian king Ceolwulf.[12] The reference to angels promotes this aim, symbolically affiliating the Anglo-Saxon church with Rome. When Gregory announced that the people of Anglia, represented by angelic youth, were ready to be changed into "fellow-heirs of the angels in heaven," a new age—the history of Bede's own beginnings—came into being. But these unhappy boys were not its heralds, any more than they were angels. Other messengers— missionaries brought to England by Augustine at Gregory's command, long after the boys had been forgotten—were charged with bringing the faith to the Anglo-Saxons. That the boys could be compared to angels was not testimony to their proximity to the divine, a role Bede reserved for real angels, but to the angel-like state of their descendants, who would be newly baptized, newly converted, and newly saved.

The boys, Bede notes, were "put up for sale." Gregory saw them amid stacks of other merchandise. What were they doing there? Peter Hunter Blair warned that readers should not "jump to the romantic conclusion that the boys whose purchase was envisaged by Gregory were English slaves on sale in a market-place." The boys might also have been held in service, he suggested, as four English boys were held in the service of Jews at Narbonne, or prisoners of war, mercenaries, or "merely young men in some way bound to the soil on Merovingian estates."[13] A letter survives from Gregory to the priest Candidus (written in September 595), asking him to buy "English boys who are seventeen or eighteen years old, that they may be given to God and educated in the monasteries" ("pueros Anglos qui sunt ab annis decem et septem vel decem et octo, ut in Monasteriis dati Deo proficiant comparet").[14] The boys Gregory sees in the marketplace are not destined for education, and clerical status, however. Those who have looked closely at the episode, including Bertram Colgrave, R.A.B. Mynors, and David Pelteret, identify the boys as slaves—although Bede does not—and relate the episode to the well-documented practice of slavery by the Anglo-Saxons.[15] "The custom of buying or ransoming slaves to turn them into missionaries was known," according to Colgrave, and both Aidan and Willibrord observed it.[16]

In the later Anglo-Saxon period opposition to slavery seemed to intensify. In 1014 Wulfstan denounced those who sold their children into foreign servitude.[17] But foreign trade in slaves persisted until the Norman Conquest, after which opposition to slavery continued. The Council of London of 1102 criticized the custom, even as servile tenure was becoming a more prevalent form of bondage.[18] In almost all cases in Anglo-Saxon sources the slaves in question are penal slaves forced into slavery because they could not pay debts or because they were being punished for some offense. The boys' status depended on their age; if they were seventeen or eighteen, they could have been sold as slave labor. But it is also possible that the boys Gregory saw in Rome were captives who were too young to be penal slaves and who merely represented a benign and neglected heathendom. Bede's narrative exalted their innocence, youth, and beauty, even though its real subject was their race, their nation, and Ælle, their king. What was their value in the market place? Ruth Mazo Karras points out that sexual exploitation was among the many unfortunate facts of life for women slaves. It is possible that boys were also sexually exploited and that their commercial value was directly related to their beauty and fairness, underscored by Gregory's focus on their faces (they are "bright of face," they have "the face of angels").[19] The boys would have been exploited by men, obviously, a kind of same-sex sex that, as we saw in chapter 4, was of particular concern to the Anglo-Saxons.

Any sexual resonance in the anecdote is, of course, suppressed by Bede and, in turn, by all those who retold the episode after him. In the version found in Laȝamon's *Brut*, the "angli" are men, not boys, whose response anticipates Gregory's discovery and spoils the drama of his curiosity and his good heart. "We are heathen men," they say, "and have been brought here, and we were sold in England, and we seek baptism from you if you would only free us" ("We beoð heðene men and hider beoð iladde, / and we weoren ut isalde of Anglene lond; / and fulluht we to þe ȝeorneð ȝef þe us wult ifreoiȝen," 14707–9). Gregory's reply is obliging. "[O]f all the peoples who live on earth, you English are assuredly most like angels; of all men alive your race is the fairest" ("Iwis ȝe beoð Ænglisce englen ilicchest / of alle þan folke þa wunieð uppen uolde; / eouwer cun is feȝerest of alle quike monnen," 14713–15).[20] Neither Laȝamon's nor other versions subsequent to Bede's include all of the episode's verbal play. Instead these versions overtly state points implied in Bede's account, showing, first, that the Angli desired baptism and requested it of Gregory, and, second, that they were captives who yearned to be free. But an ironic reading is also possible. Laȝamon's version, which makes nothing of Gregory's insight, might suggest that the Anglo-Saxons use the pope to effect a cynical exchange of baptism for freedom; conversion is their idea, not his.

The first modern reader to comment on the sexual subtext of Bede's story was John Boswell, who documented the Church's concern that abandoned children would be sold into slavery and used for sexual purposes. Some writers protested this practice, but not for the reasons we might expect. Their concern was that fathers who abandoned their children might later accidentally buy them as slaves and commit incest by having intercourse with them. Boswell noted that the public sale of slaves continued in Rome long after the empire was Christianized and illustrated the practice with the episode as Bede recounted it.[21] In the 1540s, some seven hundred years after Bede's death, Boswell's point was vividly anticipated by a remarkable figure

named John Bale, the first reader to see a same-sex shadow in the story that
has charmed so many.

BEDE AND BALE

Bale (1495–1563) was a Carmelite priest who left the Church of Rome in the
1530s. The author of several large-scale surveys of English authors and the
first biographer of Chaucer, Bale was also a collector of early manuscripts,
including those in Anglo-Saxon.[22] According to John N. King, Bale was "the
most influential English Protestant author of his time."[23] He was also a
prodigious instrument in the propaganda efforts of Thomas Cromwell.[24]
Bale recounted the episode of Gregory and the slave boys in a revisionist
narrative of English ecclesiastical history called *The Actes of Englysh Votaryes*.

> And as thys Gregorye behelde them fayre skynned and
> bewtyfullye faced, with heare upon their heades most comelye,
> anon he axed, of what regyon they were. And answere was made
> hym, that they were of an yle called Englande. Wele maye they
> be called *Angli* (sayth he) for they have verye Angelych vysages.
> Se how curyose these fathers were, in the wele eyenge of their
> wares. Here was no cyrcumstaunce unloked to, perteynynge to
> the sale. Yet have [has] thys Byshopp bene of all writers reckened
> the best sens hys tyme.[25]

Bale mockingly urged his readers to "[m]arke thys ghostlye mysterye, for the
prelates had than no wyves." He plainly implied that Gregory had sexual
designs on the boys. "[T]hese fathers" were "curyose" in the "wele eyenge"
of the boys as "wares," he wrote, using an expression with strong sexual
overtones. In sixteenth-century English, "ware" could mean "piece of goods"
(an expression "jocularly applied to women," according to the *OED*) and "the
privy parts of either sex."[26] Because priests were unmarried, Bale observes,
with much sarcasm, "other spyrytuall remedyes were sought out for them by
their good prouvders and proctours, we maye (yf we wyll) call them apple
squyres." "Apple-squires," according to the *OED*, means "pimp" or
"panderer," thus further underscoring Bale's sexual innuendo. Stressing that
this sale was not unique, Bale produces another witness, Machutus, who saw
a similar event in Rome in AD 500 and bought the boys to protect them (23a).
We are meant to conclude that Gregory, deprived of a wife by the Church's
demand for clerical celibacy, sought out "other spyrytuall remedyes" by
purchasing boys for sex.

Bale's rewriting of the story of Gregory and the Anglian boys takes place in the context of an elaborate revision of England's Anglo-Saxon Christian history proposed in *The Actes of Englysh Votaryes* and *The Image of Bothe Churches*. In *The Actes of Englysh Votaryes* Bale boldly revised English history in order to describe the nation's struggles against the corrupt influences of the Church of Rome. The chief instrument of Roman domination, Bale argued, was clerical celibacy, which permitted the clergy to degrade marriage and advocate virginity, all the while using its own religious houses for immoral purposes. Bale vigorously defended the right of the clergy to wed and believed that the Roman clergy who claimed to be celibate had in fact indulged in every form of sexual corruption. In *The Image of Bothe Churches*, Bale set forth a thesis about the Church in England that, as it was later developed by his better-known contemporary, John Foxe, became a foundational strategy for Reformation anti-Roman polemic.[27] Bale argued that the Church had been divided during the reign of Constantine and that the See of Saint Peter stemmed from the corrupt division, while an isolated community of the faithful, who retained belief in the true Church, reestablished the true Church in England. Bale argued that the false Church of Rome had taken on the image of the true Church of antiquity and that from the time of St. Augustine's mission to the English (597) to the rejection of papal authority by Henry VIII (1533) the Church in England had been corrupt. Bale was among the historians who looked back to the Anglo-Saxon period, skipping over an internal period in which they perceived England as dominated by the Church of Rome to a point that they erroneously saw as a free, "native," English church unencumbered by Roman influence. This was an exercise in self-justification. Having recently thrown off Roman rule itself, the new "English" or "Anglican" church was searching for its origins in the Anglo-Saxon period, which was perceived as another time when England's Christians governed themselves justly and righteously.

For Bede, the mission of Augustine marked the permanent conversion of Britain. Bale reversed the significance of this event. He claimed that the English church had survived pure and uncorrupted until the coming of Roman missionaries. With them they brought pernicious doctrines such as clerical celibacy, and as a result they transformed the once-pure land and its church into a new Sodom. Seeking to open his readers' eyes to the false miracles used by "obstynate hypocrytes" still living under the pope's rules, Bale wrote *The Actes of Englysh Votaryes* in order to accuse Catholics of portraying "whoremongers, bawdes, brybers, idolaters, hypocrytes, traytors, and most fylthye Gomorreanes as Godlye men and women" (2a). His diatribes are laced with references to Sodom and Gomorrah. Although his definitions of the sins of these unholy places remain vague, they encompass theological error as well as sexual excess, including, at certain points, male homosexual intercourse.

Marriage, Bale wrote in *The Actes*, was the "first order of religion," created in order to protect against "beastlye abusyons of the fleshe that shuld after happen" if men and women disobeyed God's command to increase and multiply (76). The Church sought to dissuade holy men and women from marriage, broke up existing marriages, venerated only unmarried saints, and demonized women as "spretes" ("sprites," 3a); these were the acts of "the Sodomytycall swarme or brode of Antichrist" (4a). According to Bale's extraordinary revision of the history of Anglo-Saxon holy men and women, clergymen fornicated with cloistered nuns and produced a race of bastards who were then venerated as saints, Cuthbert, Dunstan, Oswald, Anselm, and Becket among them (2b). Some did worse, since they refrained from women but "spared not to worke execrable fylthyness among themselves, and one to pollute the other," an obvious reference to male homosexual acts (12b). Devout in his praise of Mary, Bale was eager to insist that she was not abused by the clergy and that she was not a professed nun, "as the dottynge papystes have dreamed, to couer their sodometrye with a most precyouse coloure, but an honest mannys wyfe" (13a). Bale attacked "spirituall Sodomytes and knaves" who wrote the lives of these sinful saints (18a): "Come out of Sodome ye whoremongers and hypocrytes, popysh byshoppes and prestes" (186). Bale used "sodometrie"—an obsolete word for sodomy, first used in 1530, according to the *OED*—to attack clergy who took the required vows of celibacy but who were unable to remain celibate: either men who had sex with each other because they could riot have sex with women, or men who did have sex with cloistered nuns who were virtually the male clergy's sexual slaves. Shortly before he recounts the story about Gregory, Bale tells of a large group of women who joined a pilgrimage only to find that they had been taken from England to be forced to prostitute themselves to the clergy on the Continent (21a).

In leading up to his account of the boys, Bale followed Geoffrey of Monmouth, who embroidered Gildas's account into a claim that sodomy was pervasive among the early Britons, practiced by two of their kings (Malgo and Mempricius) and the cause of their overthrow by the Saxons. Gildas's version contains no hint of sexual slander, as we saw in chapter 5. Bale wrote that Malgo, who was possibly fashioned on William Rufus, was "the most comelye persone of all hys regyon," someone to whom God had given great victories against the "Saxons, Normeies, and Danes." But he was a sodomite. He imitated the ways of his predecessor Mempricius, who was "geuen to most abhomynable sodometrye, which he had lerned in hys youthe of the consecrate chastyte of the holie clergye" (21b–22a).[28] Thus the British were weak and were easily conquered by the Saxons. Bale believed that Roman Christianity entered England with the Saxons, who renamed the land England. "Then came therein a newe fashyoned christyanyte yet ones agayne from Rome with many more heythnysh yokes than afore." Bale then immediately introduced Gregory and told the story about the boys (22a–b, a section entitled "The Saxons entre with newe Christyanyte").

Elsewhere Bale underscored the charges of sodomy among Catholic clergy made in *The Image of Both Churches*. In his *Apology against a Rank Papist* (1550), Bale asked, "Whan the kynges grace of England by the autorite of Gods wurd, discharged the monkish sectes of his realme, from their vowed obedience to the byshop of Rome, did he not also discharge them in conscience of the vowe of Sodometry, whyche altogether made them Antichristes creatures?" Catholic clergy had set marriage and virginity "at variance" and replaced them with "two unhappy gestes, called whoredom and buggery."[29] In *The Pageant of Popes*, published in 1574 (after Bale's death), Bale recounted visitations to monasteries ordered by Henry VIII, which found "such swarmes of whoremongers, ruffians, filthie parsouns, giltye of sinne against nature, Ganimedes, and yet votaries and unmaryed all, so that thou wouldest thincke that there were a newer Gomorrah amonge them." At Battle Abbey, according to Bale, there were nearly twenty "gilty of sinne against nature" (their crimes included bigamy and adultery); at Canterbury there were eleven.[30] *The Pageant of Popes* shows that Bale saw another side to Gregory, casting him as the creator of a policy opposing clerical celibacy (no one could ever accuse Bale of consistency). Gregory was informed that priests "accompanied not only with virgins and wyves, but also even with their owne kindred, with mankind, yea and that whiche is horrible to be sayde, with brute beastes." ("Accompanied" is an obsolete euphemism for "cohabit with," according to the *OED*. Note that Bale regards bestiality as worse than same-sex acts.) Appalled at this conduct, Gregory revoked the canon requiring that priests not marry.[31] Gregory was given credit for being "the best man of all these Romaine Patriarkes, for learning and good life," and Bale praised his humility and his learning.[32]

Like many polemicists, Bale was an idealist. His attack on the Roman clergy can be explained by his high regard for marriage and his ardent defense of women's position. When he was a Carmelite priest, in the 1520s, Bale carried out extensive research into Carmelite archives and took special interest in the Church's view of women, in part at least because of his interest in Mary, the patron of the Carmelite order.[33] His recruitment to the Church of England came in the 1530s, when he lived in London and could see the drastic impact of Henry's marriage and decrees on all monastic orders, including his own. It was also at this time—in 1536—that Bale married, and undoubtedly this change in his life fueled his polemics about the Roman Church's demand for clerical celibacy.[34] Bale identified the ideal of marriage for the clergy as an Anglo-Saxon custom that had been brought to an end with the Norman Conquest. "I omit to declare for lengthe of the matter," he wrote in *Apology against a Rank Papist* (xiii), "what mischefe and confusion, vowes [vows] brought to this realme by the Danes and Normannes, whan the lyves of the vowers in their monasteries were more beastlye than eyther amonge paganes or Turkes." Bale, who was unaware that the Danes were not Christian, believed that the monks and clergymen, once forced to give up wives, turned to "bestlye" lives worse than those lived by pagans or Turks. In other words, he thought they had become sodomites.

Sodomy also figured in Bale's plays, his best-known works. In *A Comedy concernynge Thre Lawes, of Nature, Moses, & Christ, Corrupted by the Sodomytes, Pharysees, and Papystes* (1538), written before the historical studies just sampled, Bale created a character named Sodomismus, an allegorical figure unique in sixteenth-century English drama.[35] Sodomismus is one of six vice characters in the play. Attired "lyke a monkw of all sectes," according to Bale,[36] Sodomismus repeatedly associates himself with both monks and the pope.

> I dwelt amonge the Sodomytes,
> The Benjamytes and Madyantes
> And now the popish hypocrytes
>   Embrace me every where.
> I am now become all spyrytuall [i.e., taken over by spiritual
>   leaders],[37]
> For the clergye at Rome and over all
> For want of wives, to me doth fall,
>   To God they have no feare. (2:571–78).

Pederastic unions are listed among the forms of sodomy he promotes.

> In Rome to me they fall,
> Both byshopp and cardynall,
> Monke, fryre, prest and all,
>   More ranke they are than antes.
> Example in Pope Julye,

Whych sought to have in hys furye
Two laddes, and to use them beastlye,
   From the Cardinall of Nantes. (2:643–50).

Had he known about Gregory's letter to Candidus, Bale would have had an even more pertinent example of how a Roman pope allegedly abused innocent boys.

In *King Johan*, which casts the king as an opponent of clerical corruption, the king speaks for Bale's position. Johan (King John) regrets that the clergy

Shuld thus bynd yowre selfe to the grett captyvyte
Of blody Babulon the grownd and mother of whordom—
The Romych Churche I meane, more vyle than ever was
   Sodom.[38]

For Bale, "sodomites" were not only the unjust and impious but also those who turned from the lawful union of marriage and had illicit intercourse either with the opposite sex or with their own. In *A Comedy concernynge Thre Lawes*, Sodomismus claims to have inspired all manner of sexual sinners, ranging from the fallen angels who fornicated with the daughters of men (Genesis 6:1–4) to Onan (Genesis 38:9; see *A Comedy*, 580–610). The offense that seems most closely connected to sodomy in Bale's mind is idolatry, represented in the play as Idolatria, an old woman. Idolatria is the companion of Sodomismus, who speaks to her in terms of endearment, calling her "myne owne swetehart of golde" (481). Sodomismus is sexually profligate, not exclusively or even primarily interested in same-sex intercourse. His accusations against monks and popes, however, conform precisely to those Bale himself made in his nondramatic works.

The inference that Bale had accused Gregory of sodomy was drawn by Bale's Catholic opponent, who recognized the unacknowledged source of Bale's story in Bede's *Ecclesiastical History*. In 1565, in the first translation of Bede's *Ecclesiastical History* in modern English, Thomas Stapleton listed "a number of diuersities between the pretended religion of Protestants, and the primitive faith of the english Church" (he counted forty-five points of difference in all). Stapleton contrasted the authority of Bede, who wrote without prejudice, with that of Bale, Foxe, and other "pretended refourmers." Stapleton discussed the episode involving Gregory and the Anglian boys in his preface. Bede, who was close to this event, had told a story contrasting outer beauty with inner lack of belief. Bale had deliberately misread the event in order to charge Gregory "with a most outrageous vice and not to be named." Stapleton obviously understood Bale to have accused Gregory of sodomy. Bede was a bee who made honey (beautiful meaning) out of this episode, said Stapleton, but Bale was a "vemmous spider being filthy and uncleane himself," an "olde ribauld," and "another Nero" who found "poisonned sence and meaning" therein.[39]

To be fair, Bale's interpretation, admittedly harsh, is somewhat better than Stapleton allowed. Bale forces us to reconsider Bede's treatment of the anecdote and calls our attention to its dark side, its shadow. The episode about Gregory and the boys is animated by the contrast between light and dark, outside and inside. Gregory calls Satan "the author of darkness" who holds "men so bright of face in his grip." He finds the Anglians "devoid of inward grace" while admiring their "graceful ... outward form[s]." Gregory's language clearly recognizes that physical and moral beauty exist in close proximity to the evil and the ugly. Bede did not look beyond Gregory's words for these malignant forces. Instead he saw the brightness of the episode, which marked the "Angli" as a people elevated by their likeness, at least in Gregory's mind, to angels. Bale saw around Gregory's words and, like Gregory himself, recognized how near evil was to the good. But Bale reversed the field of Gregory's vision, casting Gregory into the darkness where Gregory himself saw Satan. What lived in that darkness was same-sex desire, the unholy appetite of Gregory and other reluctant celibates for the sexual favors of young Englishmen. Such shadows, dark places of evil and corruption, are not the only kind of shadows where same-sex relations can be seen. They are not the kinds of shadows I think of when I think of the presence of same-sex love in a heterosexual world. All the same, Bale's vision of the shadow, however distasteful it might seem, is, in context, accurate. The sexual abuse of young boys was a danger to which life in the monastery exposed them, as the penitentials show. Slavery was another danger, not unrelated, that lurked in the episode Bede describes. It is difficult to deny that the shadows seen by Bale are places where "the author of darkness," as Gregory called him, held sway.

Bale's recasting of Anglo-Saxon history had a prominent sexual aspect, if not a primary sexual character. He saw the Anglo-Saxons as a people who naturally observed God's lawful commandment to be fruitful and multiply. Their Roman oppressors, on the other hand, were those who denied clergy the right to marry and, as a result, spread sexual corruption wherever they were to be found. Gregory's "wele eyenge" of the slave boys' "wares" vividly emblematizes this exploitation and situates it in the heart of Rome. For Bale, Anglo-Saxon identity was continuous with British identity that predated the arrival of the Anglo-Saxons. English identity emerged out of this combined British-Anglo-Saxon identity in a struggle against the enslaving bonds of Roman and then Norman domination. Racial differences are but vaguely registered by Bale, and his chronology, not unexpectedly, is confused. Malgo won victories over "Saxons, Normeies, and Danes," for example, even though it was the Saxons who subverted the realm (22a). Bale's historical discourse, punctuated with numerous references to Sodom and allegations of homosexual acts among the clergy, is entirely free of allegory (his plays, obviously, are not). Bale did not need a figurative discourse about angels or origins to celebrate what was, for him, the distinguishing feature of his sources. His sense of who was Saxon, Norman, or Dane was imprecise, but Bale unquestionably understood that Gildas, Bede, Geoffrey of Monmouth, Chaucer, and others, were not mythical figures but were instead his predecessors, righteous as he was himself.[40] He was sure that the history he chronicled was as English as he was. His association of corrupt sexual practices with foreign powers—Roman and Catholic especially—is therefore easily explained, however disagreeable we find it. His polemical use of sodomy strongly resembles that of the Anglo-Norman historians and chroniclers on whose work he drew. But whereas they directed their diatribes against their own princes and rulers, Bale directed his at the princes of the Catholic Church. Among their agents he numbered the Norman conquerors of England, the despoilers of the True Church of the British.

ANGELS AND ANGLI

Another polemicist and dramatist with a vague sense of the Anglo-Saxon past and strong views on its significance is Tony Kushner. His celebrated two-part drama, *Angels in America: A Gay Fantasia on National Themes*, approaches the Anglo-Saxons through the stereotype of the WASP. Kushner correlates same-sex relations with racial stereotypes and national heritage and makes revealing use of Anglo-Saxon culture that is seldom noticed by the play's admirers. Kushner's AIDS-infected hero is the play's only WASP, the thirty-second Prior Walter in a line traced to the Norman Conquest so that it can represent the Anglo-Saxon hegemony of the West. But *Angels* reverses a dynamic that operates in all the other texts I have examined throughout this study. Anglo-Saxon penitentials, histories, poems, and commentaries ultimately side with the angels. And so, for that matter, do Chaucer and Bale, Custance being Chaucer's angel, the English boys being Bede's and Bale's. Angels are pure, either above sex or, if involved with sexual relations, chastely married; they are on the side of order. Sodomites, however they have been defined, are not. They and same-sex relations are stigmatized and repressed because they subvert order, lack shame, and threaten to lead others into sin.

In order to express Kushner's millennial vision, *Angels in America* rewrites the social history of England (and America) in order to enable a new era in which same-sex relations thrive while heterosexual relations wither. Kushner does not take the side of the angels but rather represents them as weak, lost, and prejudiced. Amid their confusion, paradoxically, their saving grace is that they retain their sexual prowess. The Angel of America, as she will be known, enters the play as a messenger to a white, Anglo-Saxon, Protestant but exits taking advice because the WASP is also a PWA, a "person with AIDS," prophet of a new homosocial order and herald of a revolution so sweeping that it offers redemption even for angels.

Rich in references to migratory voyages and the Chosen People, *Angels in America* advances a broad argument about history and progress. The play is a multicultural juxtaposition of WASP, Jewish, black, and Mormon traditions, among others. David Savran has argued that the "spiritual geography" of Mormonism is central to the play's "conceptualization of America as the site of a blessed past and a millennial future." Savran demonstrates that Mormonism was among the evangelical, communitarian sects formed in reaction to the individualism fostered by Jacksonian democracy and the ideology of Manifest Destiny.[41] A key element in the racial basis of Manifest Destiny, which claimed for the chosen people "a preeminent social worth, a distinctively lofty mission, and consequently unique rights in the application of moral principles,"[42] is Anglo-Saxonism. The premise of Anglo-Saxonism (familiar in earlier forms in the works of Gildas, Bede, Chaucer, and Bale, as we have seen, and many others, of course) is that the English are a Chosen People and a superior race.[43] Numerous nineteenth-century accounts used the racial purity of the Anglo-Saxons to justify westward expansion and empire building. Anglo-Saxon culture was thought to have been inherently democratic and the Anglo-Saxons egalitarian, self-governing, and free. The descendants of a people who so perfectly embodied the principles of American democracy had, it appeared, natural rights over lesser peoples and their lands. Anglo-Saxonism enters *Angels in America* through the lineage of Prior Walter. He is a token of the WASP culture—the only white Anglo-Saxon Protestant in the play, according to Kushner[44]—against which the oppressed peoples of the play, Jews and blacks in particular, strive.

The Anglo-Saxon subtext of *Angels* emerges in both parts of the drama, *Millennium Approaches* and *Perestroika*, through the association of Prior Walter with the angel. Kushner locates Prior's origins in the mid-eleventh century, but the Anglo-Saxon characteristics that Prior represents are prior to the Normans, whose conquest of England constitutes a particularly troubled originary moment for the chief Anglo-Saxon of the play. An early scene in each of the three acts of *Millennium Approaches* reveals something about Prior's Anglo-Saxon identity (act 1, scene 4; act 2, scene 3; and act 3, scene 1). In the first of the scenes about his lineage, Prior jokes with Louis, his Jewish lover, after a funeral service for Louis's grandmother. Prior comments on the difficulties that their relatives present for gay men: "Bloodlines," he says. "Jewish curses are the worst. I personally would dissolve if anyone ever looked me in the eye and said 'Feh.' Fortunately WASPs don't say 'Feh'" (1:20).[45] A few moments later he reveals his first AIDS lesions to Louis, who is horrified both by the lesions and by Prior's mordant jocularity about them. This scene establishes Prior's AIDS status and his WASP identity and introduces the largest of the cultural themes of *Angels in America*: the resistance that biological descent and inherited tradition, embodied here in the body of the WASP, pose to political change. Bloodlines are curses because they carry the past into the present, creating resistance to the possibilities of change that the present raises. WASP blood resists change because WASPs, as they are presented in this play, exist in a culture of stasis, while other races and creeds, denied that stability and permanence and driven by persecution and need from place to place, have developed migratory and transitional cultures open to, and indeed dependent on, change.

Having inherited a distinguished past, Prior faces an uncharacteristically grim future (for a WASP) because he carries a fatal new element in his bloodline, AIDS. The virus paradoxically reverses the deadening flow of WASP tradition and prepares for a new social order whose values the WASP himself will eventually espouse. The virus he bears is both literal (HIV) and figurative; it is eventually identified as "the virus of time," the "disease" of change and progress. The angel who appears to Prior at the end of *Millennium Approaches*, and who punctuates the play with intimations of her arrival, claims to herald a new age. When Prior receives his first intimation of the angelic, a feather drops into his room and an angelic voice ("an incredibly beautiful voice," the text specifies) commands, "Look up! ... Prepare the way!" (1:34–35). But the side of the angels is not what we expect it to be. The angel is not pointing to a new age but instead calling for a return to a previous one. The tradition and stasis that constitute Prior's Anglo-Saxon heritage draw her. She believes that Prior will be a worthy prophet precisely because he is a worthy WASP.

Kushner happened on Prior's name when looking "for one of those

WASP names that nobody gets called any more." Discussing Walter
Benjamin with a friend so interested in the philosopher that she sometimes
"thought she was Walter Benjamin reincarnated," Kushner referred to the
real Benjamin as the "prior" Walter.[46] The significance of Prior's name
unfolds in a subsequent dialogue between Louis and Emily, a nurse, after
Prior has been hospitalized. "Weird name. Prior Walter," says Emily. "Like,
'The Walter before this one.'" Louis replies: "Lots of Walters before this
one. Prior is an old old family name in an old old family. The Walters go
back to the Mayflower and beyond. Back to the Norman Conquest. He says
there's a Prior Walter stitched into the Bayeux tapestry" (1:51). The oldest
medieval record mentioned in *Angels in America*, the tapestry would seem
designed to surround Prior's origins with an aura of great antiquity.

The appearance of Prior Walter's name on the tapestry validates
Louis's claim that the Walter name is indeed an "old old" one. But the
Bayeux tapestry is a record of the political and military events surrounding
the Norman Conquest of Anglo-Saxon England in 1066. The tapestry
testifies to the subjugation of the Anglo-Saxons and marks the point at which
the government and official vernacular language of England were no longer
English. Generations of Anglo-Saxonizing historians and writers regarded
the arrival of the Normans as the pollution of the pure stock of the race.[47]
Thus Kushner's announced aim of portraying Walter as a WASP is more
than a little complicated by this decision to trace Walter's ancestry to a
tapestry long accepted as a lucid statement of Norman claims to the English
throne.[48] Notoriously ironic throughout *Angels in America*, Kushner might
have chosen the tapestry to register precisely this compromised aspect of
Prior's lineage.[49] But one's view of that lineage would seem to depend on the
uses to which it is put in *Angels in America*, where it seems intended to
represent the Anglo-Saxons as a monolithic, triumphant culture that has
reached a symbolic end point in Prior's blood.

Emily (played by the actress who plays the angel) is somewhat baffled
by Louis's high regard for Prior's ancient name and for the tapestry itself.
Louis believes that the queen, "La Reine Mathilde," embroidered the
tapestry while William was away fighting the English. In the long tradition
of French historians and politicians who used the tapestry to arouse public
sentiment to support nationalistic causes, including the Napoleonic wars
against the English,[50] Louis pictures Mathilde waiting at home, "stitch[ing]
for years," waiting for William to return. "And if he had returned mutilated,
ugly, full of infection and horror, she would still have loved him," Louis says
(1:52). He is thinking penitently of Prior, who is also "full of infection and
horror," whom Louis will soon abandon for Joe, the married Mormon lawyer

with whom Louis has an affair. Louis's view of when and where the tapestry was made is popular, but wrong. The tapestry was made in England, under the patronage of William's half-brother Odo, bishop of Bayeux and vice-regent of England, within a generation of 1066, not during the Conquest itself, and then taken to the Bayeux Cathedral.[51]

Kushner's mistaken ideas of when, where, and by whom the Bayeux tapestry was made have significant implications for his definition of "WASP." Kushner invokes the Conquest as if its chief force were to certify the antiquity and authenticity of Prior's Anglo-Saxon credentials and heritage, a point of origin for *English* identity, although, as I have shown, it traditionally represented the very betrayal of the racial purity that "Anglo-Saxon" came to represent. Louis's assertion that the name of a "Prior Walter" is stitched into the tapestry is also without foundation. Only four minor characters are named in the tapestry, none of them Anglo-Saxons ("Turold," "Ælfgyva," "Wadard," and "Vital"). The rest are important figures (Harold, William, and others), most of them Norman and well-known from contemporary sources.[52] If Prior Walter were an Anglo-Saxon, it is highly unlikely that he would be commemorated in the tapestry, although it is possible he could have been an English retainer of Harold (who was defeated by William).

But "Prior Walter" is a singularly inappropriate name for an Anglo-Saxon. It strongly suggests an ecclesiastical, monastic context, as if "Prior Walter" were "Walter, prior of" some abbey, instead of the secular and heroic ethos usually called to mind by "Anglo-Saxon." Apart from the tapestry, there is no evidence either for or against an argument about Prior's origins. Although it is possible that his ancestors were Anglo-Saxon, it is more likely that they were Normans who, after the Conquest, settled in England and established the line from which the Walters descended. Few Anglo-Saxons would expect to find their ancestors mentioned in the tapestry, while Normans would want to boast of this testimony to a family's distinguished history. The original Prior Walter might have been a Norman who took part in the conquest of the English. His family would have been prosperous. As we saw in the last chapter, the Anglo-Saxons were less well-to-do than their conquerors and resented the superiority of French into the fourteenth century. If so, as the last in a line of thirty-one men of the same name (or, by an alternative count, if bastard sons are included, thirty-three [1:86]), Prior Walter claims Norman rather than Anglo-Saxon ancestry, or, more likely, a heritage in which Norman and Anglo-Saxon blood is mixed-in other words, Anglo-Norman. His long genealogy, to which Louis proudly points, is hybrid at its origins. Kushner's stereotype of the WASP is itself a further hybrid, obviously, since it is a post-Reformation construct in which P

("Protestant") is a new element. WASP, we can see, is not only a recent
vehicle for the representation of "Anglo-Saxon" culture, but an exceedingly
shallow one.[53]

We learn more about Prior's ancestry at the start of the third act, when
two prior Priors appear to him in a dream (1:85–89). The first to appear, the
"fifth of the name," is the thirteenth-century squire who is known as "Prior
1." He tells of the plague that wiped out whole villages, the "spotty monster"
that killed him (1:86). (This is another sign of Kushner's shaky historical
sense; the first outbreak of the Black Death in England was a century later,
in 1348.)[54] They are joined by "Prior 2," described as "an elegant 17th-
century Londoner" (1:86), who preceded the current Prior by some
seventeen others and also died of the plague, "Black Jack." Priors 1 and 2 are
not merely ancient ancestors, however. They are also the forerunners of the
angel whose arrival spectacularly concludes the play. To "distant, glorious
music," they recite the language later used by the angel; her messengers, they
are "sent to declare her fabulous incipience." "They [the angels] chose us,"
Prior 2 declares, "because of the mortal affinities. In a family as long-
descended as the Walters there are bound to be a few carried off by plague"
(1:87). Neither Prior 1 nor Prior 2 understands why Prior is unmarried and
has no wife, although the second Prior understands that the plague infecting
Prior is "the lamentable consequence of venery" (1:87). Only later, when
they see him dancing with Louis, does Prior 1 understand: "Hah. Now I gee
why he's got no children. He's a sodomite" (1:114). Prior Walter is,
therefore, the end of his line. After him the WASP hegemony of the Walters,
apparently unbroken from the mid-eleventh century to the present, will
cease to exist.

The vague and portentous sense of these genealogical relations is
clarified in the next scene (1:89–96), in which Louis engages in a long,
confused, and painfully naive monologue about race and identity politics in
America, much to the disgust of his friend Belize, a black nurse and ex-drag
queen.[55] Louis describes a difference between American and European
peoples that encapsulates the tension between Anglo-Saxons and other races.
"Ultimately what defines us [in America] isn't race, but politics," he says.
"Not like any European country where there's an insurmountable fact of a
kind of racial, or ethnic, monopoly, or monolith, like all Dutchmen, I mean
Dutch people, are, well, Dutch, and the Jews of Europe were never
Europeans, just a small problem" (1:90). Significantly, Kushner chooses
England as site for a scene in which, according to Louis, the "racial destiny,"
not the "political destiny," matters (1:91). A Jew in a gay bar in London,
Louis found himself looked down upon by a Jamaican man who still spoke

with a "lilt," even though his family had been in England for more than a century. At first this man, who complained that he was still treated as an outsider, struck Louis as a fellow traveler: "I said yeah, me too, these people are anti-Semites." But then the man criticized British Jews for keeping blacks out of the clothing business, and Louis realized how pervasive racial stereotypes could be (1:91). In America, Louis believes, there is no racial monopoly; in America the "monolith is missing," so "reaching out for a spiritual past in a country where no indigenous spirits exist" is futile (1:92). The native peoples have been killed off "there are no angels in America, no spiritual past, no racial past, there's only the political and the decoys and the ploys to maneuver around the inescapable battle of politics, the shifting downwards and outwards of political power to the people" (1:92). Wiped clean of its indigenous spirits, the nation as Louis sees it would seem to be a blank slate not unlike England before the Anglo-Saxons, ready for migratory peoples (including Jews and Mormons) who bring their past with them as they seek to build a new future. Belize holds Louis's liberal interpretation of American government and culture in utter contempt. Kushner ensures that the naiveté of the Jew's liberalism will be exposed and contained by Belize's furious reply that in America race is more important than anything else.

Louis's speech reveals the meaning of Anglo-Saxon that is encapsulated in Prior's WASP identity. Even though Prior's mixed Norman and Anglo-Saxon genealogy contradicts Louis's point about the monolith of racial purity that the WASP supposedly represents, Prior is singled out as the recipient of the angel's visit because he is made to represent the cultural monolith of WASP America, fixed and unchanging, embodying what Louis calls "an insurmountable fact of a kind of racial, or ethnic, monopoly, or monolith" (1:90). WASP heritage stands conveniently juxtaposed both to Louis's vision and to Louis's own heritage of many small groups, "so many small problems" (1:90). Although Kushner might have wished to represent the Anglo-Saxons only as a hybrid people, and hence introduced evidence that points to the eleventh-century intermingling of Norman blood, it seems evident to me that the racial dynamics of the play require that the Anglo-Saxons represent the "monolith" about which Louis speaks. Only then can other races and groups be set up in opposition to them.

Indeed, even in motion, the Anglo-Saxons of *Angels in America* are oppressors. One of the most harrowing moments in *Millennium Approaches* is Prior's account of his ancestor, a ship's captain, who sent whale oil to Europe and brought back immigrants, "Irish mostly, packed in tight, so many dollars per head." The last ship he captained sank off Nova Scotia in a storm; the crew loaded seventy women and children onto an open boat but found that it was overcrowded and began throwing passengers overboard: "They walked up and down the longboat, eyes to the waterline, and when the boat rode low in the water they'd grab the nearest passenger and throw them into the sea" (1:41). The boat arrived in Halifax carrying nine people. Crewmen are the captain's agents; the captain is at the bottom of the sea, but his "implacable, unsmiling men, irresistibly strong, seize ... maybe the person next to you, maybe you" (1:41–42). The agents of the Anglo-Saxons arbitrarily decide the fates of the Irish in their care The episode is a stark political allegory, a nationally rendered reminder of the rights of one group to survive at the expense of another, a deft miniature that reveals the power of the conquerors over the conquered, the interrelation of commerce and the immigration patterns of impoverished nations, and, most of all, "unique rights in the application of moral principles," a signature belief of Manifest Destiny.[56]

The point of the association of stasis with Anglo-Saxon heritage—the grand design of *Angels in America*—emerges fully in *Perestroika*, when the Angel of America articulates her ambitions for the WASP and discloses the assumed affiliations between the Anglo-Saxons and the angels. The angel attempts to persuade Prior to take up her prophecy. "I I I I / Am the Bird of America," she proclaims, saying that she has come to expose the fallacy of change and progress (2:44), "the Virus of TIME" that God released in man (2:49), enabling humans to explore and migrate. Angels do not migrate; instead, they stand firm (2:49). God himself found time irresistible and began to prefer human time to life in heaven. The angel says:

> Paradise itself Shivers and Splits
> Each day when You awake, as though WE are only
>   the Dream of You.
> PROGRESS! MOVEMENT!
> Shaking *HIM*. (2:50)

A few moments later She shouts, "You *HAVE DRIVEN HIM AWAY!* YOU MUST STOP MOVING!" (2:52). God became so bored with the angels that he abandoned them on the day of the 1906 San Francisco earthquake. And who could blame him? In the one scene that Kushner gives performers the permission to cut, if only in part (act 5, scene 5; see 2:9), the angels are shown sitting around heaven listening to a malfunctioning 1940s radio over which they hear the broadcast of the meltdown of the Chernobyl reactor. Their real concern, however, is the radio's malfunctioning vacuum tube (2:130). They are a picture of feckless paralysis, obviously unable to respond to the changes forced on them by human or heavenly time. "More nightmare than utopia, marooned in history," Savran writes, "Heaven commemorates disaster, despair, and stasis."[57] The purpose of the angel's visitation is to recruit Prior as the angels' prophet on earth. Angels, we see, are not messengers from the divine or heralds of change, although that is how we conventionally think of them, and how Kushner and the play's publicity represent them. Angels are instead associated with stasis and with the power of ancient spirits to resist change. Opposed to the flow of power "downward and outward," as Louis puts it, of "power to the people," the angels want God to return to his place so that they can return to theirs.

The angel's visit is not intended to save Prior from his disease but to use his disease against him, to try to persuade this "long descended" man (like the angel in this) to stop the phenomenon of human progress, to get him to turn back the clock. The angel says to him that she has written "The End" in his blood. This could mean that the AIDS virus is supposed to ensure his desire to stop time—stop the progress of the disease—and prompt him to proclaim her message (2:53), although what is written in his blood could also be his homosexuality, which writes "The End" in a different sense, since it means that he is the last of his line. Later in the scene in which the angel commands Prior to stand still, symbolically appealing to his Anglo-Saxon love of stability and tradition, Belize dismisses the vision as Prior recounts it: "This is just you, Prior, afraid of the future, afraid of time. Longing to go backwards so bad you made this angel up, a cosmic reactionary" (2:55). Prior and Belize were once lovers; Belize knows him well. Like Prior, three other figures—the angel, Sister Ella Chapter (a friend of Joe's mother in Salt Lake City), and the nurse (all played by the actress who plays the angel)—are fearful of movement. Emily does not want Louis to leave the hospital room (1:52). Before Joe's mother moves to New York to help Joe cope with his schizophrenic wife, Harper, Ella reminds her that Salt Lake City is "the home of the saints" and "the godliest place on earth," and then cautions, "Every step a Believer takes away from here is a step fraught with peril" (1:83). But Ella's is not a view that the play endorses. Joe's mother leaves anyway. All the chosen people do.

Like her, Prior rejects the advice to stay put. He ignores the angel's command precisely because "The End" is written in his blood. He interprets these words as the angel's wish that he die: "You want me dead" (2:53). No longer the Prior who joked fatalistically about his lesions outside the funeral home in act 1 of *Millennium Approaches*, he refuses to die. Because he has contracted "the virus of time, the WASP, who has the most to lose, turns from the past to the future. All the "good" characters in the play are already on the move, already evolving, even Joe's drug-maddened wife, just as all the valorized nations and races in the play have migrated. The prominence of migration and the movement away from racial purity are basic elements of Kushner's thesis about change, which is based on an idea of the Anglo-Saxons, the WASPS, as static, permanent, and fixed. Politics change racial makeup and break down pure races and their racism. Kushner explains:

> Prior is the only character in the play with a Yankee WASP background; he can trace his lineage back for centuries, something most Americans can't reliably do. African-American family trees have to start after ancestors were brought over as slaves. Jews emigrated from a world nearly completely destroyed by European genocide. And most immigrant populations have been from poor and oppressed communities among which accurate genealogy was a luxury or an impossibility.... a certain sense of rootlessness is part of the American character.[58]

Anglo-Saxon history prior to the Normans shows that "a certain sense of rootlessness" is also part of the Anglo-Saxon character. American rootlessness was inherited from the nation's Anglo-Saxon founders; the Anglo-Saxons in America were hardly a people who wanted to stay put. It is because of their restlessness and their desire to move westward that Louis, as Kushner's surrogate, can assert that there are no angels in America.[59]

Kushner's association of WASPs with stasis is his most interesting—but least accurate—reinterpretation of the historical record. Kushner seems to think that Anglo-Saxons—WASPs at least—are not a migratory people. At this point his play helps us see a truth in Bede's *Ecclesiastical History* that Bede himself did not acknowledge. Bede reported that after the migration of the Angles to Britain, the land of "Angulus" remained empty "from that day to this." Are there no angels in America? There are no angels in Angulus, either, because the entire population moved to Britain. Thus the Angles took *their* ancient spirits with them, just as did blacks, Jews, and other migrant peoples. Already in the eighth century the immigrants to Britain were known as Anglo-Saxons.[60]

Louis's tendentious view of history is easily discredited, and not only by Belize. The intermarrying of Anglo-Saxon and Norman families ended the pure monolith of "the English" that Prior Walter supposedly represents. What is true of Prior Walter and all WASPS was true for people in England even before the Conquest. "Apartheid is hard enough to maintain," Susan Reynolds writes, "even when physical differences are obvious, political control is firm, and records of births, deaths, and marriages are kept. After a generation or two of post-Roman Britain not everyone, perhaps comparatively few people, can have been of pure native or invading descent. Who can have known who was descended from whom?" Reynolds draws the inescapable conclusion that "those whom we call Anglo-Saxons were not consistently distinguishable from everyone else."[61] After the Conquest, of course, the Anglo-Saxons became less "Anglo-Saxon" than they had been earlier, but at no time were bloodlines in Anglo-Saxon England pure; like most bloodlines, they were even then more the consequence of politics than they were of race.

This severing of biological descent and culture is a denial of the power of race to unify a people. That is the good news of *Angels in America* for homosexuals, the new Chosen People of this epic (what epic does not have one?). Like Mormons, Jews, and other racial groups, gay people too are oppressed, without a homeland, and on the move. But unlike those groups, gays are, first of all, a *political* people, not bound by nation or race. They have no common descent; there is no link between their sexual identity, which the play sees as their central affiliation, and either their biological or their cultural ancestry. So seen, gays serve as a perfect prophetic vehicle for Kushner's new multicultural America. Prior succeeds in subverting the angels' design and persuading them to become his messenger; he has refused to become theirs. Their message is that the clock should be turned back to old values and stasis, staying put. His message is that change is good. Won over to humanity's view of time and place, the angels sue God, resorting to time-bound human processes (litigation) to redress grievances. The joke apparently is that the angels' heavenly wishes are inferior to the desires of humanity. The new angels of America know better than the Angel of America because Prior, their WASP spokesman, resoundingly refutes the angel's call for stasis. God, however, will probably win; his lawyer is Roy Cohn, the demon in *Angels*. Discredited at this point, God is a disloyal lover who has abandoned his angels for (the men of?) San Francisco. The angels, in turn, are also discredited, for they have accepted Prior's suggestion that those who abandon their lovers should not be forgiven, just as Prior will not forgive or take back Louis (2:133, 136).

So Prior moves ahead, not in spite of AIDS but rather *because* of AIDS. The "virus of time" has jolted him out of torpor and self-pity and eventually transforms him into the play's strongest character, a position from which he waves an affectionate goodbye to the audience. This is an AIDS play with a difference—with a happy ending.[62] Because he is a WASP the angel singled him out, but because he is a PWA he rejects her. In *Angels in America*, AIDS retains its deadly force (Cohn and others die of it) without killing the play's central character. Obviously weakened, but strong nonetheless, Prior survives. Having been visited by an angel, Prior all but becomes one. "You are fabulous creatures, each and every one," he says to the audience. "And I bless you: *More Life*. The Great Work begins" (2:148). He recapitulates the last lines of Millennium Approaches, in which the Angel declares, "Greetings, Prophet. The Great Work begins. The Messenger has arrived" (1:119). Another messenger has arrived at the end of Perestroika, and his name is Prior Walter. Prior's farewell to the audience, however moving, is a remarkable banality to which I will return.

Savran argues that the play, like *The Book of Mormon*, "demonstrates that there are angels in America, that America is in essence a utopian and theological construction, a nation with a divine mission.[63] It is possible to suggest that Bede and Kushner share a political purpose, which is to create the idea of a unified people. Bede does this with the term—the concept— "Angli," which comes to mean "the English," a people elevated by their likeness to angels. Like Chaucer and Bale, Kushner is also out to unify a people, but more ambitiously and inclusively, and not a people to be compared to angels, but a people to replace them. The threat that unifies the English in Bede's work is the heathen past. The same might be said for Chaucer's ancient British Christians, at least as the Man of Law imagines them. Bale too imagined the British as overwhelmed by Roman Catholicism as brought by the Anglo-Saxons; he saw the British of his own time triumphing over the same evil force. The threat that unifies Kushner's new angels is not AIDS, which only menaces a small percentage of them, but the old regimes of race that divide and weaken people and prevent change, the very forces of conservative national and religious identity that Bede, Chaucer, and Bale advocated so powerfully. Those forces are routed at the end of *Angels in America*, and the boards are clear for a new age. The promised land of *Angels in America* is a multicultural, tolerant world in which biological descent counts for little (there are no successful marriages in the play) and cultural inheritance imparts defining characteristics to people without imposing barriers among them.

MILLENNIUM APPROACHES

I began thinking about this study in 1993, when I saw *Angels in America* for the first time. I was troubled by the conflation of Anglo-Saxon and Norman identities and unclear about how Kushner meant to align his vaguely sketched history of Prior's family with the play's sexual politics. It seemed obvious that he had merely used the WASP as a rhetorical trope and that he had not thought about the Anglo-Saxonism contained in that acronym or how Anglo-Saxonism might be related to his historical thesis about Mormons or, for that matter, angels in America. Kushner ignored the hybrid nature of WASP identity. Likewise, he missed the prominence of same-sex friendships in the nineteenth-century Mormon tradition. D. Michael Quinn has noted that Mormons, although sometimes seen as clannish and isolated, participated fully in what Quinn describes as the "extensive homocultural orientation among Americans generally" a century ago.[64] Same-sex relations, sexual and otherwise, figure prominently in the history of early Morinon leaders, male and female alike. Kushner's representation of the Mormons would lead one to believe otherwise, however, since his Mormons seem hardly aware that homosexuality exists.

In not knowing much about the Anglo-Saxons, Kushner shares a great deal with the authors I have examined in part 3 of this book. The Anglo-Norman chroniclers knew next to nothing about the Anglo-Saxons that they did not get from Bede's *Ecclesiastical History*. A few later writers, including thirteenth-century scholars, struggled to recover the Anglo-Saxons' language, but their efforts mostly reveal how quickly knowledge of the Anglo-Saxons' culture, even their ecclesiastical culture, had faded. Chaucer and his contemporaries knew even less, relying again on French chronicles to conjure images of the Anglo-Saxon past. For all his testy and repetitive declarations, Bale was closer than any of his predecessors to real knowledge of the Anglo-Saxons. Despite his errors and confusion, his knowledge of a continuous historical tradition and its sources shames both earlier and especially later efforts. The "scholarly recovery" of Anglo-Saxon language and texts advanced rapidly after Bale's time but did not, for many years, produce a representation of Anglo-Saxon culture any more accurate than his.

Kushner, unfortunately, did no better than the other authors I have named. I take *Angels in America* as a reasonable, if regrettable, reflection on popular understanding of Anglo-Saxon culture. Kushner seems to be more respectful of Mormon traditions than of Anglo-Saxon traditions. The play contains a diorama portraying the Mormons' westward journey but nothing about the migration of the Anglo-Saxons (2:62–72). Mormon culture seems alien to him and hence multiculturally significant; its history needs to be recaptured and represented. WASP culture, evidently, is familiar and does not need to be elaborated. But at least in the extended historical sense that Kushner evokes through his use of the Bayeux tapestry, WASP culture too is alien to him. Its multicultural significance is ignored, homogenized into stereotypical patterns and ideas. Absent the oversimplified WASP, would *Angels in America* have had a culture to demonize and denounce?

Angels in America is unique among the works I have discussed in not taking the side of the angels. More important, it is also unique in its perspective on same-sex love. As I showed in part 1, it is possible to glimpse satisfying moments of same-sex love—if not same-sex sex—in opera and dance, and even in a few Anglo-Saxon narrative texts. Gays and lesbians hoping to find representations of love as they know it can find it in these works, sometimes at a small cost (i.e., closing our eyes at the opera), often at no cost. But when we go to *Angels in America*, we have no need to deprive our senses in any way. This is a work that, like many others, not only aims to show gays and lesbians what the author assumes we want to see but even blesses its audience for showing up. There are many differences between the power of such a work and that of *Dido and Aeneas*, as danced by Mark Morris, and the power of *Der Rosenkavalier*, with its use of the convention of the trouser role. The central difference, it seems to me, conforms to the difference between liberation and legitimation as approaches to gay and lesbian rights. Kushner and Morris liberate a same-sex perspective; they emphasize the sexual—the homosexual—in a transgressive manner. That is one way to see homosexual sensibility in the modern world, demanding its due. But finding same-sex love in works that are not about homosexual desire—for example, in operas using trouser roles—also legitimates same-sex love by pointing out that it can exist, plainly if unobtrusively, as the shadow of heteronormative desire.

The second time I saw *Angels in America* was New Year's Eve, 1995. My partner and I had bought tickets at a premium because the theater advertized a "party" to follow the performance, which concluded shortly before midnight. The "party" turned out to be glasses of cheap fizzy wine hurriedly passed out by staff members eager to clear the house. The cast reappeared to mock the management's fleecing of the audience and to lead us in "Auld Lang Syne," gracefully lifting the occasion above the circumstances provided for it. Shortly before midnight, in a light snowfall, we walked down a street filled with people who were rushing into bars and restaurants. It was a relief to board the train. The cars were also full—some couples, some groups, some singles, some straight, some gay—but oddly quiet, a capsule of greater Chicago heading to parties or to bed. Between one stop and another the new year arrived. The car's little communities acknowledged the moment without ceremony. Gay, straight, alone, together, we rode happily along. For me the calm—the indifference—made a welcome change from the excitement and intensity of the play and the hustle of the street. No angels crashed through the roof, no heterosexuals were chastised, no homosexuals turned into saints (or demons), no call to a great work of liberation sounded. This is all right,

I thought to myself. This is how the millennium, Kushner's and any other, will come, and go.

That is also how I think same-sex love goes along in the world, how it works best for some of us at least—love that belongs in the picture, always there, an ever-present shadow. Political and social work will always be needed to win equal treatment for gays, lesbians, bisexuals, and others who make up sexual minority groups. But there are many ways in which that work can be undertaken. I know that many activists cannot see themselves resting until the difference between heterosexual and homosexual is obliterated and such institutions as marriage and the family are transformed and open partnerships and public sex become the new norms. These people see no reason why the institutions of heterosexual desire should be their institutions. Neither do I. Nor do I see why the institutions of homosexual desire should be mandated for all. My vision of same-sex love might seem tepid and diffuse, devoid of passion and revolutionary fervor, not queer enough. Perhaps it is. But I strongly believe that same-sex love cannot be reduced to genital sex, and I will always believe that life is more interesting, pleasurable, and meaningful if its erotic potential can be realized across a spectrum that includes but is not restricted to the sexual. A world that slowly gets used to that idea would seem a better home to me than any queer planet I have yet to see described.

NOTES

1. See Robert P. Miller, ed., *Chaucer: Sources and Backgrounds* (New York: Oxford University Press, 1977), 484. On the narrator's many apostrophes, see the explanatory notes by Patricia J. Eberle in Geoffrey Chaucer, *The Riverside Chaucer*, ed. Larry D. Benson; 3d ed. (Boston: Houghton Mifflin, 1987), 856–58. Innocent's treatise was addressed to a deposed cardinal; Chaucer reported that he had translated this work himself. See the G Prologue to the *Legend of Good Women*, lines 414–15, in Benson, *Riverside Chaucer*, 600.

2. References to *The Man of Law's Tale* are given by line number from *Riverside Chaucer*, 89–103.

3. For an analysis of hagiographical tropes in *The Man of Law's Tale*, see Melissa M. Furrow, "The Man of Law's St. Custance: Sex and the Saeculum," *Chaucer Review* 24 (1990): 223–35.

4. Æthelburh was allowed to marry Edwin because he promised to allow her to worship as she wished and agreed to consider accepting her faith as his own. Eventually he did so, but only after letters to him and his wife from Pope Boniface and persuasions of other forms, including victory over his assailants, a vision, and the sage counsel of his wise men. See Bertram Colgrave and R.A.B. Mynors, eds. and trans., *Bede's Ecclesiastical History of the English People* (Oxford: Oxford University Press, 1969), book 2, where the saga of Edwin's conversion occupies chaps. 9–14, pp. 162–89.

5. Colgrave and Mynors, *Bede's Ecclesiastical History*, book 2, chap. 9, pp. 162–63.

6. Some of the Anglo-Saxon evidence discussed in this chapter appears in my essay "Bede and Bawdy Bale: Gregory the Great, Angels, and the 'Angli,'" in *Anglo-Saxonism and the Construction of Social Identity*, ed. Allen J. Frantzen and John D. Niles (Gainesville: University of Florida Press, 1997), 17–39.

7. Colgrave and Mynors, *Bede's Ecclesiastical History*, book 2, chap. 1, pp. 132–35. Gregory's puns were not original with Bede; a version of the story is found the anonymous Whitby, *Life of St. Gregory*, probably written between 704 and 714 but unknown to Bede when he finished the *Ecclesiastical History* in 731. See Bertram Colgrave, ed. and trans., *The Earliest Life of Gregory the Great* (Cambridge: Cambridge University Press, 1985), 49, 144–45.

8. Gildas, *The Ruin of Britain and Other Documents*, ed. and trans. Michael Winterbottom (London: Phillimore, 1978). See Nicholas Howe, *Migration and Myth-Making in Anglo-Saxon England* (New Haven: Yale University Press, 1989), 33–49, for a discussion of Gildas and the pattern of prophetic history.

9. Colgrave, *Earliest Life*, 144–45 note 42. See "Angles" and variants in the index to Colgrave and Mynors, *Bede's Ecclesiastical History*, 596. Recent studies on the meaning of "angli" in Bede's *Ecclesiastical History* do not discuss Gregory's role in choosing the name, presumably because it is seen as merely symbolic. See D.P. Kirby, *The Earliest English Kings* (London: Unwin Hyman, 1991), 13–15; and H.E.J. Cowdrey, "Bede and the 'English People,'" *Journal of Religious History* 11 (1981): 501–23. See also Patrick Wormald, "Bede, the *Bretwaldas*, and the Origins of the *Gens Anglorum*," in *Ideal and Reality in Frankish and Anglo-Saxon Society*, ed. Patrick Wormald with Donald Bullough and Roger Collins (Oxford: Basil Blackwell, 1983), 121–24.

10. Colgrave and Mynors, *Bede's Ecclesiastical History*, book 1, chap. 15, p. 51. For an analysis of the ethnography operating in Bede's analysis, see John Hines, "The Becoming of the English: Identity, Material Culture, and Language in Early Anglo-Saxon England," *Anglo-Saxon Studies in Archaeology and History* 7 (1994): 49–59.

11. Colgrave and Mynors, *Bede's Ecclesiastical History*, book 5, chap. 24, pp. 566–67. Although Bede clearly wished to present the Angles (the angels) as the primary group in the migration, there was never a consensus about which group, the Angles or the Saxons, was primary, or even about where in England they settled. D.P. Kirby notes that Gregory believed that the Saxons settled in the north and the Angles in the south, reversing the usual assumptions about the pattern of distribution and pointing to its arbitrary nature. *The Life of Wilfrid*, who came from York, describes him as a Saxon bishop. See Kirby, *Earliest English Kings*, 12–13.

12. Colgrave and Mynors, *Bede's Ecclesiastical History*, preface, 2–3.

13. Peter Hunter Blair, *The World of Bede* (Cambridge: Cambridge University Press, 1970), 45. See also Hunter Blair, *An Introduction to Anglo-Saxon England* (Cambridge: Cambridge University Press, 1956), 116–17.

14. Colgrave and Mynors, *Bede's Ecclesiastical History*, 72 note 1; the letter is found in Arthur West Haddan and William Stubbs, eds., *Councils and Ecclesiastical Documents Relating to Great Britain and Ireland*, 3 vols. (Oxford: Clarendon, 1871), 3:5 (quoted here), and is translated in Dorothy Whitelock, ed., *English Historical Documents, c. 500–1042* (London: Eyre Methuen, 1979), no. 161, p. 790.

15. David Pelteret, "Slave Raiding and Slave Trading in Early England," *Anglo-Saxon England* 9 (1981): 104. See also Pelteret, *Slavery in Early Mediaeval England: From the Reign of Alfred until the Twelfth Century* (Woodbridge, Suffolk: Boydell Press, 1995).

16. Colgrave, *Earliest Life*, 145 note 43.

17. Dorothy Whitelock, *The Beginnings of English Society* (Harmondsworth, Middlesex: Penguin, 1952), 111. The church allowed penitents to free or manumit slaves as a form of penance or as an act of mercy.

18. On the Council of London of 1102, dominated by Anselm, see the discussion in chapter 6. On the question of selling women who were wives of the clergy into slavery, see A.L. Poole, *From Domesday Book to Magna Carta, 1087–1216*, 2d ed. (Oxford: Oxford University Press, 1955), 40. The Normans' decrees did not affect the status of those who were already slaves, and it continued to be possible for individuals to voluntarily surrender their freedom when compelled by necessity to do so; see Marjorie Chibnall, *Anglo–Norman England, 1066–1166* (Oxford: Basil Blackwell, 1986), 188.

19. Ruth Mazo Karras comments on prostitution and female slaves in "Desire, Descendants, and Dominance: Slavery, the Exchange of Women, and Masculine Power," in *The Work of Work: Servitude, Slavery, and Labor in Medieval England*, ed. Allen J. Frantzen and Douglas Moffat (Glasgow: Cruithne, 1994), 16–29. See also Elizabeth Stevens Girsch, "Metaphorical Usage, Sexual Exploitation, and Divergence in the Old English Terminology for Male and Female Slaves," in *Work of Work*, 30–54. I raise the possibility that the Anglian boys were intended for sexual purposes in *Desire for Origins: New Language, Old English, and Teaching the Tradition* (New Brunswick: Rutgers University Press, 1990), 47.

20. G.L. Brook and R.F. Leslie, eds., *Laȝamon: "Brut,"* 2 vols., EETS, OS, 250, 277 (London: Oxford University Press, 1963, 1978), 2:770. For commentary on versions of the anecdote by Wace and Geoffrey of Monmouth, see Lawman, *Brut*, trans. Rosamond Allen (London: Dent, 1992), 463, notes to lines 14695–923.

21. John Boswell, *Christianity, Social Tolerance, and Homosexuality: Gay People in Western Europe from the Beginning of the Christian Era to the Fourteenth Century* (Chicago: University of Chicago Press, 1980), 144.

22. For an informative survey of Bale's achievement, see Leslie P. Fairfield, *John Bale: Mythmaker for the English Reformation* (West Lafayette, Ind.: Purdue University Press, 1976). See also Hugh A. MacDougall, *Racial Myth in English History: Trojans, Teutons, and Anglo-Saxon* (Hanover, N.H.: University Press of New England, 1982), 33–37. On Bale's Anglo-Saxon manuscripts, see David Dumville, "John Bale, Owner of St. Dcinstan's Benedictional," *Notes and Queries* 41 (1994): 291–95.

23. John N. King, *English Reformation Literature: The Tudor Origins of the Protestant Tradition* (Princeton: Princeton University Press, 1982), 56. For recent commentary on Bale in the context of Renaissance humanism, see Alan Stewart, *Close Readers: Humanism and Sodomy in Early Modern England* (Princeton: Princeton University Press, 1997), 38–83.

24. See Fairfield, *John Bale*, 55–56, 121.

25. John Bale, *The Actes of Englysh Votaryes* (London, 1548), 22a–22b. Stewart comments briefly on this episode, *Close Readers*, 42.

26. Contemporary sources invite wordplay on "Angles" and "Ingles." In the sixteenth century "Ingles" meant both "English" and "a boy-favourite (in bad sense): a catamite" (*OED*), and was used to pun both on "angle" and on "angel." "Ingle" was also a term of abuse for boys who played women on the stage. See Patricia Parker, *Shakespeare from the Margins: Language, Culture, Context* (Chicago: University of Chicago Press, 1996), 143–46.

27. John Bale, *The Image of Bothe Churches* (Antwerp, 1545 or 1546). For Foxe's views, see William Haller, *The Elect Nation: The Meaning and Relevance of Foxe's "Book of Martyrs"* (New York: Harper and Row, 1963).

28. Ultimately these stories derive from Geoffrey of Monmouth, *History of the Kings of Britain*, trans. Sebastian Evans, revised by Charles W. Dunn (New York: Dutton, 1958), book 11, chap. 7, p. 238, for Malgo. Bale indicates a variety of sources, ranging from Gildas to Geoffrey of Monmouth, "Florence" (John) of Worcester, and others, including William Tyndale (22a). Bale's immediate source is probably the *Nova legenda Angliae* of John Capgrave, whose narratives of saints' lives he grossly distorted. See Fairfield, *John Bale*, 114, 121–22.

29. John Bale, *Apology against a Rank Papist* (London, 1550), xxvii, xii (v).

30. John Bale, *The Pageant of Popes* (London, 1574), 36.

31. Bale cites Gregory's "Epistle to Nicolas" (*Pageant of Popes*, 34v–35r).

32. Bale, *Pageant of Popes*, 32.

33. Fairfield, *John Bale*, 17–18, 42–43.

34. This summary is based on Fairfield's analysis, *John Bale*, 31–49.

35. Donald N. Mager, "John Bale and Early Tudor Sodomy Discourse," in *Queering the Renaissance*, ed. Jonathan Goldberg (Durham: Duke University Press, 1994), 141–61. See also Stewart, *Close Readers*, 52–62.

36. John Bale, *A Comedy concernynge Thre Lawes, of Nature, Moses, & Christ, Corrupted by the Sodomytes, Pharysees, and Papystes*, ed. Peter Happé, in *The Complete Plays of John Bale*, 2 vols. (Cambridge: D.S. Brewer, 1986), 2:65–121. References to act and line number are for quotations from this text. On the attire for Sodomismus, see 121.

37. See Happé, *Complete Plays of John Bale*, 165, note to line 575.

38. Bale, *King Johan*, lines 368–70, in Happé, *Complete Plays of John Bale*, 1:39.

39. Thomas Stapleton, *The History of the Church of England Compiled by Venerable Bede, Englishman* (1565; reprint, Menston, England: Scolar, 1973), 3b. Stapleton's translation is used in the Loeb Classical Library, *Baedae opera historica*, ed. J.E. King (New York: Putnam, 1930).

40. John Bale, *Scriptorum illustrium Maioris Brytanniae* ("Ipswich," but really Wesel, 1548). For a list of Bede's works, including an English translation of the Gospel of John ("in patriam transtulit linguam"), see 50v–52r; for Chaucer's, see 198, unhelpfully alphabetized under *G* for "Galfridus Chaucer").

41. David Savran, "Ambivalence, Utopia, and a Queer Sort of Materialism: How *Angels in America* Reconstructs the Nation," *Theatre Journal* 47 (1995): 218. Some of the following material appears in my essay "Prior to the Normans: The Anglo-Saxons in *Angels in America*," in *Approaching the Millennium: Essays on Tony Kushner's Angels in America*, ed. Deborah A. Geis and Steven F. Kruger (Ann Arbor: University of Michigan Press, 1997), 134–50.

42. Manifest Destiny had its roots in a theory of natural rights for a particular race that translates into nationalism and then imperialism. See Albert K, Weinberg, *Manifest Destiny* (1935; reprint, Chicago: Quadrangle, 1963), 8 (for the quote), 41.

43. Reginald Horsman, *Race and Manifest Destiny: The Origins of American Racial Anglo-Saxonism* (Cambridge: Harvard University Press, 1981); the phrase "Manifest Destiny" was not coined until 1845; see 219. On Anglo-Saxonism, see Frantzen, *Desire for Origins*, 15–18, and 27–61, where I comment on the phenomenon as a force in Anglo-Saxon studies from the Renaissance to the present.

44. Tony Kushner, "The Secrets of 'Angels,'" *New York Times*, 27 March 1994, H5.

45. Tony Kushner, *Angels in America: A Gay Fantasia on National Themes*, part 1, *Millennium Approaches* (New York: Theatre Communications Group, 1993); part 2,

Perestroika (New York: Theatre Communications Group, 1994). References to volume and page number are given in the text (vol. 1 for *Millennium Approaches* and vol. 2 for *Perestroika*).

46. Savran, "Ambivalence," 212 note 14.

47. For an excellent summary of this issue, see Clare A. Simmons, *Reversing the Conquest: History and Myth in Nineteenth-Century British Literature* (New Brunswick: Rutgers University Press, 1990), 13–41.

48. The earl Harold was elected king of England at the death of Edward the Confessor in 1066; he was said to have given an oath of allegiance to William, duke of Normandy, and betrayed that oath when he claimed the throne of England. Harold was defeated at the Battle of Hastings by William the Conqueror. See Frank Stenton, *Anglo-Saxon England*, 3d ed. (Oxford: Oxford University Press, 1971), 576–80.

49. According to Savran, "The opposite of nearly everything you say about *Angels in America* will also hold true" ("Ambivalence," 208; see also 222).

50. David J. Bernstein, *The Mystery of the Bayeux Tapestry* (Chicago: University of Chicago Press, 1986), reports that Hitler, like Napoleon, studied the tapestry when he contemplated an invasion of England, 28–30.

51. Bernstein, *Mystery of the Bayeux Tapestry*, 8, 14.

52. Bernstein, Mystery *of* the Bayeux Tapestry, 30.

53. The term was originally used to describe American Protestantism. See E. Digby Baltzell, *The Protestant Establishment: Aristocracy and Caste in America* (New Haven: Yale University Press, 1964). Kushner's elaborate genealogy for Prior Walter attaches a far more ambitious historical and international sense to the term.

54. May McKisack, *The Fourteenth Century, 1307–1399* (Oxford: Oxford University Press, 1959), 219.

55. See Savran, "Ambivalence," 223–24, for an analysis of Kushner's treatment of identity politics and race in this scene.

56. Weinberg, *Manifest Destiny*, 8.

57. Savran, "Ambivalence," 213.

58. Kushner, "Secrets of 'Angels,'" H5.

59. Several reviewers have commented on the identification of Louis with Kushner's own views. See, for example, John Simon, "Angelic Geometry," *New York*, 6 December 1993, 130. Savran says that Louis is "constructed as the most empathetic character in the play" ("Ambivalence," 223).

60. Susan Reynolds, "What Do We Mean by 'Anglo-Saxon' and 'Anglo-Saxons'?" *Journal of British Studies* 24 (1985): 397–98.

61. Reynolds, "What Do We Mean by 'Anglo-Saxon'?" 402–3.

62. On the need for narratives that reverse the usual trajectory of the experience of AIDS, see Steven F. Kruger, *AIDS Narratives: Gender and Sexuality, Fiction and Science* (New York: Garland, 1996), 73–81.

63. Savran, "Ambivalence," 222–23.

64. D. Michael Quinn, *Same-Sex Dynamics among Nineteenth-Century Americans: A Mormon Example* (Urbana: University of Illinois Press, 1996), 2.

JONATHAN FREEDMAN

Angels, Monsters, and Jews: Intersections of Queer and Jewish Identity in Kushner's Angels in America

The foreignness of Jews is a kind of difference unlike others. They are "those people" whom no label fits, whether assigned by the Gaze, the Concept or the State.... [F]or Jewishness, the type is the exception and its absence the rule; in fact you can rarely pick out a Jew at first glance. It's an insubstantial difference that resists definition as much as it frustrates the eye: are they a people? a religion? a nation? All these categories apply, but none is adequate in itself.

—Alain Finkielkraut (164)

The French Jewish critic Alain Finkielkraut neatly encapsulates the conundrum that Jews have long posed to the imagination of the West. Jews are doubtless different—but somehow differently different, in ways that differ markedly over time. To sample just a few of the major Western understandings of the Jew is to see how diverse and contradictory models of Jewish identity have been. Installed since biblical times in a position of national marginality, constructed by medieval theologians as outsiders to revealed truth, persecuted in the early modern period as usurers or pawnbrokers (from whom governments did not hesitate to borrow), defined by eighteenth-century philosophers as members of a debased tribe in need of cultural improvement, and viewed by nineteenth-century ethnologists as an irrevocably inferior race whose members should be deported, sequestered, or

From *PMLA* 113, no. 1 (January 1998). © 1998 by The Modern Language Association of America.

ultimately exterminated, Jews have historically been defined as many contradictory things (Arendt; Langmuir; Poliakov; Rose). And as a new generation of critics has powerfully argued, this multiply constructed figure has an additional property. Although essential to the many different categories by which human difference has been constructed, the Jew challenges the coherence of these classifications (Cheyette; see also Boyarin and Boyarin). If Jews are a race, why do they look so different from one another? If they constitute a religion, how are they to enter the secular nation-state? And if a nation is defined by shared language and culture, how can these people who speak numerous languages and who cleave stubbornly to a culture of their own belong?

Nowhere have both these properties of the Jew—giving a shape to otherness and calling such constructions into question—been more evident than in images of sexual transgression, especially in the later nineteenth century, when entirely new classifications of sexual deviance were elaborated: the degenerate, the pervert, the homosexual. For as Sander Gilman and others have argued, these powerful but unstable models of deviance were built on that shifting figure of all-purpose alterity—the Jew—often, to add to the irony, by assimilating Jewish intellectuals like Max Nordau, Cesare Lombroso, and Freud (Gilman, *Case* and *Jew's Body*; Pick; Harrowitz). The figure of the monstrous Jewish pervert became a staple of anti-Semitic propaganda first in Europe, then in the United States in the late nineteenth century, but the link between the Jew and the sexual other had been forged in the imaginative literature of Europe and England long before—for instance, in medieval mystery plays, which emphasized the Jew's sexual ravenousness and extrahuman powers. Shakespeare's Shylock is a figure metonymically connected with that other merchant of Venice Antonio, whose homoeroticism echoes and is echoed by the Jew's supposed appetite for unnatural reproduction in the form of usury. (According to the medieval philosopher Nicole d'Oresme, for example, "[i]t is monstrous and unnatural that an unfruitful thing should bear, that a thing specifically sterile, such as money, should bear fruit and multiply of itself" [Shell 51].) And Dickens's Fagin is simultaneously a classic Jewish monster with supernatural powers (Fagin does not leave footprints on marshy ground) and one of the first and most fearsome representatives of the child molester, that new figure of sexual pathology in the late nineteenth century. In a more positive vein, Proust's *A la recherche du temps perdu* can be read as a lengthy attempt to play images of the "race maudite" 'damned race,' the Sodomites, against an equally othered race, the Jews (520). The Jewish other and the sexual other were thus frequently placed in vibrant contiguity in the literary traditions of the West well before sexologists or psychologists or race theorists codified that relation.

And yet the overlapping and mutually constitutive discourses on the Jew and the sexually perverse generate questions about each other that disrupt established categories. Shylock's rapacious Jewishness and Antonio's noble homoeroticism measure each other in a way that undermines any simple characterization of Jewish vice or Christian virtue. And in contrast to Dickens's use of anti-Jewish sentiment to enhance the evil of a perverse villain, the dazzling interplay of images of sexual deviance and Jewish otherness in Proust works to undo any stable code of identity, whether rooted in the faubourg Saint-Germain or the rue du Temple.

This categorizing tradition and its destabilizing work superintend my inquiry into the most powerful recent attempt to interrogate the complex interrelation between inscriptions of Jewish and sexual otherness: Tony Kushner's "gay fantasia on national themes," *Angels in America*. Kushner's two-part epic-comic-tragic-fantastic drama has since its first performances in 1991 and 1993 been received with equal doses of critical praise and audience enthusiasm. *Angels* restored to American theater an ambition it has not enjoyed since the days of Eugene O'Neill or Arthur Miller, even though Kushner's syncretism extends the theatrical medium in ways unimagined by his predecessors, conjoining recent American political history, gay male identity politics, Brechtian alienation devices, Mormon mythmaking, Broadway schtick, and cabalistic lore. Along with many other projects, the play undertakes an extensive mapping of the place where figurations of the Jew meet figurations of the sexual other, the deviant, the queer.[1] No other text since *Sodome et Gomorrhe* in *A la recherche* has given such sustained and sympathetic attention to both sides of this complex and long-standing conjuncture. But the disappointment of the play, its flawed conclusion, follows ineluctably from Kushner's need to collapse this parallel and to affirm a vision neither queer nor Jewish. For Kushner desires a dramatic form and an understanding of transcendence that allow a space for queer citizenship in a culture obsessed with the mythography of rebirth and the inevitability of miracle. Much is imaginatively and culturally gained thereby, but it is my doleful task here to suggest that much is lost as well and that what is lost is almost exclusively on the Jewish side of the equation. The play collapses into a traditional assimilationist answer to the questions of Jewish identity it has bravely raised: the price of achieving political efficacy in a Christian-centered culture turns out to be the abandonment of Jewish difference to affirm other forms of difference. In conclusion, I compare Kushner's vision of utopian identity with Walter Benjamin's in "Theses on the Philosophy of History," one of Kushner's inspirations. For in the very text Kushner invokes stands a version of the utopian project that eliminates this kind of Hobson's choice in favor of a politics inspired by but not limited to the definitionless difference culturally inscribed in the figure of the Jew.

The unstable and shifting equation between the sexual transgressive and the Jew is established in *Millennium Approaches*, the first part of *Angels in America*. The play begins with Rabbi Isidor Chemelwitz's eulogizing Louis Ironson's grandmother Sophie in front of Louis and his lover, Prior; one scene later, Prior reveals that he has a Kaposi's sarcoma lesion, "the wine-dark kiss of the angel of death," and proclaims, "I'm going to die" (*Millennium* 21). The fate of Sophie Ironson in America—that "melting pot where nothing melted"—chimes with and ironically foreshadows Prior's, and it is a reminder that his death is too early and starkly inevitable. And the words that Rabbi Chemelwitz speaks of Sophie resonate directly in Prior's experience: "You can never make that crossing that she made, for such Great Voyages in this world do not any more exist. But every day of your lives the miles that voyage between that place and this one you cross. Every day. You understand me? In you that journey is." Although the syntax is stage Yiddish, the language is rich with implication for the two gay men: the archetype for the transformation of identity, which is the mark of queer experience and survival in the play, is the wandering, rootless, shape-shifting Jew who never finds a home. "You do not live in America," claims the Rabbi. "Your clay is the clay of some Litvak shtetl, your air the air of the steppes" (10). The fate of the Jew, like that of the queer, is to be eternally other even in the utopian land that proclaims itself a haven for all aliens. At the end of the play, Prior proclaims, "We will be citizens," underlining his own alienness even in the quest to overcome it (*Perestroika* 148).

Although Kushner emphasizes the contiguity between the Jew and the queer, he does not insist on positing their common alterity. Instead, he uses each as a metonym for the other, creating an interplay of similarity and difference that conspicuously resists reduction into identity. Early in *Millennium Approaches*, for example, Mormon Joe's homoerotic desire is articulated by his dream of Jacob wrestling with a "golden-hair[ed]" angel, an image both of male–male desire and of the struggle between prophetic vocation and queer identity that resonates throughout the play. The dream vision insists on multiplicity and struggle, even in its articulation of a sexually charged oneness—not only in the homoerotically inflected wrestling match between Jacob (soon to be Israel) and an Aryanized angel but also within Joe, whose identifications are multiple. "I'm … It's me. In that struggle," Joe tells his wife, Harper, suggesting that he can be or wants to be both a new Jacob wrestling with the angel for prophetic power and an angel yearning to press his body against a Jewish man's (49).

In yet another important instance of the queer–Jew conjunction, Louis Ironson becomes aware of himself as a Jew only after he encounters anti-Semitism from a Jamaican-born black man in a London gay bar; he says, "I feel like Sid the Yid, you know I mean like Woody Allen in *Annie Hall* with the payess and the gabardine coat" (91). His Jewishness is spotlighted for him—and for the audience—when it comes into contact with the politics of otherness in the gay community. Kushner does not specify which kind of alterity might be more privileged, preferring instead to ironize all possible forms of difference through Louis's experience of their clashing interplay.

Although the richness of this interplay is a tribute to Kushner's skill as a dramatist and cultural critic, that process has a darker, more complex side as well. For at the imaginative center of the play stands its most daring and conflicted representation of the queer–Jew interrelation: Roy Cohn, Kushner's at once most historically specific and most stylized character. The real Roy Cohn was of course a perennially controversial figure in American politics, from his days as chief aide to Joseph McCarthy to his career as a politically connected power broker with ties to right-wing politicians, the mob, and the Catholic Church (see Von Hoffman). He was also a spectacularly self-denying gay man, simultaneously the object of homophobic innuendo by his political opponents and, as one of the first public victims of the AIDS virus, an object lesson to the gay male community of the perils of internalized self-hatred (Cadden). An anonymously contributed panel in the Names Project AIDS memorial quilt expresses this conflation of qualities; it reads, "Roy Cohn. Bully. Coward. Victim." Kushner cites this panel as the source of his interest in Cohn: "I was fascinated [by the panel].... People didn't hate McCarthy so much—they thought he was a scoundrel who didn't believe in anything. But there was a venal little monster by his side, a Jew and a queer, and this was the real object of detestation" (Lubrow 60). And throughout the play, Kushner not only notices but also exploits the process by which Cohn was constructed in the culturally sedimented image of the monstrous Jewish pervert—a "venal little monster ... a Jew and a queer."

Well before Cohn's opponents invoked the stereotype of the venal little monster, the monstrous Jewish pervert had assumed a specifically American embodiment. For between 1880 and 1920—a time of extensive eastern European immigration, economic upheaval, and class warfare—anti-Semitism entered the American political arena on a massive scale. After the financier Joseph Seligman was barred from hotels in Saratoga, many other Jews were excluded from resorts and vacation hotels; Ivy League universities began establishing quotas for Jewish students; and the eugenicist Anti-Immigration League, which worked to establish the quota-setting Immigration Restriction Act of 1924, grouped Jews with other southern and eastern Europeans (as well as Asians and other "undesirables"). In addition, a flood of books, broadsides, and periodical articles in the mainstream and the more popular (if not populist) press rechanneled the anti-Semitic calumny that permeated Europe—many of the anti-Semitic French journalist Edouard Drumont's most extreme animadversions, for example, were directly reprinted in the anti-Semitic tract *The American Jew* (1888); later, the *Protocols of the Elders of Zion* (c. 1905), a notorious forgery by the Russian secret police, was circulated in the 1920s by no less a figure than Henry Ford. These texts put into American circulation the familiar figure of the Jewish pervert.

These slurs sutured the Jew both to sociopolitical power and to nonprocreative sexual practices. It was as if the perverse political power of the Jew could be expressed only by that figure's indulgence in deviant forms of sexuality. Thus *The American Jew* follows claims about the Jews' financial power with assertions that Jews imported sexual perversion into an otherwise pristine America: "Those certain hideous and abhorrent forms of vice, which have their origin in countries of the East, and which have in recent years sprung into existence in this country, have been taught to the abandoned creatures who practice them, and fostered, elaborated, and encouraged, by the lecherous Jew!" (Selzer 49). The speech of Jews is said to be as disgusting as their behavior:

> The average Jew is disgustingly bawdy in his talk, and interlards his conversation with filthy expressions and obscene words. On the verandas of summer resorts, in hotel corridors, in the lobbies of theaters, on steamboats, on railway cars, and in public places in general, the Jew indulges in this repulsive peculiarity, to the great annoyance and disgust of respectable Christian women and decency-loving Gentile men. This was one of the habits that made him so objectionable at summer resorts, and has led to his practical exclusion at every first-class summer hotel in the land. (50)

This image of the licentious or lascivious Jew was rapidly inscribed in narratives of female exploitation, either as an instigator of white slavery or as an exploiter of female workers. A 1909 article in *McClure's* claimed that a cadre of mysterious Jews controlled the prostitution industry in New York—largely by selling their own daughters—and that "one half of all the women ... in the business ... started their career in New York" prostitution (Turner 58). *The American Jew* extended the concern to gentiles: "In many of the factories operated by Jews throughout the country, the life of an honest girl therein employed is made simply a hell, by reason of the Jews' predominant lechery" (Selzer 53). These fears exploded when Leo Frank, a Jewish factory owner falsely accused of raping a young female worker, was lynched by an Atlanta mob in 1915—an event that is generally considered the worst anti-Semitic incident in United States history and that was made possible by the network of associations I have cited above. At his trial, Frank was constructed as sexually perverse: a known sodomite in Georgia, a state whose antisodomy laws have remained notorious, Frank favored oral intercourse, his chief accuser testified. This testimony was relevant because the victim, Mary Phagan, died with her hymen intact. Frank was cast by his chief public antagonist, the populist politician Tom Watson, in the image of the gentile-mad Jewish pervert: "[a] typical young libertine Jew ... dreaded and detested by the city authorities of the North [for] utter contempt of law and a ravenous appetite for ... the girls of the uncircumcised" (Frey and Thomson-Frey 126; see also Dinnerstein 180). It was on these multiple grounds—as capitalist, despoiler of young gentile women, pervert, and Jew—that Frank was lynched.[2]

Hyperphallic but abjuring the proper exercise of the phallus, politically and economically empowered but turning to the seduction of innocent American virgins, the Jewish male thus enters the American populist imaginary as a peculiar amalgam of sexual and political power, perverting gentile bodies and the body politic with a single gesture. For example, in *McClure's* Turner argued that Jewish control of the prostitution industry was the basis for "a system of political procurers" that buttressed Tammany Hall and thereby polluted the national political process (60). This image is imported into *Angels* through Roy Cohn, one conduit for populist paranoia in the 1950s. "[H]e's like the polestar of human evil, he's like the worst human who ever lived, he isn't human even ...," Louis cries out when he hears of Cohn's death (*Perestroika* 95). Although usually attentive to the signs of anti-Semitism, Louis participates in the suturing of Cohn and anti-Semitic images of Jewish monstrosity. Kushner's iconography here is quite precise. "Playing the phone" with what the stage directions call "sensual abandon," Cohn cries, "I wish I was an octopus, a fucking octopus. Eight loving arms and all those suckers" (*Millennium* 11). Through the magic of theatrical transformation, he metamorphoses into that very inhuman figure. Fixing cases, buying Broadway seats, cheating clients, Cohn seems to extend his tentacles everywhere.

Indeed, Kushner's Cohn corresponds with uncanny accuracy to one of the most powerful images of anti-Semitic propaganda, which I label, with a nod to Sander Gilman's anatomization of the Jew's body, the Jew's tentacles. In anti-Semitic discourse of the later nineteenth and early twentieth centuries, the Jew's monstrosity is performed by the transformation of the hand—the emblem of warmth, love, and pleasure—into bat wings, vampire talons, spider legs, or octopus tentacles. For example, a late-nineteenth-century illustrated anatomy of the Jew includes not just standard anti-Semitic attributes—"restless suspicious eyes," "curved nose and nostrils," "ill-shapen ears of great size like those of a bat"—but also "long clammy fingers" that reach out to clutch or caress (Selzer, following 108). In much classic anti-Semitic propaganda, these corpse-like fingers extend in a monstrous way that connotes social or sexual power. "The Jew's soft hands and curved fingers grasp only the values that others have produced," claims *The American Jew* (Selzer 99), and according to T.T. Timayenis's *The Original Mr. Jacobs* (1888), "the soft hand almost melting with the hypocrisy of the traitor" is a sign of "physical degradation," which "closely follows upon moral degradation. This is strongly remarked among Jews who, of all the races of men, are the most depraved" (21). Among visual representations that use this trope is Gustave Doré's famous caricature of Mayer Rothschild, *Dieu Protège Israel*, which represents the banker holding the globe and defiling it with his long, batlike talons. In George Du Maurier's *Trilby* (1894), the hypnotizing musician Svengali is represented as a spider filling Trilby's dreams with images of monstrous pestiferousness. Illustrated covers of the *Protocols of the Elders of Zion* depict a brutish Jew pawing a bleeding, violated globe or a spider covering the world with its all-encompassing legs.

Kushner's trope of the octopus functions with particular brilliance in this context: it conjoins an image of the Jew as hyperphallic monster with one that stresses the perverse dimensions of that figure. Indeed, it is the second image that constitutes Kushner's most original addition to the tradition. An octopus, like a spider, has "eight loving arms," but it also has "all those suckers": the multiplication of phalli suggested by the arms is reoriented by the trope of the suckers, which unites implications of cheating, vampirism, and fellatio in a vivid image of monstrosity that is both recognizably Jewish and demonstrably queer.[3] The figure of Cohn thus represents an audacious attempt to think through to the center of anti-Semitic imagery, to the cultural queering of the Jew, and finally to the representation of the Jew as at once monstrous, empowered, and perverse—an image Kushner then installs at the center of the play's most malignant icon of queer-Jewish identity.

Kushner invokes this anti-Semitic iconography throughout the play with amazing accuracy. Cohn is foul-mouthed:

ROY. Christ!
JOE. Roy
ROY (Into receiver). Hold. (Button; to Joe) *What?*
JOE. Could you please not take the Lord's name in vain?
    (Pause.)
    I'm sorry. But please. At least while I'm ...
ROY (Laughs, then). Right. Sorry. Fuck.
                                    (*Millennium* 14; ellipsis in orig.)

Cohn seduces an innocent gentile, Joe Pitt, whom he tempts first into big-city life and then into homosexual practices and a homosexual identity (to Cohn's hypocritical chagrin). Cohn embodies stereotypical Jewish lasciviousness and greed by hogging a cache of AZT—one he procures, as anti-Semites might imagine, thanks to his possession of secrets about affairs of state. But the idea of the sexually transgressive is never far from the malign Jew, and when anti-Semitic language surfaces in the play, it is sutured to the notion of queerness. For example, when Belize confronts Cohn about this selfish appropriation of a drug that can help prolong, if not save, Prior's life, Cohn refuses to share, then launches racist epithets at Belize. Belize responds with a string of his own imprecations: "shit-for-brains, filthy-mouthed selfish motherfucking cowardly cocksucking cloven-hoofed pig" (*Perestroika* 61). At once homophobic and anti-Semitic, Belize's curse points to self-hatred among both Jews and queers in a society suspicious of its manifold others. But to call Cohn a "cloven-hoofed pig" is to curse him for being both Jewish and nonkosher: cloven-hoofed animals are kosher; pigs are not. The curse thus echoes the common anti-Semitic habit of conflating Jews with that which they abjure, but it also ironically suggests that Cohn has taken as his totem animal the octopus, a beast as forbidden to observant Jews as the pig. The octopus-loving Cohn proudly casts himself the same way that Belize casts him, as forbidden, taboo, *treyf* in a self-negation that contravenes both his sexual and his religious identity.[4]

This construction of Cohn confronts the most regressive element of the right with a reminder that one of its cynosures was also one of its biggest bogeymen, the perverse Jewish power broker. It also outs Cohn in terms that he would have resented. But Kushner evinces a profound fascination with this character, one that lends *Angels* a remarkable inner tension. For while Kushner keeps killing Cohn off, Cohn keeps rising from the dead, like a zombie or golem. Cohn's death dominates *Perestroika*, all the more so because it seems to occur three or four times. The first instance is the memorable scene in which Cohn fakes his death in front of the ghost of Ethel Rosenberg. By tricking the ghost, Cohn achieves a Nietzschean triumph over the dead even though he cannot beat death. Cohn dies a few moments later, and the play even manages to have him properly mourned. Discovering Cohn's body while sneaking in to steal his AZT, Belize urges Louis to remember his grade-school Hebrew and say kaddish, the Jewish prayer for the dead. The ghost of Ethel Rosenberg, hovering by the bedside, prompts Louis when he forgets, then comically has him add a curse:

> LOUIS. Oseh sholom bimromov, hu ya-aseh sholom olenu v'al
>   col Yisroel ...
> ETHEL. V'imru omain.
> LOUIS. V'imru omain.
> ETHEL. You sonofabitch.
> LOUIS. You sonofabitch.
>   (*Perestroika* 126; ellipsis in orig.)

Blessed and cursed, mourned and mastered, Cohn returns again as a ghost that haunts Joe Pitt. He kisses Joe on the mouth in a moment of overt sexuality that pays tribute to Joe's nervously asserted "outness": "Show me a little of what you've learned, baby Joe. Out in the world." Then Cohn announces his departure to the afterlife with a Shakespearean flourish: "I gotta shuffle off this mortal coil. I hope they have something for me to do in the great Hereafter, I get bored easily" (127). Even after this final appearance, Cohn is brought back yet again when Prior, retreating from heaven, sees Cohn agreeing to take on God as his client. And Cohn is in a sense killed again by the excision of this scene from the Broadway and national touring productions of the play.[5]

These remarkable cursings and blessings, ritualized slayings and compulsive revivals turn Cohn into a great vaudevillian in the twilight of his career making one farewell appearance after another before being dragged offstage in mid-shtick. But they also endeavor to bring Cohn's uncanny power under authorial control. As with that other stage Jew Shylock, the energies gathered in Cohn exceed his author's attempts to order and organize them. The persistence of these efforts to kill Cohn, mourn him, revive him, then kill him again attests to the power he continues to exert over his author.

It is also a sign of Kushner's need to master Cohn and all that Cohn allegorically incarnates: homophobia, the most invidious forms of right-wing populism, and McCarthyism. Indeed, the symmetry of the two plots of the play suggests that Cohn functions as the objective correlative of the AIDS virus: he infects Mormon Joe with his political vision just as the virus infects Prior.[6] But Cohn's persistence in the face of multiple deaths suggests that he enacts another allegory as well: that of Jewish power. The fantasy culturally inscribed in the supposed monstrosity of the Jew, after all, is that these persistently marginalized members of a Christian-centered culture possess the greatest amount of what Cohn calls "clout" (*Millennium* 45), a secret power all the more insidious because it is hidden, one that has persisted over the passage of centuries despite all efforts to eradicate it. This phantasmic image of the Jew with power both attracts and repels Kushner, as his representation of Cohn reveals.

In *Angels*, the emblem of ambivalence about Jewishness is Louis, another queer Jew. But Louis is also a neurotic nebbish. Cohn energizes this ambivalent image by refusing to be a nebbish and by arrogantly asserting the voracious, phallic power ascribed to the Jew under the sign of monstrosity. Cohn's willingness to embody this image, to be the Jew with tentacles, palpably attracts Kushner and also leads to Kushner's equally powerful need to master Cohn dramaturgically—to mourn or to kill him. For to affirm the play's ideological commitment to the full assimilation of queer citizens into an ideal body politic, Kushner must eliminate Cohn and all the phallic aggression he represents. At the end of the play, there is room for angels and angelic queers in a utopian America, but there is no place for monsters.

Cohn's ejection from the play, then, is not to be read as a function of some putative self-hatred[7] but an inevitable aspect of Kushner's social and political program. I am deeply sympathetic to Kushner's politics, but their inscription in *Angels* has disturbing dramatic and ideological consequences. As *Perestroika* lurches toward its climax (like Cohn, it seems to end several times), a Christian thematic surfaces that stresses grace and rebirth. And along with this thematic comes a classic form of emplotment—Shakespearean comedy—that affirms regeneration through the creation of a new, redeemed community. Both these forms have notorious difficulties in reckoning with the figure of the Jew.

Like *Twelfth Night*—or, more relevantly, *The Merchant of Venice*—Kushner's play ends with the evocation of a community as a newly formed, extended, inclusive family, albeit a family with a difference. Composed of various forms of otherness, this family is a redeemed version of the community of others that Louis seeks in the gay bar in London: a Mormon with recently discovered lesbian tendencies, a Jew, and a black male drag queen, all presided over by a WASP man living heroically with AIDS. But given the play's preoccupation with the queer–Jew equation, it is disturbing that Louis, the Jewish member of this queer family, should be represented as querulous and ineffectual. The queer Jew enters the postnuclear family, that is to say, not only as a cultural stereotype (albeit one depicted with some affection) but as a particularly disempowered one. More troubling still is the absence of Cohn and anyone associated with him from this community—for Joe Pitt, too, is banished from the final scenes. Shylock, at least, gets to leave the stage under his own power; no such agency, not even negative agency, is granted to either Cohn or his surrogate son. This elision pushes the play into a more explicitly Christian narrative: it emphasizes the near-miraculous rebirth of Prior after his fever-induced dream vision, for he lives on thanks to the AZT stolen from Cohn's deathbed by Belize and Louis. Cohn dies, it seems, so that Prior might live to preside over the new queer postnuclear family, at least for the space of the theatrical enactment.

The turn to Christian thematics suggested by the privileging of the Prior plot is confirmed by the imagery and action of the play's final section. At Central Park's Bethesda Fountain, Prior has Louis begin the story of the biblical pool of Bethesda and directs Hannah and Belize to complete it. This moment is undeniably moving, but when considered under the sign of Jewishness it remains deeply problematic. Prior asks Louis to perform an act at once typical and typological, to submerge his own Jewish voice in a chorus of Christian ones. The story of Bethesda that Louis tells has distinctly anti-Jewish overtones in the Book of John, where it precedes Christ's healing of a lame man (Prior walks with a cane as a result of his disease). The miracle increases the persecutorial furor of the Jews, already aroused by Christ's performing such miracles as bringing back the dead (Belize mentions Lazarus earlier in the play). But Christ announces that he is the fulfillment of the Old Testament prophecy to the Jews: "Had ye believed Moses, ye would have believed me, for he wrote of me" (5.46). Needless to say, Christ's words fall on deaf ears. These implications were, I suspect, absent from Kushner's consciousness as he wrote; however, they animate the cultural text to which he is clearly referring, and at this point in the play, that passage is writing him. Louis performs the act that, in the biblical passage Kushner alludes to, Jews exist to accomplish: announcing the new Christian dispensation, then getting out of the way.

The Bethesda angel that hovers over the play's conclusion seems to derive more from Marianne Williamson than from Walter Benjamin, and I want in conclusion to suggest why. This turn to the Christian grows out of the play's most powerful and moving political aspirations. The particular success of *Angels*, after all, is to speak at once to multiple audiences—gay and straight; highbrow and middlebrow; socialist, Democratic, and even Republican—and to argue to those audiences for a mode of civic identity that includes rather than excludes, that creates rather than denies community. To David Savran, this enterprise is problematic, for it recapitulates the liberal pluralist ideology that Kushner has explicitly disavowed.[8] Yet as Savran grudgingly admits, the play's breadth of appeal and generosity of address is the source of its efficacy in a public sphere dominated for several decades by conservative ideologies that articulate the utopian longings historically central to the construction of a distinctive American identity:

> What is most remarkable about the play is that it has managed, against all odds, to amass significant levels of both cultural and economical capital.... It does so ... by its skill both in reactivating a sense (derived from the early nineteenth century) of America as the utopian nation and mobilizing the principle of ambivalence— or, more exactly, dissensus—to produce a vision of a once and future pluralist culture. (225)

The evocation of the queer family at the end of *Angels* is a perfect example of this utopian vision of union by dissensus and of the political ends to which Kushner attempts to turn this vision. He offers the image of redeemed community in the guise of a utopian Americanness in which the nation is reconstituted in the image of a postnuclear family made up of quarreling outsiders—in Savran's terms, the very embodiment of union by dissensus. That Kushner is echoing a problematic nationalist discourse is ultimately less important than his appropriation of it for a frankly queer political project—and of the family-as-nation metaphor for a nonprocreative notion of both family and nation that includes all forms of family in a new national narrative. When Prior, the reluctant prophet, having wrestled with his own angels, announces his apocalyptic revelation, he intends to include all the members of the audience in this new union, which is more perfect because it is still divided:

> The world only spins forward. We will be citizens.
>   The time has come.
> Bye now.
> You are fabulous creatures, each and every one.

And I bless you: *More Life.*
The Great Work Begins. (*Perestroika* 148)

Prior predicts that "we"—the members of the queer family—"will be citizens," but to achieve this status, "each and every one" must devise a new form of citizenship and work to construct a redeemed America that can gather gay and straight, black and white, Mormon, Christian, and Jew into a collective identity precisely through the act of quarreling over that identity.

But herein lies the problem with Kushner's achievement, at least when considered from a point of view that stresses the different difference that is Jewish difference. To affirm this project, Kushner must speak in the idiom of mainstream culture while criticizing that culture: he must evoke a utopian ideal of America that exerts political and imaginative power in the social arena but that is substantially less than ideal. As Sacvan Bercovitch has suggested, this American ideal of utopia presents the nation as a perfected version of its flawed predecessors just as in the versions of Protestant theology adopted by American Puritans the Christological narrative serves as a fulfillment of its Jewish antecedents.[9] Ironically, this utopian understanding of America has served for many Jewish intellectuals—including Kushner (and perhaps Bercovitch as well)—as a vector of assimilation into a national drama that had excluded them. "It was impressed upon us," writes Kushner of his childhood, "as we sang America the Beautiful at the Seder's conclusion, that the dream of millennia was due to find its ultimate realization not in Jerusalem but in this country" (*Thinking* 5). But according to Bercovitch, the deployment of a typological schema in the construction of an American national utopia ultimately swallows up the narrative of Jewish history that serves as its antecedent and gloss. Jewish difference becomes not only one part of an ethnic panoply—of a vision of union by ethnic dissensus—but also the shadowy type whose truth is named America (Bercovitch 73–81). In such a schema, the narrative of the biblical Hebrews and even that of the Jewish people may be privileged, but by the very conditions of that privilege, their difference—that which marks them as Jews—is extinguished.

To be sure, Kushner invokes the rhetoric of an American utopia not to elide Jewish difference but to intervene on behalf of a queer politics in a cultural debate over the national destiny: to queer the Puritan, as it were. However, the narrative schema he deploys situates his endeavor on a firmly Christian terrain in an overtly typological way. This effect becomes clearest in the play's final foray into the typological imaginary, the concluding speech of Prior. Prior the arch-WASP reverses Louis's anticipation of the Christian dispensation and speaks a Jewish blessing, marked as such by Kushner in his commentary on the play: "More Life."[10] But the reversal cannot be complete; although the Protestant imaginary can contain Jewishness under the logic of typology, Jewishness is granted no such power vis-à-vis the Christian. Prior's articulation of a Jewish blessing thus continues and indeed confirms the absorption of Jewish type into Christian fulfillment instead of breaking or reversing that pattern. It is troubling that a play beginning with a rabbi's voice extolling "the melting pot that does not melt" ends with the subordination of the Jew to Christian emplotment. But Kushner is determined to find a place for angels in America—somehow.

Is there a way of conceptualizing the utopia *Angels* evokes that would not amalgamate otherness into a culturally palatable unity? Benjamin, one of Kushner's major sources for the play, thought so, and his writings suggest a different model for the consolations *Angels* offers. As I have suggested, Benjamin is everywhere in Kushner's play, from its imagery of apocalypse to its angelic iconography. But Benjamin's presence is felt most powerfully in the final scene. When Prior cries, "The world only spins forward" (a false claim, since the world, which spins on its axis, could be said in that sense to be moving nowhere), his speech alludes to the moment in the "Theses on the Philosophy of History" when Benjamin defines his own utopian vision through the image of a Klee drawing, the *Angelus Novus*:

> His face is turned towards the past. Where we perceive a chain of events, he sees only one single catastrophe which keeps piling wreckage upon wreckage and hurls it in front of his feet. The angel would like to stay, awaken the dead, and make whole what has been smashed. But a storm is blowing from Paradise; it has got caught in his wings with such violence that the angel can no longer close them. This storm irresistibly propels him into the future to which his back is turned, while the pile of debris before him grows skyward. This storm is what we call progress. (257–58)

Kushner invokes Benjamin but ignores the complexity of his argument. With its audacious conflation of the angelic and the monstrous, Klee's image serves as a reminder that the difference between angel and monster is often just a matter of perspective. This is the chastening recognition that Kushner's utopianism conspicuously lacks, especially when compared with Benjamin's muted (in Benjamin's word, "weak" [254]) messianism. That the angel is propelled forward by the wind from paradise is less important than the text's clear distinction between the beholder of the angel and the vision the angel experiences. The same nonidentity exists within the collective subject who is the implicit addressee of Benjamin's text. This storm may be what "we" call progress—but Benjamin leaves thoroughly and disturbingly open-ended the questions of who that "we" is and what the relation is between what "we" see and what "we" want to see.

In the space created by that opening lies a less amalgamative, more open-ended model of collective identity that creates a place for divergent understandings of history, progress, paradise, and utopia—even of America.[11] That space provides an escape from the impulse to amalgamate—to assimilate?—the various sorts of otherness that Kushner's utopian project ultimately embodies, despite his juggling of multiple models of alterity until the last act of the play. The beauty and brilliance of *Angels* is that the play points beyond itself—and so imposes hard questions about the nature of identities, Jewish and queer alike, that a less insistent, more troubled vision of utopia would leave in its wake.

NOTES

In writing and revising this essay, I have profited from the advice and counsel of Sara Blair, Philip Blumberg, Daniel Boyarin, Jonathan Boyarin, Bryan Cheyette, Daniel Itzkovitz, Anita Norich, Joseph Roach, and David Scobey. After I had written the piece, I read an excellent essay on the same topic by Alisa Solomon that reaches precisely opposite conclusions.

1. In this essay I distinguish *sexually perverse*, *deviant*, and *other* from *queer*. The first three terms are labels imposed on those whose sexual practices are considered outside the norm; the last is used by those who are so labeled to define themselves in a way that contests such categorization (see Warner and Berlant xxvi).

2. Itzkovitz (esp. 178–79) suggested the relevance of Frank to my argument.

3. Fellatio and Jewishness are explicitly linked elsewhere in the play; Harper attempts to win Joe back to her bed by telling him that "Mormons can give blowjobs." She learns how to do so not in her temple, however, but from "a little old Jewish lady with a German accent" on the radio (*Millennium* 27).

4. The real Cohn seems to have felt no need to apologize for or conceal his Jewishness even though he worked for most of his adult life on the fringes of the American fight most closely affiliated with anti-Semitism. That Cohn does not represent simple Jewish self-hatred makes the network of ironies radiating from the cloven-hoofed pig and octopus images an even more powerful expression of Kushner's imaginative conflicts and investments.

5. The scene appeared in the 1988 production at the Mark Taper Theater, which Kushner considers definitive. But its excision in middlebrow venues like Broadway suggests an act of cultural omission that is consistent with Kushner's political project.

6. It was Kushner's explicit intention to draw this parallel, according to Oskar Eustis, who commissioned *Angels*, served as a sounding board during its composition, and directed the definitive production.

7. Kushner is not a self-denying or self-hating Jew, despite his investment in Louis, who he claims dictated the text of *Angels* to him when he was blocked in the early stages of composition (Lecture). Kushner is involved in projects that affirm a cultural Jewishness: he has worked on an adaptation of the Yiddish play *The Dybbuk* and is currently planning a version of *The Golem* as part of a trilogy on the intertwining of race and power in the modern world.

8. For Kushner's repudiation of liberalism, see *Perestroika* 158.

9. It can be argued that there are ample doctrinal continuity and shared eschatology in the Christian and Jewish traditions. But as Langmuir observes, typological thinking in the Middle Ages made a primary theological point of the historical insufficiency of the Jews. This view persists in American versions of covenant theology, as Bercovitch shows, and in eighteenth- and nineteenth-century Enlightenment philosophy, as Rose argues. More to the point, Kushner alludes to a biblical passage suggesting the historical supersession of the Jewish people by Christian revelation. According to Ruether, such biblical passages make anti-Judaism (and hence, later in time, fully racialized anti-Semitism) a vital part of the Christian tradition rather than a blot on an otherwise sympathetic vision.

10. Here is Kushner's account of the origin of the blessing: "The play is indebted, too, to writers I've never met. It's ironical that Harold Bloom ... provided me with a translation of the Hebrew word for 'blessing'—'more life'—which subsequently became key to the heart of *Perestroika*. Harold Bloom is also the author of *The Anxiety of Influence*, his oedipalization of the history of Western literature, which when I first encountered it years ago made me so anxious my analyst suggested I put it away. Recently, I had the chance to meet Professor Bloom, and, guilty over my appropriation of 'more life,' I fled from the encounter as one of Freud's *Totem and Taboo* tribesmen might flee from a meeting with that primal father, the one with the big knife" (*Thinking* 39). Kushner's ambivalence here is palpable (and reminiscent of Louis). He strikes the culturally mediated stance of the ambivalent Jew in the very act of suggesting how culturally mediated his knowledge of Jewishness is. The same admixture of acknowledgment and disavowal is activated by another powerful Jewish father figure, Roy Cohn.

11. At the end of *The Anatomy of National Fantasy*, Berlant points to the dangers of this kind of amalgamative thinking: "[I]n the United States, power is erotically attached to America. The national frame is abstract, like a man, or a Statue of Liberty. Since that sentence is false—for a man and a statue are only abstract if you repress their conditions of production—the subject who wants to avoid the melancholy insanity of the self-abstraction that is citizenship ... must develop tactics for refocusing the articulation, now four hundred years old, between the United States and America, the nation and utopia. She must look, perhaps to her other identities, for new sources of political confederation" (286).

WORKS CITED

Arendt, Hannah. *The Origins of Totalitarianism*. 1948. New York: Harcourt, 1951.

Benjamin, Walter. "Theses on the Philosophy of History." *Illuminations*. Trans. Harry Zohn. New York: Schocken, 1969. 253–64.

Bercovitch, Sacvan. *The American Jeremiad*. Madison: U of Wisconsin P, 1978.

Berlant, Lauren. *The Anatomy of National Fantasy: Hawthorne, Utopia, and Everyday Life.* Chicago: U of Chicago P, 1991.

Boyarin, Jonathan, and Daniel Boyarin, eds. *Jews and Other Differences: The New Jewish Cultural Studies.* Minneapolis: U of Minnesota P, 1997.

Cadden, Michael. "Strange Angel: The Pinklisting of Roy Cohn." *Secret Agents: The Rosenberg Case, McCarthyism, and Fifties America.* Ed. Marjorie Garber and Rebecca Walkowitz. New York: Routledge, 1995. 93–105.

Cheyette, Bryan. *Constructions of the Jew in English Literature and Society: Racial Representations, 1875–1945.* Cambridge: Cambridge UP, 1993.

Dinnerstein, Leonard. *The Leo Frank Case.* New York: Columbia UP, 1968.

Eustis, Oskar. Personal interview. 8 Aug. 1996.

Finkielkraut, Alain. *The Imaginary Jew.* Trans. David Suchoff. Lincoln: U of Nebraska P, 1994.

Frey, Robert Seitz, and Nancy Thomson-Frey. *The Silent and the Damned: The Murder of Mary Phagan and the Lynching of Leo Frank.* Lantham: Madison, 1987.

Gilman, Sander. *The Case of Sigmund Freud: Medicine and Identity at the Fin de Siecle.* Baltimore: Johns Hopkins UP, 1993.

———. *The Jew's Body.* New York: Routledge, 1991.

Harrowitz, Nancy. *Antisemitism, Misogyny, and the Logic of Cultural Difference: Cesare Lombroso and Matilde Serao.* Lincoln: U of Nebraska P, 1994.

Itzkovitz, Daniel. "Secret Temples." Boyarin and Boyarin 176–202.

Kushner, Tony. *Angels in America: Millennium Approaches.* New York: Theater Communications, 1993.

———. *Angels in America: Perestroika.* New York: Theater Communications, 1993.

———. Lecture. Bread Loaf School of English. Middlebury. 7 Aug. 1996.

———. *Thinking about the Longstanding Problems of Virtue and Happiness: Essays, a Play, Two Poems, and a Prayer.* New York: Theater Communications, 1995.

Langmuir, Gavin. *Toward a Definition of Antisemitism.* Berkeley: U of California P, 1990.

Lubow, Arthur. "Tony Kushner's Paradise Lost." *New Yorker* 30 Nov. 1992: 59–64.

Pick, Daniel. *Faces of Degeneration: A European Disorder, circa 1848–1918.* Cambridge: Cambridge UP, 1989.

Poliakov, Leon. *Histoire de l'antisemitisme.* 4 vols. Paris: Calmann-Lévy, 1955–71.

Proust, Marcel. *Sodome et Gomorrhe.* Ed. Antoine Compagnon. Paris: Gallimard, 1989.

Rose, Paul. *Revolutionary Anti-Semitism in Germany from Kant to Wagner.* Princeton: Princeton UP, 1990.

Ruether, Rosemary. *Faith and Fratricide: The Theological Roots of Anti-Semitism.* New York: Seabury, 1974.

Savran, David. "Ambivalence, Utopia, and a Queer Sort of Materialism: How *Angels in America* Reconstructs the Nation." *Theater Journal* 47 (1995): 207–27.

Selzer, Michael. *Kike!* New York: World, 1972.

Shell, Marc. *Money, Language, and Thought: Literary and Philosophic Economies from the Medieval to the Modern Era.* Berkeley: U of California P, 1982.

Solomon, Alisa. "Wrestling with *Angels*: A Jewish Fantasia." *Approaching the Millennium: Essays on Angels in America.* Ed. Deborah Geis and Steven Kruger. Ann Arbor: U of Michigan P, 1997. 118–33.

Timayenis, T.T. *The Original Mr. Jacobs.* New York: Minerva, 1888.

Turner, George Kibbe. "The Daughters of the Poor." *McClure's* Nov. 1909:45–61.

Von Hoffman, Nicholas. *Citizen Cohn*. New York: Doubleday, 1988.
Warner, Michael, and Lauren Berlant. Introduction. *Fear of a Queer Planet: Queer Politics and Social Theory*. Ed. Warner and Berlant. Minneapolis: U of Minnesota P, 1993. vii–xxxi.

BENILDE MONTGOMERY

Angels in America *as Medieval Mystery*

Although highly praised in the popular press when it first appeared and officially canonized soon thereafter by Harold Bloom,[1] Tony Kushner's *Angels in America* has now come under the scrutiny of critics of a more suspicious gaze. Among these less than enthusiastic critics are the notorious Arlene Croce, who, if only indirectly, includes *Angels* as an instance of "victim art"; Leo Bersani, who finds the play "muddled and pretentious"; and David Savran, who unravels the play's ambivalences to show not only that it is seriously at odds with its own apparent intentions, but that its immense popularity can be accounted for in the way it supports the "binary oppositions" of the status quo and thereby implicitly supports the Reaganite agenda that it would otherwise subvert.[2] More positively, however, Savran also notes that "the play deliberately evokes the long history of Western dramatic literature and positions itself as heir to the traditions of Sophocles, Shakespeare, Brecht, and others."[3] Among these others, I suspect that an important tradition to which Kushner is also the heir is that of the medieval mystery cycles. To read *Angels in America* in the light of this tradition may help dispel Savran's suspicion that Kushner is as much the victim of Enlightenment categories as are his political enemies.

It should first be noted that although Kushner was a student of medieval culture (he graduated from Columbia with a degree in medieval

From *Modern Drama* 41, no. 4 (Winter 1998). © 1998 by the University of Toronto.

studies),[4] he has little interest in the specific Christian contents of the cycles. Indeed, in an early interview with Savran, Kushner makes his ambivalence about the Middle Ages clear. On the one hand, he dismisses them as "of no relevance to anything" only to praise them later on for the "great richness [that] can come from societies that aren't individuated."[5] Kushner's use of the Corpus Christi plays in *Angels in America* is consistent with this ambivalence. While he is interested in the cycle plays because of their dramatic structure and internal form, his own agenda demands that he distance himself from their theological contents in favor of what appears to be a highly secularized humanism. To use Thomas M. Greene's language, Kushner "force[s] us to recognize the poetic distance traversed"[6] between the hierarchic world of the cycles and our own postmodern experience.

If, as Savran suggests, Walter Benjamin's "Theses on the Philosophy of History" (an essay written in 1940 in an attempt to account for the emergence of Hitler's new order) is "the primary generative fiction for *Angels in America*,"[7] we have an important instance of Kushner's abiding interest in the question of redemptive history, an interest first apparent in his *A Bright Room Called Day* (1985). Kushner himself admits that his protagonist, Prior Walter, is named for Benjamin and that his angel is modeled on Paul Klee's painting *Angelus Novus*, discussed in Benjamin's essay. Significantly, however, the medieval mystery cycles are also attempts to come to terms with questions similar to those raised by Benjamin and of interest to Kushner. Developed in the late fourteenth and fifteenth centuries, during what Martin Stevens calls "some of the most disruptive upheavals of the social order," including economic depression and plague, the mystery cycles developed when, not unlike Benjamin four hundred years later, medieval Christians were reexamining the nature and meaning of redemptive history in an effort to redefine their own newly emerging social order. The plays helped, as Stevens suggests, to create "a reinvigorated sense of morality."[8] As such, the cycles would seem to be particularly hospitable to Kushner's postmodern didactic project, written at the end of the millennium and during the age of AIDS.

Moreover, Benjamin's theory of redemptive history is similar to that expressed in the medieval cycles. A student of Jewish mysticism, Benjamin felt that "the moral duty of criticism was to 'redeem' the past, to save it from oblivion by revealing its concealed truth."[9] Once revealed, the truth of the past, particularly as it is embodied in the "oppressed," might then provide some hope for the future. "The past," Benjamin says, "carries with it a temporal index by which it is referred to redemption." He notes that "for the Jews ... every second of time was the strait gate through which the Messiah might enter." In his scheme, the contemplation of the whole of tradition "teaches us that the 'state of emergency' in which we live is not the exception but the rule."[10] No doubt selected in a way that would distress Benjamin, the events of the mystery plays show, nonetheless, the world in a similarly constant state of "emergency." These "emergencies" (the fail, a fratricide, the flood, the murder of children, etc.) are, moreover, presented in a way that links past "emergencies" to present realities. In the mysteries, each past event conceals some sign of Christ's redemptive action: an action made necessary by the initial cosmic emergency," the fall of men and angels, with which the cycles begin; made possible by the death of Jesus, the central and ubiquitous emergency of the cycles; and, for those who have heeded the prefigurements, fulfilled in the ultimate emergency of "Doomsday."

While Kushner's use of multiple locations is obviously consistent with medieval practice, his arrangement of incidents in *Angels in America* closely imitates the structural outline of the mystery cycles. As the cycles trace an arc from Genesis to Doomsday, so, too, does Kushner's play. As the cycles begin with the Creation and Fall, Kushner's play also begins with allusions to a more perfect and, significantly, Jewish past, now fallen from grace. At the funeral of Sarah Ironson, Rabbi Chemelwitz notes that her grandchildren "with the goyische names" have become so assimilated into the modern world, a world fallen from the primal Eden of "the clay of some Litvak shtetl," that they are no longer capable of embarking on a "Great [Voyage]."[11] Moreover, as in the cycles, the individual incidents of *Angels in America* culminate in an epilogue whose apocalyptic imagery suggests the "doomsday" scenes of traditional mystery cycles. In Kushner's final scene, dominated by a statue of an angel, Hannah and Prior speak of a time "[w]hen the Millennium comes"—"[n]ot the year two thousand, but the Capital M Millennium" (II, 147). The scene focuses on another family, now newly constituted and prepared to do what the old Rabbi despaired of: to begin again, "to go out into the world" (II, 147). Sarah is replaced here by a new matriarch, Hannah, named for the Biblical prophet who praises Yahweh for defeating the powerful and raising up the poor and oppressed.[12] This newly constituted family has been gathered and redeemed not, as in the medieval cycles, because they have been chosen by Christ, but rather because its members have loved Prior Walter—the "prophet" of the new postmodern times whose wounded and dying body dominates each part of *Angels in America* as ubiquitously as the body of Christ dominates "every second of time" of the Corpus Christi cycles.

As in the cycles, all other action takes place within this Biblical arc, an arc that encompasses all time and understands it as redemptive history. In setting out the genealogy of Louis Ironson (grandson of Sarah, son of Rachel), Kushner positions one of his principal characters within the Biblical narrative of the Ur-family. In fact, Louis, full of self-loathing, later identifies himself with Cain ("now I can't see much and my forehead ... it's like the Mark of Cain" [I, 99]), and he is the one character whose name and genealogy are invoked by the Rabbi at the "Fall" in scene one and who reappears throughout the play until the "Doomsday" of the final scene.

Among the other characters are, of course, angels, and also a devil, a devil whose particular traits are rooted in medieval practice. Even in George C. Wolfe's very un-medieval New York production, few critics failed to recognize the devil in Ron Liebman's out-of-sync performance as Roy Cohn.[13] While in the cycle plays Lucifer's fall generally precedes Adam and Eve's, Kushner's devil appears first in the second scene, but is very much like the Lucifer of the Chester plays. There the devil sits in God's throne exclaiming, "Here will I sitt nowe in this steade, /... / Behoulde my bodye, handes and head— / the mighte of God is marked in mee."[14] Similarly, Cohn sits in a throne of his own invention wishing he were a formidable monster: "an octopus, a fucking octopus. Eight loving arms and all those suckers" (I, 11). Like the Lucifer of York who gloats in a power that "es passande my peres" (is passing my peers),[15] Cohn claims, like God, to "see the universe" (I, 13), curses all with "God-fucking-dammit to hell" (I, 14)), blesses chaos (I, 15), and, in a temptation scene (I, 52–58), tries to lure the faithful Christian, Joe, with the promises of similar power: "Let nothing stand in your way" (I, 58). By his own admission, he's "an absolute fucking demon with Family Law" (II, 138).

To counterbalance the devil, Kushner's principal angel, who may owe some inspiration to Benjamin's "Angelus Novus,"[16] also bears some additional resemblance, as Rob Baker points out, to the angels of medieval alchemy whose "Great Work" is to transform by fire base lead into pure gold.[17] Kushner's text, however, also associates his angels with Biblical angels. Perhaps playing with the frequent use of "Mary" in gay parlance, Kushner writes an "Annunciation" scene in which Prior exclaims, just before a Gabriel-like angel appears, "Something's coming in here, I'm scared, I don't like this at all, something's approaching and I.... OH! [...] God almighty ..." (I, 118, stage directions omitted). Most frequently, though, Kushner associates his angel with Jacob's angel in Genesis 32. First, Joe, a closeted Mormon homosexual, alludes to Jacob's angel when he defends himself to his wife: "Jacob wrestles with the angel. [...] The angel is not human, and it holds nothing back, so how could anyone human win [...]?" (I, 49–50). Despairing of spiritual victory, Joe, who, nonetheless, had desired to be "Blessed" (I, 54), then seeks the approval of the angel's opposite. On his deathbed, Roy Cohn blesses Joe:

> ROY [...] You don't even have to trick it out of me, like what's-his-name in the Bible.
> JOE Jacob.
> ROY [...] A ruthless motherfucker, some bald runt, but he laid hold of his birthright with his claws [...] (II, 82–83)

Under the tutelage of Joe's Mormon mother, however, Prior, fully human and living with AIDS, literally "wrestle[s]" with the angel and wins, demanding, "bless me or whatever but I will be let go," after which he "*ascends*" to heaven on a "*ladder of[...] light*" (II, 119–20).

More importantly, the correspondence Kushner establishes between Prior Walter and Joe around their relationship to the Jacob story is typical of the kind of "[i]nterconnectedness" (to use Hannah's word [II, 146]) that characterizes the internal structure of the entire play. Specifically, these correspondences might more properly be named "analogies," and they, like the structuring arc of the play, further situate *Angels in America* within a medieval dramatic tradition, a tradition developed when "resemblance ... organized the play of symbols, made possible knowledge of things visible and invisible, and controlled the art of representing them."[18] David Tracy, a modern theorist of "analogy," defines it as "a language of ordered relationships articulating similarity-in-difference. The order among the relationships is constituted by the distinct but similar relationships of each analogue to some primary focal meaning."[19] Here, Prior and Joe are not simply opposites, as Savran's observations about "binary oppositions" would suggest. At one and the same time, they are both similar (in their homosexuality and their need of a blessing) and different (in that [a] one is closeted and the other is out and [b] one wrestles with the angel, the other spars with the devil). As analogues rather than paired opposites, each relates in a unique way to the story of Jacob's redemption. This pattern of relationships is precisely the kind that V.A. Kolve notes at work in the cycles. Like Erich Auerbach, who notes that medieval "figural interpretation changed the Old Testament from a book of laws and a history of the people of Israel into a series of figures of Christ and the Redemption,"[20] Kolve shows how events and characters in the "Old Testament" plays (Noah's flood, the sacrifice of Isaac, for example) prefigure events and characters of the "New Testament" plays (John the Baptist, the crucifixion of Jesus, for example). He notes further that this prefigurement occurs in such a way that "the differences between figure and fulfillment are as important as the similarities."[21] In other words, the ordered relationships among events and characters in the cycles preserve the principle of analogy: their similarity-in-differences is maintained, each achieving significance from a common relationship to some prime analogue. In the cycle plays, the prime analogue is Jesus Christ; in *Angels in America* it is, of course, Prior Walter.

Although analogy is most clearly evident in the "split scenes" placed strategically throughout the play, Kushner uses analogy most significantly as the metaphoric expression of the profound similarities-in-difference that his meditation on contemporary politics and AIDS has led him to discover abounding in all reality. Like Louis and Joe, Prior (male, gay, worldly) and Harper (female, straight, Mormon) only seem opposites. Meeting around a common table, they recognize each other at "the very threshold of revelation" (I, 33). They soon speak in parallel sentences ("I'm a Mormon"; "I'm a homosexual"; "[Mormons] don't believe in homosexuals"; "[Homosexuals] don't believe in Mormons"). They share not their partners' disembodied and "Enlightened" myth of progress but a more concrete understanding of human finitude and a conviction that imagination is limited because bound to memory. They so clearly comprehend each other that they can reveal truths about the one that the other did not suspect: Prior can tell Harper that Joe is gay; Harper can tell Prior that his "most inner part" is "entirely free of disease" (33–34). Significantly, following these specific revelations and the larger implicit revelation that characters as diverse as Harper and Prior are not simply independent and opposing characters but fully implicated in each other's lives, the angel manifests itself for the first time.

Further, Kushner's analogies create an ordered series of relationships among God, self, and world and thereby give shape to the otherwise disparate elements of the play. If in the Corpus Christi plays the prime analogue is the suffering body of Christ, in *Angels in America* the prime analogue is the suffering body of Prior Walter. Both bodies dominate their plays not simply as graphic images of physical pain and suffering but primarily as interpretive paradigms. Positing the wounded body of Christ as an analogue for, among other things, the woundedness of the social body, of the body politic, and of the individual physical body, the cycles teach that the destinies of these separate bodies are in fact interconnected. As each of these bodies (social, political, individual) suffers in its own way, its suffering also participates in Christ's suffering and in that participation achieves a significance inaccessible to the same suffering considered in isolation: as Christ must die to rise again, so too must all else that is. As the analogical design of the medieval plays redefined their own emerging new social order, so the similar design of *Angels in America* helps to redefine whatever sense of order Kushner sees emerging not only from the AIDS pandemic but also from the collapse of modernism itself. Rather than only exploring AIDS and its metaphors, as Susan Sontag does,[22] Kushner offers AIDS as the primary analogue by means of which he seeks to recover meaning not only in the wake of AIDS but also out of the ruins of the entire postmodern collapse.

When Roy Cohn's doctor says that in the "presence" of the HIV virus, "[t]he body's immune system ceases to function" (I, 42), he is describing for a single human body the woundedness that, by analogy, is typical of all the defenseless bodies in what Kushner's Angel calls a "Universe of Wounds" (II, 54). As Prior's body can no longer defend itself against death, Harper notices from the outset that all around her

> beautiful systems [are] dying, old fixed orders spiraling apart ...
> [...] everywhere, things are collapsing, lies surfacing, systems of
> defense giving way.... (I, 16–17)

During the wrestling match with Prior at the end of the play, the angel remarks on the same events:

> The slow dissolving of the Great Design, / The spiraling apart of
> the Work of Eternity, / The World and its beautiful particle
> logic/All collapsed. (II, 134)

The separate elements in Kushner's design of a "Universe of Wounds" are the individual, the nuclear family, the American justice system, international diplomacy, the physical integrity of the planet, and the Judeo-Christian tradition itself.

In Kushner's design, these separate wounds form an ever-widening series of concentric circles radiating from a single wounded center, Prior Walter. In a vision of his own family history (I, 85–89), for example, the prior Priors teach him that "[i]n a family as long-descended as the Walters there are bound to be a few carried off by plague." While Prior's AIDS remains unique, suffering from plague, pestilence, "[t]he spotty monster," he learns, has an analogue in the common suffering of all that is human (86–87). Prior understands himself not only as an isolated, purely psychological entity, but as a member of the human family. On the other hand, Roy Cohn, unlike Prior, remains trapped in a thoroughly modern and "monological consciousness."[23] His disease, like Joe's homosexuality, must remain a secret, private, "closeted" business. Like Dante's Satan, he is the ultimate isolationist and last appears "*standing waist-deep in a smoldering pit, facing a volcanic, pulsating red light*" (II, 138). Moreover, the body of the traditional family is also wounded: Sarah Ironson's grandchildren have become assimilated; Joe's father could not love him (I, 76); Joe abandons Harper; Roy's "fathers" are "Walter Winchell, Edgar Hoover. Joe McCarthy most of all" (I, 56); even the Reagans are "not really a family [...] there aren't any connections there, no love, they don't ever even speak to each other except through their agents" (I, 71). In addition, like Prior, the body politic is wounded: justice is confused with power; "ipso facto secular humanism" has given way to "a genuinely American political personality. Modeled on Ronald Wilson Reagan" (I, 63); Washington is a "cemetery" (I, 23); "The whole Hall of Justice," Joe fears "it's empty, it's deserted, it's gone out of business. Forever. The people that make it run have up and abandoned it" (I, 72). After "Perestroika" and the fall of the Berlin Wall, "the World's Oldest Living Bolshevik" decries the present as a "Sour Little Age" and regrets the loss of any "Grand" and "comprehensive [Theory]" to guide a new revolution (II, 13–14). Further, the planet is also wounded: "the Chernobyl Power Plant in Belarus is already by leagues the greatest nuclear catastrophe" (II, 129); Libby fears the radon escaping in Hannah's basement (I, 82); and Harper learns early on about "holes in the ozone layer. Over Antarctica. Skin burns, birds go blind, icebergs melt. The world's coming to an end" (I, 28).

As all these wounded bodies are analogues to the wounded body of Prior Walter, so too is the great wound in the body of the Judeo-Christian tradition: like Louis and Joe, who abandon their lovers, and those others who have abandoned the Halls of Justice, God has also abandoned the universe. The primal covenant is broken, and heaven "*has a deserted, derelict feel [...] rubble is strewn everywhere*" (II, 121). In a scene inspired perhaps by the "Parliament of Heaven" episode in the N-Town plays,[24] the angels announce that they have become mere "impotent witness[es]" longing for the return of God (II, 130–31). But while the N-Town Daughters of God prepare for the coming of Christ, Kushner's angels, like mouthpieces for the Religious Right, foresee a future filled with chaos, a chaos that can only be averted by embracing stasis. Here Kushner makes most evident that although the structure of his play is similar to that of the cycles, it is also quite obviously different. Instead of imitating the cycles in a slavish way, thereby producing only similarity, something "of no relevance to anything," Kushner imitates them so as to announce at the same time his distance from them. Rather than create something absolutely "new," Kushner keeps faithful to the principle of analogy: quite deliberately, and like Prior Walter, he enters into a conversation with his own usable (prior) past. Unlike his modernist monster, Roy Cohn, whose death is hastened by his uncompromising defense of utter difference ("Roy Cohn is a heterosexual man, Henry, who fucks around with guys" [I, 46]), Kushner shares with Prior and Harper (and, it might be added, with most medieval descriptions of the imagination)[25] the belief that because imagination is always in a conversation with memory, it "can't create anything new [...] It only recycles bits and pieces from the world and reassembles them into vision" (I, 32).

Distancing himself from the theological assumptions of the medieval cycles to comment on contemporary reality, however, does not necessarily make Kushner the unwitting heir of the Enlightenment, as Savran suggests. To see *Angels in America* built around "a host of binary oppositions," as Savran does, ignores the complexity of Kushner's fully analogical imagination and fails to consider what Tracy calls "that dialectical sense within analogy itself."[26] What Savran reads as an "elaboration of contradictions" ("heaven/hell ... communitarianism/individualism, spirit/flesh," etc.)[27] Kushner's imagination holds in balance as dialectically aligned pairs. In his last scene, his "Doomsday," Kushner embodies the concordance of opposites, rather than their contradiction, in the Bethesda Fountain, "Prior's favorite place in the park" (II, 94), whose statuary angel dominates the scene. While Louis identifies the fountain as a monument to the "Naval dead of the Civil War" (II, 94), Belize sees it as a source of healing. Prior, the prophet of the impending age, however, sees it as both: "[it] commemorate[s] death but [...] suggest[s] a world without dying. [It is] made of the heaviest things on earth, stone and iron, [it] weigh[s] tons but [it is] winged" (II, 147). Incapable of understanding himself as independent of his body, and joined analogically to the community around him, Prior, unlike Roy Cohn and the ever-closeted Joe, is no representative of the detached, enlightened ego. Rather, more like a medieval holy man, Prior sees death not as the opposite of life, but as its complement and fulfillment. Conceived so, Prior's impending death, like the death of Christ in the mysteries, is not the occasion of despair but rather the springboard of hope.

Moreover, membership in the family which gathers around Prior at the end is dependent on a similar dialectical vision. Although Harper is absent, she is finally no more "pathologized" than is Prior Walter. She is clearly not the heir of Mary Tyrone and Blanche DuBois, as Savran suggests.[28] Unlike theirs, her disease and Prior's do not lead to isolation. Just as their diseases can never be understood in isolation from each other, disease itself roots them in a fragile and complex human condition that Joe and Roy, both absent from the final scenes, take great pains to deny. Moreover, for both Harper and Prior, disease can never be understood as independent of vision: her straight, Mormon, female vision always and everywhere the complement of his gay, secularist, male one. As she flies to San Francisco in a plane that also weighs tons and is winged, she has her own vision of apocalypse: "the souls of these departed joined hands, clasped ankles, and formed a web, a great net of souls, and the souls were three-atom oxygen molecules, of the stuff of ozone, and the outer rim absorbed them, and was repaired" (II, 144). If Roy and Joe are ineligible for membership in the new human family, it is precisely because they have failed to transcend Savran's binary oppositions: Joe's homosexual body remains the enemy of his Mormon spirit; Roy dies cursing life, gloating in the triumph of his will over Ethel Rosenberg (II, 115). Yet those who have loved Prior and join him around the Bethesda Fountain share in his analogical vision: while each remains independent of the other, they understand that the future of Prior's body is also their own. White, black; gay, straight; Jewish, Mormon; male, female: they retain their identities but share a common fate. While this final scene is indeed "utopian," it is not simply an image of an American utopia that "diffuse[s] or deflect[s] dissent," as Savran suggests.[29] It is, rather, an image of the new Jerusalem, which preserves the principle of analogy and where similarity and difference persist in constant and open conversation.

The credibility of this brief exploration of some medieval aspects of *Angels in America* was, unfortunately, nowhere supported by George C. Wolfe's New York production. Several foreign directors, however, seem to have appreciated the play's relationship to its medieval past. In doing so, they mounted productions that distanced themselves from the misguided attempts at psychological realism that marred Wolfe's production and thereby obscured Kushner's vision. Such a style could hardly convey what Bent Holm suggests is the play's "allegorical nature" or support his view of the play as a "wake-up call to The Theater's 'reality.'"[30] In Neil Armfield's September 1994 Australian production, on the other hand, "all ropes and pulleys were clearly visible and almost every stage object was on wheels enabling the cast members to smoothly and swiftly run them in and out."[31] Most tellingly, at the Avignon theater festival in summer 1994, Brigitte Jacques staged the first part of the play outdoors in the medieval Cloître des Cannes. In a manner consistent with Kushner's original stage directions that the play be "actor-driven" (I, 5), French street kids visibly moved set pieces on and off stage in a production that one critic called "not only minimalist but basic."[32] Such a basic production, it seems to me, embodied the kind of interconnectedness the play longs for.

NOTES

1. Harold Bloom, *The Western Canon: The Books and School of the Ages* (New York, 1994), 567.

2. Arlene Croce, "Discussing the Undiscussible," *New Yorker* (26 December 1994/2 January 1995), 55; Leo Bersani, *Homos* (Cambridge, MA, 1995), 69; David Savran, "Ambivalence, Utopia, and a Queer Sort of Materialism: How *Angels in America* Reconstructs the Nation," *Theatre Journal*, 47:2 (1995), 207–27.

3. Savran, "Ambivalence," 209. See note 1.

4. Arthur Lubow, "Tony Kushner's Paradise Lost," *New Yorker* (30 November 1992), 61.

5. Tony Kushner, "The Theatre of the Fabulous: An Interview with Tony Kushner," interview by David Savran, in *Essays on Kushner's Angels*, ed. Per Brask (Winnipeg, 1995), 134–35.

6. Thomas M. Greene, *The Light in Troy: Imitation and Discovery in Renaissance Poetry* (New Haven, CT, 1982), 40.

7. Savran, "Ambivalence," 211. See Walter Benjamin, "Theses on the Philosophy of History," in *Illumination*, ed. Hannah Arendt, trans. Harry Zohn (1968; rpt. with omissions, New York, 1969), 253–64.

8. Martin Stevens, "Medieval Drama: Genres, Misconceptions, and Approaches," in *Approaches to Teaching Medieval English Drama*, ed. Richard K. Emmerson (New York, 1990), 45–46.

9. David Stern, "The Man With Qualities: The Incongruous Achievement of Walter Benjamin," *The New Republic* (10 April 1995), 32.

10. Benjamin, 260, 254, 264, 257. See note 7.

11. Tony Kushner, *Angels in America: A Gay Fantasia on National Themes, Part One, Millennium Approaches* (hereafter I) and *Part Two, Perestroika* (hereafter II) (New York, 1992, 1994), I, 10. Subsequent references appear parenthetically in the text.

12. 1 Sam. 2: 1–10.

13. For example, Andrea Stevens, "Finding a Devil within to Portray Roy Cohn," interview with Ron Liebman and Ron Vawter, *New York Times* (18 April 1993), Arts and Leisure sec., i. See also John R. Quinn, "Corpus Juris Tertium: Redemptive Jurisprudence in *Angels in America*," *Theatre Journal*, 48: 1 (1996), 85: "the corporeality of Cohn and of Cohn's law are also inverted representations of the new law, a sort of Satan resurrected."

14. *The Fall of Lucifer* (The Tanners), Play I of *The Chester Mystery Cycle*, ed. R.M. Lumiansky and David Mills, Early English Text Society (London, 1974), II. 186–89.

15. *The Creation and the Fall of Lucifer* (The Bartiers), play I of *York Plays*, ed. Lucy Toulmin Smith (1885; rpt. New York, 1963), 156.

16. Savran, introduction to "Theatre of the Fabulous," 131. See note 5

17. Rob Baker, *The Art of AIDS* (New York, 1994), 214.

18. Michel Foucault, *The Order of Things: An Archaeology of the Human Sciences* (New York, 1970), 17.

19. David Tracy, *The Analogical Imagination: Christian Theory and the Culture of Pluralism* (New York, 1981), 408.

20. Erich Auerbach, "Figura," trans. Ralph Manheim, in *Scenes from the Drama of European Literature* (New York, 1959), 52.

21. V.A. Kolve, *The Play Called Corpus Christi* (Stanford, CA, 1966), 67.

22. See Susan Sontag, *AIDS and Its Metaphors* (New York, 1989).

23. Charles Taylor, "The Dialogical Self," in *The Interpretive Turn: Philosophy, Science, Culture*, ed. David R. Hiley, James F. Bohman, and Richard Shusterman (Ithaca, 1991), 52.

24. See *The Parliament of Heaven; The Salutation and Conception*, play XI of *The N-Town Plays*: Cotton MS Vespasin D.8, ed. Stephen Spector, vol. 1, Introduction and Text, Early English Text Society (Oxford, 1991), ll. 1–216.

25. See, for example, the discussion in Richard Kearney, *The Wake of Imagination: Toward a Postmodern Culture* (Minneapolis, MN, 1988), 115–138.

26. Savran, "Ambivalence," 212–13; Tracy, 413 (see note 19).

27. Savran, "Ambivalence," 212.

28. Ibid., 215.

29. Savran, "Ambivalence," 224, quoting Sacvan Bercovitch, "The Problem of Ideology in American Literary History," *Critical Inquiry*, 12:4 (1985–86), 644.

30. Bent Holm, "Flying in Different Directions: American Angels in Denmark," trans. Per Brask, in Essays on Kushner's Angels, 30–31.

31. Ian Olorenshaw, "*Angels* in Australia," *Essays on Kushner's Angels*, 73.

32, Laszlo Szekrenyi, "*Angels* in Avignon," *TheaterWeek* (5–11 September 1994), 37.

JAMES FISHER

The Progress of Death in the Land of Pure Delight: Hydriotaphia, or The Death of Dr. Browne

And here in Heaven
I will never die.
I can say that
And not feel
I'm telling
A lie.
In Heaven I will never die.
Never
Never
Never
Die.

—Browne's *Soul*, *Hydriotaphia, or*
The Death of Dr. Browne (53)

Political upheavals and the horrors of evil pervade the grim, sensual *A Bright Room Called Day*, but death dominates Kushner's next play, *Hydriotaphia, or The Death of Dr. Browne*, subtitled "An Epic Farce About Death and Primitive Capital Accumulation." Kushner wrote the play in 1987, but it underwent a significant revision prior to its first professional productions a decade later. Kushner frequently points out that "the moments in history that interest me the most are of transition" (Mader 1), something

From *The Theater of Tony Kushner: Living Past Hope*. © 2001 by Routledge.

he vividly demonstrates in *Bright Room*. Kushner locates another historical transition in *Hydriotaphia*—one somewhat more obscure but, in its own way, no less important.

Through his imaginative rumination on the life of Sir Thomas Browne in *Hydriotaphia*, Kushner imagines the period in which capitalism was born. Although his interest in historical transitions binds *Bright Room* and *Hydriotaphia* together, there is little else that connects these two plays. In place of the frighteningly real grimness of *Bright Room*, Kushner creates a wild flight of theatrical and intellectual fantasy in *Hydriotaphia* that results from "a certain fascination that I've always had with death and dying, and I've been intrigued by the fact that it seems like a very lively kind of fascination" (Mader 1). *Bright Room*'s Agnes certainly fears death in much the way that Browne does in *Hydriotaphia*, but instead of the titanic evil that afflicts Agnes, Browne is in a far more personal struggle with the imminence of his death, the subtler avarice and brutality of his own soul, the greed of his unloving family members and friends, and the ignorant and superstitious time in which he lives. In this play, Kushner asks: what is the effect of unchecked acquisitiveness on an individual's soul, on those around him, and on the society of which he is an integral part? These and related questions are tied to a meditation on the meaning of death, both in its scientific reality and in its spiritual possibility.

Hydriotaphia depicts, with grotesque foreboding, the last day in the life of Sir Thomas Browne (1605–82), a noted seventeenth-century writer and physician and, in Kushner's imagination, a seminal capitalist. This multipronged play mingles the metaphysical with the mundane, explores the complexities of existence and the mysteries of the afterlife and, as such, anticipates themes Kushner explores in more contemporary terms in *Angels*.

The real Sir Thomas Browne was born in London, the son of a successful merchant. His first significant literary work, *Religio Medici* (c. 1635), written sometime before Browne began practicing medicine in Norwich around 1637, was published in 1642 without his consent. *Religio Medici* demonstrates that Browne was a premodern man of science who, despite education at Oxford, Montpelier, and Padua, and a probing intellect, was still bound to many of the superstitions of his day. Three years after its publication, the Catholic Church prohibited the reading of *Religio Medici*, but others, including John Dryden, imitated its style. Browne's contemporaries compared him favorably with Shakespeare, although this comparison rapidly faded in the decades following his death.

Browne married Dorothy, daughter of Edward Mileham of Norfolk, in 1641, and they had eleven children. Following his marriage, Browne completed his most ambitious work, *Pseudodoxia Epidemica* (*Vulgar Errors*), which was published in 1646 and was followed in rapid succession during the 1650s by *The Garden of Cyrus*, *A Letter to a Friend*, and, in 1658, *Hydriotaphia* (or *Urn-burial*). Browne was knighted in 1671 by Charles II, although his selection was only by default (the mayor of Norwich had declined the honor) despite the fact that Browne had been a faithful Royalist all of his life.

Later, Browne wrote two more works that were published posthumously: *Christian Morals*, regarded by some scholars as a continuation of *Religio Medici*, and *Certain Miscellany Tracts*, a work on a wide range of topics related to human and natural history. In his *Life of Sir Thomas Browne* (1756), Samuel Johnson describes Browne's writing as "vigorous but ragged, it is learned but pedantick, it is deep but obscure, it strikes but does not please, it commands but does not allure.... It is a tissue of many languages, a mixture of heterogeneous words brought together from distant regions" ("Sir Thomas Browne" 4). His literary influence is especially evident in the works of Swift and Melville, and although Browne's "appeal has largely been because he inhabits the byways of literary discourse, not the mainroads," writes Jonathan F. S. Post, his "remarkably individual" talents as a writer are in presenting a "countervoice to the expected" in revealing "the dark mysteries of life and human potentiality" (156–57). Since these dark mysteries of life and the possibility of human progress are core themes for Kushner, he was naturally attracted to Browne's work and life.

Specifically focusing on Browne's treatise, *Hydriotaphia*, described by Post as one of "the ripest of any studies written in English" (12), Kushner invents the last day of Browne's life as a metaphor for his theories and what Browne symbolizes in the dialogue on social and economic progress. In *Hydriotaphia*, Browne went beyond the typical archaeological reporting of his day when writing of nearly fifty ancient burial urns discovered in a field near Walsingham. Browne challenges the limits of human knowledge in his treatise; pondering on the bones found in the urns, he questions man's sense of "significance and self-sufficiency" (Post 121), finding that the "certainty of death is attended with uncertainties, in time, manner, places" (*The Major Works*, 290). He also criticizes the burial practices of the ancients and his own time, focusing on "the irrationality of numerous customs and the way fictions—or glosses—of death presume to rationalize the unknown" (Post 126), concluding that God does not necessarily promise immortality to human beings:

> There is nothing strictly immortall, but immortality; whatever hath no beginning may be confident of no end. All others have a

dependent being, and within the reach of destruction, which is
the peculiar of that necessary essence that cannot destroy it self;
And the highest strain of omnipotency to be so powerfully
constituted, as not to suffer even from the power of it self. But the
sufficiency of Christian Immortality frustrates all earthly glory,
and the quality of either state after death, makes a folly of
posthumous memory. God who can only destroy our souls, and
hath assured our resurrection, either of our bodies or names hath
directly promised no duration. (*The Major Works*, 312–13)

Browne's ruminations on death, burials, and the Christian view of eternal life
are used by Kushner as a grotesque backdrop for a man facing his own
demise. Kushner employs these notions as a jumping-off point for an
irreverently whimsical, theatrically baroque exploration of life and death
through his argument with Browne's own philosophical questions about
existence and the material and spiritual aspects of death. Not binding himself
to the strict facts of Browne's life, Kushner's close encounter with Browne is
at once both outrageously comic and malevolently macabre.

When he first encountered Browne's writing, Kushner attempted to
stage the treatise *Hydriotaphia* itself, but he found that this experience instead
inspired a play. Spending three weeks writing *Hydriotaphia* in 1987 for a brief
non-Equity production, Kushner worked with the cast, including some
members of the first staging of *Bright Room*, and "it ran for one week in a tiny
theater in New York. This is a period piece with heavy costumes.... and we
ran during a very hot summer in an unair-conditioned space" (Evans, "Last
Laughs," 10). Obviously, this was not the perfect venue, but Kushner
retained an affection for the play over the subsequent years. Following the
success of *Angels*, there was a great demand for another Kushner play, so he
brought it off the shelf and began revisions.

With Kushner's cooperation, *Hydriotaphia* was given a production in
1997 at the Tisch School of the Arts at New York University, directed by
Michael Wilson. The staging led to joint productions at the Alley Theatre in
Houston, Texas (also directed by Wilson), and at California's Berkeley
Repertory Theatre in 1998. For each of these productions, Kushner made
significant revisions. Prior to the Alley's production, Kushner discussed the
play's genesis with the theater's dramaturg, Travis Mader. Calling
Hydriotaphia "semi-historical and semi-biographical," he explained that he
found in Browne's *Hydriotaphia* "some of the most beautiful prose I had ever
read," and that he particularly responded to "how obscure and strange it is—
and being fascinated with the themes it touches on, which are dying and

immortality" (Mader 1). The inevitability of death, human conceptions of the possibility of continuing life after death, and the meaning the past holds for the future are all usual Kushnerian concerns. In *Hydriotaphia* they are presented with a seemingly incompatible mixture of illusory invention, expansive humor, and highly charged drama.

Beyond a complex depiction of human existence and death, Kushner argues political and economic issues in *Hydriotaphia* through an amalgam of Brechtian and cinematic techniques. Like *Bright Room*, *Hydriotaphia* is episodic, with one scene seeming to bleed into the next and with projected titles for scenes and comments on the action. Here again, Kushner reinvigorates the Brechtian style, melding Brecht's structural foundation with his own approach to character, linguistic lyricism, and a bold theatricality. Kushner is interested in Browne's life and times as they represent the notion of the revolution of "primitive capital accumulation," a term coined by Marx, who, Kushner writes, is

> making reference to the ugly and vital process whereby a nation which is entering a capitalist phase of economic and social relations dislocates its rural populations in the course of a violent land-grab by aristocratic and entrepreneurial classes intent on accumulating, by any means necessary, the material resources which provide the bases for mercantile, manufacturing and speculatory fortunes; from the devastation consequent upon such officially sanctioned piracy, an impoverished urban and factory workforce emerges, desperate for wages: primitive capital accumulation is the nakedly brutal manner in which money was grubbed from people and land, before the banalization, the normalization of such mayhem, before we learned new words for it, like modernization, Progress, industrialization—before the invention of Spin. ("Three Brief Notes from the Playwright," 5)

Shakespeare, Kushner continues, lived through the end of the "roughest phases" of primitive accumulation in England, and he believes that Shakespeare's plays, as such, "reflect the chaos of the time, their bloodiness, their immense excitement, and the irreconcilable dissonance of such vast material appetite with Christ's asceticism, with His antipathy towards wealth and usury, Christ's preference for the poor" ("Three Brief Notes from the Playwright," 5). In Kushner's view, the resulting human misery caused by the seizure of "common lands, moors and forests, and their transformation into private property, made a social, political revolution inevitable" ("Three Brief

Notes from the Playwright," 5), one in which capital brutally triumphed. Kushner adds that Browne lived "after that revolution, during the Restoration of the Old Order Transformed (think Gerald Ford taking over after the dismissal of Nixon) (or perhaps, 'earth-friendly' Al Core replacing Monica Lewinsky's boyfriend)" ("Three Brief Notes from the Playwright," 5). The connections between the transition era in which Browne lived and that of Kushner's own life are more fully explained by Kushner:

> The play is set just after an extreme time, after Cromwell. It is very similar to the 1990s. Reaganism is to a certain extent a Restoration. Nixon began it: a certain resettling of the terms of the social contract along very conservative lines. And the social revolution of the 1960s is still with us—just witness what is happening in the White House! One wonders why Monica [Lewinsky] was keeping that dress—but let's not get into that. All of this would be inconceivable in the '60s—our blessing and our curse. The '60s were not a time about sexuality, social interrelatedness, politics. Clinton is very much a product of the '60s, as is, in his own bizarre way, Newt Gingrich. In a sense they are a reaction to the '60s. We are very much in this post-revolutionary, post-counterrevolutionary dazedness that you find in Dr. Browne's time in 17th century England. (Roca 32)

Kushner imagines Browne's era as one of transition into modern capitalism, a time in which the powerful could freely seize common lands and accumulate vast holdings of valuable property. Stressing the politics inherent in the situation, Kushner says that *Hydriotaphia* is, "about how the political and economic system we live under affects everything, including the way we die. It's about how his [Browne's] death affects the lives of, everyone in his household. It also is about the death of a writer and the ramifications of his work" (Evans, "Last Laughs," 10).

Along with the political, it is important to note the personal aspects of *Hydriotaphia*, a "dark comedy with a strain of gallows humor, a kind of madness" (Evans, "Last Laughs," 10), which was partially inspired by Kushner's response to the AIDS pandemic. The loss of many friends, as well as the death of his uncle, Max Deutscher, to whom he dedicated *Hydriotaphia*, were Kushner's first significant experiences with death. Describing himself as "an agnostic Jewish humanist socialist," Kushner's personal identification with the political issues and the unanswerable and frightening questions raised in *Hydriotaphia* leads him to depict "a society that glorifies individuality at the expense of connectedness, that makes a virtue of isolation and pathologizes connectedness, we make our deaths hard. Death is terrifying because we fear extinction, find it inconceivable" (Evans, "Last Laughs," 10). The failure of connectedness—of the denial of a society's accountability for the well-being of all of its citizens—is a theme that comes more fully to the fore in *Angels*, as well as in such later Kushner works as *Slavs!*, the one-act teleplay *East Coast Ode to Howard Jarvis*, and the as-yet unproduced opera libretto *Caroline, or Change*, and the screenplay *Grim(m)*.

Blending realistic and phantasmagoric elements in his seriocomic riff on Browne, Kushner employs human embodiments of Death, Browne's Soul, and witches who roam through this antic and chilling "epic farce" set in the plague-ridden days of the Restoration. The action is presented in Browne's sickroom on April 3, 1667 ("more or less" according to the stage directions, 39), and although *Hydriotaphia* demands no scene changes, its requirements are not minimal. The play is filled with the potential for numerous imaginative scenic and lighting effects, as when Browne's Soul attempts to ascend to Heaven on a golden ladder from above or when Death appears eerily from the shadows to lay "a chilly hand on Dr. Browne's throat" (3) while drawing a huge carving knife from his sleeve. Other visual inspirations are provided by the scene itself, with Kushner calling for a central deathbed with a marble headboard "like a tombstone" (41), and the richly appointed chamber is scattered with the attractions of Browne's life, including books, papers, scientific equipment, musical instruments, nautical tools, writing implements, human skulls, medicine bottles, and "bottles with dead things and necrotic tissues floating inside" (41).

In the play's opening image, wedding death with life, Browne lies semicomatose on his deathbed while two servants roll on the floor in passionate abandon. Browne is depicted as a grasping, emotionally barren conservative who is physically and spiritually bloated with the excesses of his life. These excesses are symbolically underscored by the bizarre clutter of man-made and natural acquisitions filling his room.

As Browne slips into and out of consciousness, lying in his own filth (he describes himself as "a blossom of putrescence" [117]), Kushner begins *Hydriotaphia* by establishing Browne as the senior partner in a limestone quarry business along with his stuttering pastor, Dr. Leviticus Dogwater, a Protestant cleric who announces to Browne's wife that "once we thought Heaven glowed with the light of divine fire, Dame Dorothy, but now we *know*—it glows with the shine of gold" (67). Dogwater mouths Christian platitudes, claims to believe in its dogmas, but his true ethos, "Accumulate, Accumulate" (143), is avidly shared by Browne.

Browne's London Limestone Quarry Company has seized some
Norfolk common lands, forcing the residing peasants off and onto the open
road. Pounding engines beat constantly in the distance as the quarry
relentlessly fills the pockets of Browne, Dogwater, and the quarry's investors,
all of whom hope to expand their holdings in similar fashion with Browne's
guidance. Dogwater anxiously monitors Browne's condition, hoping to wrest
a controlling interest in the quarry before Browne, suffering from an onion-
sized intestinal blockage, succumbs.

Grotesquely bloated from the discomforting blockage—"I'd sell my
soul for a bowel movement" (72), he cries—Browne's distension
metaphorically underscores his rampant acquisitiveness. Browne at first
denies seeing his impertinent, sometimes bawdy Soul, who waits impatiently
for his death, much in the manner of Ebenezer Scrooge denying the
existence of Jacob Marley's ghost in *A Christmas Carol*. Relations between
Browne and his Soul are, however, far more contentious. As Browne fights
off death, Soul, striving to avoid pollution from human contact, angrily tells
him, "You hoard everything. It's only justice that you should die of
constipation" (78). Browne admits glimpsing a point of heavenly light in the
blackness of his periodic comas, but Soul is annoyed that Browne, who has
shown little interest in that bit of "gold" during his life, now clings
desperately to it simply because she wants it. He battles the inevitability of
his demise, thus preventing Soul's rise to Heaven. "Redeem me then," she
demands, "DIE! I want nothing weighty, no ballast when I ascend. Nothing
you've touched and polluted. The house, the gold, the quarry, all yours. I
only want a small shard of an idea ..." (78). Death, walking the earth in the
guise of Browne's long-deceased father, who Browne bitterly remembers as
"a granite-hearted drunkard" (165), is prepared to oblige Soul by ending
Browne's life, but he is continually—and comically—interrupted as he stalks
his victim.

Browne clings to life as those around him begin a fierce battle for his
fortune. Dogwater insists, "God hates idle money as much as he hates idle
men" (68), and Browne detects "a distinctly mercenary scent in the air
tonight. This isn't me dying; it's a great deal of money rolling over" (167).
Browne's intimates are vying—through sex, lies, and avarice—for a piece of
the quarry, but his long-suffering, no-nonsense wife, Dame Dorothy, wants
nothing to do with it, explaining the essential difference between her
husband and herself by pointing out that the engines [of the quarry] give me
nightmares and headaches. But they tranquilize him" (89). The fourteen
children Dame Dorothy has borne her husband provide little comfort for her
since some have died in infancy and those who attained adulthood have been

driven away by Browne's harsh criticisms and emotional coldness. He is ultimately able to acknowledge his familial failures when he laments, "I think now I never thought enough about love" (122). This remark points to another significant thread that runs through *Hydriotaphia* and Kushner's other works.

The only small affection Browne can find comes from Babbo, his "imponderably old and faithful retainer" (76) whose "charming peasant patois" (118) provides him some measure of comfort. Babbo nursed Browne's father and his grandfather, and notes in the strange dialect Kushner invents for her that Browne's grandfather "han't bin no babbie, just lonely. He bin da most entertaining of da three" (177). As this example indicates, the unbridled anarchy of this appealingly cluttered play carries into its dialogue. To avoid the usual stilted Americanized British stage speech, Kushner creates a crazy quilt language for the play's "bumpkins" that, he writes in the stage directions, is "derived from Yorkshire, Brooklyn and also based on Krazy Kat. It is not southern American, Texan, Irish nor African American!!" adding that for the aristocratic characters, a "standard American English, crisp and clear" (42) be employed.

Babbo offers the sweet warmth and comic ribaldry of an old nurse of theatrical tradition. She occasionally falls into sexual tomfoolery with Maccabbee, Browne's horny amanuensis, who wears a tin nose in place of the real one he has lost to a virulent case of the clap. Dr. Emil Schadenfreude, Browne's German physician and resident fop, provides little comfort, matter-of-factly expressing Kushner's fascination with "life in death" (58) while finding that his difficult patient is "a regular sack of toxins" (55). Providing further comic complications in the battle for Browne's fortune is Doña Estrelita, his Spanish ex-lover. Constructed of equal parts Carmen Miranda and Eva Peron (with a little Charo thrown in), Doña Estrelita seems to genuinely care for Browne—or at least for the memory of their torrid affair twenty years before—and she wants to take his corpse with her to be buried in Spain. Also drifting in and out is Leonard Pumpkin, Browne's gravedigger, an ambitious young man who sees his way out of poverty through the sexual favors of Browne's lonely wife. Pumpkin hopes that following Browne's death Dame Dorothy will marry him and, using her inherited riches, he can seek a knighthood and leave his peasant status permanently behind him.

Another mysterious figure appears in Magdelina Vindicta, the Abbess of X, who turns out to be Browne's sister thought lost twenty years before in a shipwreck. She is now a militantly subversive nun; "I'm not at liberty to say" (141), she imperiously intones when pressed for details about her particular order. Debating with Dogwater over Browne's fortune, she indicates her disgust with the pompous moralizing masking the cleric's greed, insisting that the "Mysteries of the Faith aren't subservient to market fluctuations!" (143). She expresses a similar disdain for Dogwater's views on religion: "They should never have translated the Bible," she says, "You are the crippled progeny of that labor" (143). Despite her protestations, however, it is clear that she, like the others, has come in hope of inheriting Browne's financial empire. In one of the play's more farcical moments, the Abbess, who Browne himself describes as "ferocious" (165), beats up Dogwater as they battle to replace forged versions of Browne's will in his desk.

The play's other comedic moments emerge in various ways: Browne gives a leech to Dogwater, who shrieks and throws it into the audience—a gag set in counterpoint with the play's more serious ambitions and intended to engage the spectators more directly in the farcical spirit of the plot. There is much joking in the play about the rivalries between Catholicism and Protestantism, as well as a broadly comic scene in which Dogwater and Schadenfreude simultaneously attempt to top each other with their florid eulogies for a profoundly disinterested Browne. Much of the remaining humor involves secondary characters struggling to prevail in winning Browne's fortune. This battle of the wills causes Browne to complain, "I seem to have lost center-stage" (116); about to become "wormfood" (73), he whines that "my later is gone" (82) and realizes there is no way to change this course of events. Dogwater stutteringly comments that "Guh-God moves in mah-mysterious and sometimes ruh-rather malicious ways. To spur us. And we go on. We duh-dare not do otherwise" (208).

Kushner adds three additional characters who represent "da homeless n' afflictet" (80). Sarah, Mary, and Ruth are all members of the Ranters, a radical religious sect that formed in England during the social unrest of the mid-seventeenth century. The Ranters, who collectively called themselves "My one flesh," proposed a unity with mankind and the whole of creation and, in essence, this is how Kushner employs the three members in the play. The historical Ranters questioned God's omnipotence, wondering why He permits evil in the world. Their pantheistic/nature-based beliefs later led many Ranters to convert to Quakerism as their sect vanished. Kushner's three Ranters are among those who have been displaced by Browne's ruthless land acquisition. Dame Dorothy, as Babbo explains, is "partial to heretics" (99), so she has admitted the three women to their house, apparently not aware that one of them, Sarah, is the daughter of a woman hanged as a witch with Browne's assistance. This element of the play is also historically based; in 1664, Browne testified at the trial of two women, Amy Duny and Rose

Cullender, accused of bewitching some children. Browne was called upon as an expert witness, but, as Kushner explains, "merely stated that if we believe there is a God, we must also concede the existence of Satan and of witches. He was not attempting to sway the outcome, but to his horror, the women were hanged. There was a sense of guilt that poisoned the remaining years of his life" (Evans, "Last Laughs," 10). Those poisoned years have had a profound effect on the Browne of Kushner's play, and the Ranters are a visible reminder of Browne's culpability. They come to his home to exact revenge (while also stealing food and silver from Browne's kitchen) and provide a vivid image of those harmed, intentionally or not, by Browne's superstitions, mistakes, and acquisitiveness.

Despite the riotously lunatic comic drive of its plot, *Hydriotaphia* does not lose its focus. It is a deeply disturbing meditation on death that explains Kushner's belief in "something vital and electric in morbidity" (Mader 1). He divides the lengthy *Hydriotaphia* into three acts, and each scene is named: "Contemptus Mundis" (act 1, scene 1), "In What Torne Ship Soever I Embarke" (act 1, scene 2), "The Dance of Death" (act 2), "Who Sees Gods Face, That is Self Life, Must Die" (act 3, scene 1), and "Post Mortem" (act 3, scene 2). Although the action seems to proceed continuously, there is an episodic quality to the comings and goings of Browne's death chamber that is decidedly Brechtian.

Kushner's 1998 revision of *Hydriotaphia* strengthens the image of the central character—sardonic, querulous, argumentative, and dismissive of those around him, Browne is a forerunner of Kushner's imagining of Roy Cohn in *Angels*. Kushner characterizes both as extremely odious while still creating sympathy for their sufferings and their fundamental humanity. Browne deserves to have lost the love of his wife and absent children, admitting himself that "I did not live well" (88). He stresses, though, that "I never intended to harm. That was true" (121). His coldness—and the chill he feels from those around him—is part of his attraction to the dead, and his own disenchantment is reflected in his understanding of his archaeological work. When an ancient burial urn from the excavation of his quarry arrives, the prodigiously pedantic Browne reflects on his memories of visiting ancient Roman catacombs where "that fragile stillness" of death hovered, and where he could view the "dry, deflated bodies" and "the disappointed faces of the dead" (162). In moments like those, the play succeeds in foregrounding Kushner's belief that there is something frighteningly alive about Browne's fascination with burials and obsession with death. When Browne orders the urn to be opened, he is shaken when "a spume of dust" rises suddenly from it. Frightened, Browne notes, "See? The dead do rise" (164).

Yet Browne cannot face his own end. Prevented from being celestially freed from Browne's body, his Soul becomes increasingly human, and believes that Browne is "murdering the song" (105) of her delayed ascension. She regards Browne as dead weight that is pulling her down, so, ever the scientist, Browne orders Maccabbee to help him prove the weightlessness of the soul. Maccabbee weighs three live chickens, which are then slaughtered and weighed again. Two of the chickens weigh exactly the same as when they were alive, while the third inexplicably becomes heavier. When the expanding chicken explodes, it is discovered to be filled to overflowing with maggots, another grotesque image Kushner uses to relate Browne's physical bloat to his financial greed.

Reflecting on his own mortality, Browne laments at length on the concept of his own demise. He realizes, "Oh god I'm talking myself to death" (180). Despite a rational awareness that he is at life's final frontier, Browne cannot truly believe it. When Pumpkin arrives to discuss plans for Browne's burial, Kushner brings together many strands of Browne's persona: false modesty, arrogance, pride, morbid fascination with the rituals of death, and an abject fear of the unknown:

> I want to be buried deep. Very deep ... not too deep. Apart from the mob, but not in a lonely place. Avoid the usual cliches, no willow trees, though I'd like a view, for summer evenings. No pine box. Flimsy. Use that urne. Toss out the previous occupant, or better yet, throw me in there with him and let us mingle. (*Little pause*) No markers, or, well, maybe just a little unpretentious stone. Maybe ... "Here lies Sir Thomas Browne, scientist." "Here lies Sir Thomas Browne, who made his wife miserable," "Here lies Sir Thomas Browne, no grandchildren ... BUT A GENIUS! SHAKESPEARE HAD NOTHING ON HIM!" (*He is now bellowing at Pumpkin with wild hatred and immense pride:*) Or maybe an obelisk! Or a pyramid! A pyre! A sea-burial, or ... GET OUT OF HERE! (171)

When Pumpkin persists, Browne becomes hysterical: "I don't need you, wretch! I'M NOT GOING TO DIE. It isn't ... *conceivable*! I can't ... IF I DIE ... THE WORLD ENDS!" (171).

Dame Dorothy makes a final sad attempt at a reconciliation, telling Browne that "I never really wanted anything from you. And you leave behind you only a dreadful lot of woe" (172). Despite this, she offers to stay with him as he faces the end, but he rebuffs her in a gesture true to his basic persona.

Browne fears death, but clings to the Christian belief that the end of this life opens a door into the next. Death, comically interrupted in his prior attempts to claim Browne, finally does so in a spine-tingling scene abruptly shifting the play away from its farcical tone. Brutally strangling his helpless victim, Death points out that "there is no mystery to this. It's ugly. A simple murder ..." (181). Browne tries to see his death in more lyrical literary terms, but Kushner maintains the nightmarish reality by employing a Melvillian seafaring metaphor that is a precursor to a similar speech by Prior Walter in *Millennium Approaches*:

> The ship embarks at first wind. The mast and sails are gilded with blood, on seas of blood we sail, in search of prey. The nets hauled in by mighty hands, up from the red depths to the surface, up come the great black nets, full and heavy of the worlds riches, hauled to the stronghold, to the drybone bank of death, with a hiss and suck plucked from the waters, in a ruby mist, in a fine red rain. You ... who must live through this ... I pity you. (180)

Once dead, and following some additional machinations over Browne's will, the remaining characters come together to sing the English hymn, "There Is A Land of Pure Delight" (a mild anachronism—this particular hymn, by Isaac Watts, was not written until 1704). The lyrics suggest a beauty in the journey from life to death that is in ironic juxtaposition to its actuality:

> There is a land of pure delight
> Where saints immortal reign.
> Infinite day excludes the night
> And pleasure banish pain.
> There everlasting spring abides,
> And never-withering flowers.
> Death like a narrow sea divides.
> This heavenly land from ours. (197)

The inarticulate characters only understand death as a sad fact of life, and Babbo simply moans that Browne, "Nevah more to waket" (186), although he does speak further through his will.

In the last act, Browne's true will is finally read. Here Browne's character is illuminated clearly and simply: "My will is to eat. To greedily engorge without restraint and know not eating death" (202). Death has, in fact, devoured him despite his wishes. Babbo, reflecting on Browne's death, fancifully recounts his life and fascination with a mortality he fought unsuccessfully to defeat, concluding, "N'da kid growet up to be a fatuous doctah wif da power a life n' death, n'den ... N'den he died, a course" (186). Browne's will reveals that he has left his worldly riches to his wife after all, and, in response to the farcical connivings of the others vying for his fortune, he mocks, "So much fuss and bother ... I suppose it gave the supporting cast something to do. While waiting for the end" (202). Greedily retentive to the end, Browne refuses even to share any visionary insights with his survivors: "the future.... NO. Don't tell, them ANYTHING" (203).

Dame Dorothy, who resists the acquisitive tendencies of her late husband, sees things differently. Believing her whole generation to be "cursed by our gold" (210), and to the horror of Dogwater, the Abbess of X, and Schadenfreude, she decides to return the quarry lands "to the people" (193). She has seen too much suffering—and has endured much herself—resulting from her husband's ruthless acquisition of the land, although Kushner makes it obvious that Dame Dorothy's gesture is too little and too late. The acquisition of capital has become the order of the day, despite her resolve to resist it. Kushner's gift for rhetoric serves Dame Dorothy's explanation of her concerns for the displaced, the feelings she harbors about her life with husband, and the ravages of capitalism:

> People sleep on the open road at night. On cold mornings there's some who don't wake up. You see them, ice-crusted ... I want a thicker skin but it won't grow, at night I hear those machines in the quarry pounding and I think: it's flesh those hammers pound, its bone. We're immensely rich but we live without luxury. He can't bear to part with anything, even remorse, and I can't bear the accumulation. Thomas is lucky to die. I must live on here for a while yet, and I hate this life. In me there is a bleeding wound, and it never heals, and its full of blood, and full of light, and there's paradise in there, besieged and unreachable but always beckoning. And the more foul and ugly the world becomes the more it beckons. The more it aches. (135–36)

Browne's world collapses completely after his death when an alcohol-sotted corpse stashed in the kitchen oven by Pumpkin ignites a fire destroying part of his house. More significantly, the thunder of the quarry machines, mated to Browne's final desperate heartbeats, abruptly stops as the machines collapse into an underground catacomb. Browne's Soul enjoys a postmortem cigarette, but Dame Dorothy firmly rejects Pumpkin and resolves to make the crossing to a new—and perhaps better (or at least more hopeful)—world in America.

A primer for appreciating the style and substance of Kushner's later works, *Hydriotaphia*, like *Bright Room*, establishes his lofty ambitions for a revitalized epic theater which, as he himself explains, explores possibilities that "range from a vastly improved world to no world at all" (Mader 1). The Brechtian influences are somewhat less overt in *Hydriotaphia* than in *Bright Room* as Kushner's own aesthetic asserts itself with greater confidence, but the political message of the play seeps through the cracks of its grisly mausoleum slapstick. The episodic, cinematic qualities are also less in evidence, but there is no lessening of the grotesque phantasmagoria that is given free range thanks, in part, to the play's being set in a time of primitive premodern science. The wonders of contemporary science are viewed in their first awkward, unknowing stages and are, as such, frightening in their horrific ignorance. Browne himself is little more than a science experiment, undergoing leechings and enemas with Rube Goldberg machines belonging more to a commedia dell'arte farce than to real life, as well as various other repugnant procedures which only hasten a death that mere decades later would be treated successfully by medical science. Kushner effectively—if, in this case, with outrageous humor and ghoulish imagery—features his recurring fascination with the wrenches of transitions. It is not only the encroachment of capitalism, but also the marriage of superstition to religion and their collision with science that is also central to *Hydriotaphia*. The intersection of the macabre and the comic has not been given such free range in Kushner's subsequent work, although it is always present even if applied with more subtlety. It is, however, the excessive weirdness of *Hydriotaphia* that is its greatest strength; Kushner imagines the seventeenth century in its most backward, uncomprehending awkwardness and so creates a vision of the human condition in its basest form. Here, Restoration comedy meets a Saturday matinee horror movie, Browne meets the Marxes (Karl and Groucho), and the result is a surprisingly bracing, nightmarish romp through church, cemetery, and capitalism.

When *Hydriotaphia* was given its first professional productions, it premiered at the Alley Theatre in Houston, Texas, for a run scheduled March 27–April 25, 1998. The press opening was delayed a week as Kushner, still revising, continued to sharpen the play. According to the local Houston press, Kushner "has made extensive rewrites that will be going into the production this week, and the Alley wanted to give the cast and production crew time to accommodate the changes" (Evans, "Kushner Still Tweaking *Hydriotaphia* Script," 1C). The Houston performances were followed some months later by a September 11–November 1, 1998 run at the Berkeley Repertory Theatre in Berkeley, California, with several cast members held over from the Alley production. Both productions greatly profited from the performance of Jonathan Hadary, who had played Roy Cohn in the national tour of *Angels in America*. Hadary gave a potent performance as Browne, with one critic noting that he gave the character "a blend of mortal suffering and intellectual detachment" (Evans, "Kushner Hits Highs, Lows in Epic Farce," 1D). Other cast members appearing in both productions included long-time San Francisco Mime Troupe member Sharon Lockwood (The Abbess of X), Shelley Williams (Dame Dorothy), Charles Dean (who played Dogwater at the Alley and switched to Schadenfreude at Berkeley), Paul Hope (Death), and Delia MacDougall, Moya Furlow, and Louise Chegwidden as the Ranters.

Critics in both regions were split over the play's merits. Some reviewers felt there were too many themes to allow an audience to grasp them all. This is a frequent criticism of Kushner's plays. Others disagreed on the success with which the balance of farce and seriousness was presented, with one Houston critic describing Kushner's "wildly erratic" and "irreverent" play as abounding "in bright, whimsical ideas" and with a production that was "ingenious, well-paced and full of neat visual effects" (Evans, "Kushner Hits Highs, Lows in Epic Farce," 1D). Others were less impressed, finding it merely a "mildly interesting entertainment, but the play fails as craft, as social commentary and as a measure of Kushner's formidable talent" (Halverson). Another critic stressed that *Hydriotaphia* contained "some very, very funny moments and has a lovely visual, if occasionally visceral, impact," but found the script "wordy" (Arenschieldt 19).

California critics concurred with those in Texas, with one reviewer appreciating the play's "bubbly, profound, historically rooted Monty Python-meets-Ben Jonson tribute to writing. And he [Kushner] has disguised it as a comedy about thanatology, the study of the experience of dying and bereavement" (De La Viña 29). Another reviewer groused about the play's three-and-a-half-hour length, finding that the play was "as bloated as its protagonist," but that it was "eminently worth watching" and that the "heady result is what might have emerged had Bertolt Brecht and Joe Orton collaborated on a Restoration comedy" (Rosenstein). The comparison to Restoration comedy is apt, but another California critic compared the "often smart and funny" play with George Bernard Shaw's *Heartbreak House*, feeling that it also seemed "static and redundant, an ambitious, anxious work by a writer who was warming up to write a masterpiece" (Winn C1). Other critics stressed *Hydriotaphia*'s contemporariness, with one writer arguing that *Hydriotaphia* is "utterly current in its portrayal of the spiritual corruption that can slowly infect the noblest of souls," despite the play's seventeenth-century setting, adding that "the theater world is never more effectively subversive than when making stinging observations about our world through the lens of another" (Stearns 4D). Most critics commented in some way on "Kushner's deep, playful love of language" (De La Viña 29), and even those finding faults with aspects of *Hydriotaphia* felt it was evidence of Kushner's ability to deliver on his impressive ambitions as a playwright.

Kushner himself felt that *Hydriotaphia* is "in some ways the most heterogeneous play I have written, really sprawling. Even for me" (Roca 32). Reflecting on the play in performance, Kushner stressed "it really is about what the subtitle says, about death and primitive capital achievement. But the longer I have been listening to it, the more I realize it is a play about writing" (Roca 32). Whether Kushner means to suggest that he, as a writer, is able to debate with Browne the writer, or that he admires Browne's ability to capture in prose the mysteries of life and death, is unclear, but for Kushner *Hydriotaphia* prefigured his move toward writing about those aspects of human experience not easily grasped and that may never be understood or articulated by the living, despite our innate awareness of things beyond our comprehension.

In fact, *Hydriotaphia* is, like all of Kushner's major works, overflowing with themes and is illustrative of the author's daring as a writer. Kushner's excess and fearlessness may be viewed as virtues or flaws by audiences and critics, but either way *Hydriotaphia*, in its earliest form and as revised, moved Kushner closer to a fuller explication of themes and growth as a dramatist that would permit him to revitalize late-twentieth-century American theater with *Angels in America*.

WORKS CITED

Arenschieldt, Rich. "Theatrical 'David and Goliath,'" *Houston Voice*, April 17, 1998, pp. 19–20.
Browne, Sir Thomas. *The Major Works.* Edited with an introduction and notes by C.A. Patrides. London and New York: Penguin Books, 1977.
———. *The Works of Sir Thomas Browne.* Edited by Geoffrey Keynes. Second Edition. Four Volumes. London: Faber & Faber, 1964.
De La Viña, Mark. "Kushner's Farce is a Mortal Cinch," *San Jose Mercury News*, September 18, 1998, pp. 29–30.
Evans, Everett. "Kushner Hits Highs, Lows in Epic Farce," *Houston Chronicle*, April 10, 1998, p. D1.
———. "Kushner Still Tweaking *Hydriotaphia* Script," *Houston Chronicle*, March 30, 1998, p. C1.
———. "Last Laughs," *The Houston Chronicle*, March 29, 1998, pp. 10, 20.

Halverson, Megan. "Farce Creatures," *Houston Sidewalk*, April 17, 1998, n.p.

Kushner, Tony. *Death and Taxes. Hydriotaphia and Other Plays*. New York: Theatre Communications Group, Inc., 2000.

———. "Three Brief Notes from the Playwright," *Performing Arts*, September 1998, pp. 5–6.

Mader, Travis. "Tony Kushner and Dr. Browne," *Alley Theatre Newsletter*, spring 1998, p. 1.

Post, Jonathan F.S. *Sir Thomas Browne*. Boston: Twayne, 1987.

Roca, Octavio. "Kushner's Next Stage," *San Francisco Chronicle*, September 6, 1998, p. 32.

Rosenstein, Brad. "Unblocked," *San Francisco Bay Guardian*, September 23–29, 1998, n.p.

"Sir Thomas Browne" *Alley Theatre Newsletter*, spring 1998, p. 4.

Stearns, David Patrick. "Kushner's Latest Less Substance Than Style," *USA Today*, September 29, 1998, p. 4D.

Winn, Steven. "Kushner Overreaches In Ambitious But Static *Hydriotaphia*," *San Francisco Chronicle*, September 18, 1998, p. C1.

JAMES RESTON, JR.

A Prophet in His Time: Premonition and Reality in Tony Kushner's Homebody/Kabul

Early in the second act of *Homebody/Kabul*, Tony Kushner's brilliant play about Afghanistan, I gave up on my quest for a purely artistic evening. Foolishly, I had tried to imagine what this theatrical experience might have been if Sept. 11 had never happened; if America had not gone to Afghanistan—in truth and in its mind—through the fall of 2001; if I personally had not been so transfixed and paralyzed and fascinated by the faraway events, so that nothing else from September to January had seemed so important as to read every story about "the war," every profile about the innocent, vaporized victims, every new attempt to explain the mind of Osama bin Laden and the wrath of Islamic radicals against the West.

But it was no use. The connection of this play to the Recent Past (to borrow one of its early lines), was too intense, too immediate. Neither Kushner nor his audience could escape reality. There was no way to move back into the mind-set of just another evening out at the theatre. Much more than mere art was in play here.

"The Present is always an awful place to be," the loquacious British woman of a certain age known as the Homebody says at the play's beginning. And so it was: In early January, as *Homebody/Kabul* had just opened, Osama bin Laden and Mullah Omar were still at large. The flag-draped caskets of the first American casualties of war were coming home. The warlords and

From *American Theatre* 19, no. 3 (March 2002). © 2002 Theatre Communications Group.

the thieves had taken over again, and the poppy fields were back in business, foreshadowing a flood of cheap Afghan heroin on American streets next year. The calls for more American troops to engage in more dangerous operations, over a longer period of time, were growing more persistent, and the White House was talking about building permanent bases in central Asia.

No exit from this dreadful place is in sight.

The barren landscape of that tortured land had begun to look more and more like the quagmire that I had expected it would become from the beginning. Afghanistan was, had been, is and would always be in the future, "a populated disaster." But we were there, and it was here, everywhere. We could not avoid it.

"We shudder to recall the times through which we have lived," the wonderful, frumpy Homebody says as she sits next to her frilly lampshade, "the Recent Past, about which no one wants to think." We did not want to think about it, but we could think of nothing else. The blow had sucked all the wind out of us, and we were still gasping for breath months later. It had been hard to reach out for entertainment. Escapist distractions had seemed too trivial, and until this play, there had been few connections, few insights to this benighted, corrupt place halfway round the world with which suddenly our immediate destiny seemed intertwined.

To write so many prescient lines completely out of one's imagination, and then for colossal, unforeseen world events to impart such resonance to them ... what an accomplishment! My admiration for the playwright soars. I am envious.

The day before my night at the theatre, I had contributed further to undermining my artistic evening. I thought it would be good preparation to see Mohsen Makhmalbaf's film *Kandahar*. There on the big screen was the real Afghanistan of sand dunes and jagged, desolate mountains, of chaos and thievery, of birdlike women behind their blue pleated bird-cage costumes, of primitive mullahs and hate-filled madrassases, of transportation by horse cart and bare feet, of bewildering, unfathomable, warring tribes—Tajiks, Uzbeks, Hazaras, Pashtunes—of ever-shifting loyalties, of mines and Mujahadeen, of bombed-out towns whose mud brick ruins are only suggested by the set of *Homebody/Kabul*.

So I bring the baggage of reality to the theatre on West 4th Street; but who in this theatre can leave that baggage at home? Toward the end of the play when the corrupted diplomat Quango says, "Have you noticed, nearly every other man you meet here is missing pieces?", the vision of the stumps of mine-shattered legs and arms that I had seen in *Khandahar* flashed into my mind.

And it is this populated disaster, this mutilated hand of a country that America has committed itself to embrace and to civilize and (could it really be?) to democratize. The Homebody uses the wonderful phrase "Universal Drift." But this is more about the American Drift. And our open-ended commitment as a nation to this terrible place is made by a president who had been elected on the platform that we could not go everywhere in the world as its policeman.

"I hold on tight to his ruined right hand," the Homebody says in her fantasy, "and he leads me on a guided tour through his city." And then a few lines later, once you understand the metaphor of the grossly dismembered hand, she says, "Would you make love to a stranger with a mutilated hand if the opportunity was offered to you?" And then, as if it were Bush or Rumsfeld answering: "Might do."

Kushner and I share an unusual bond. As he had written his play about an obscure place of medieval attitudes and barbaric practices that suddenly and unexpectedly became germane to a new American "war on terrorism," so I had written a book about an obscure 800-year-old story of a medieval crusade that had reportedly become required reading in the Bush White House. For, in his diatribes from the caves of Tora Bora, Osama bin Laden had railed against the "Jewish-Christian crusade" against Islam and all Arab peoples. In his construction, this was a struggle of believers versus infidels, East versus West, Christianity versus Islam, Godless secularism versus spiritualism, the United States versus al Qaeda. In his megalomania and narcissism, bin Laden had succeeded in personalizing the struggle. And President Bush had helped the villain mightily on Sept. 16 by declaring that America's struggle was a "crusade" against terrorism. Bush would use the word only once, but once was enough. It was a gift to bin Laden. Now it was bin Laden versus Bush.

And so people have been saying to me that, after reading about the 12th-century conflict in the Third Crusade between Richard the Lionheart and Saladin in *Warriors of God*, they understand the situation in the Middle East much better.

As I left the theatre after *Homebody/Kabul*, I overheard people saying the same thing. But what did they understand better? What insights did they glean after 3 hours and 45 minutes in the theatre? What could a stage play convey that we didn't already know from the newspapers and the television?

It begins with the power of romance. In her dusty and musty London flat, the Homebody sits alone in the absence of her waspish, uptight, priggish scientist-husband Milton and her screwed-up daughter Priscilla (in whose adolescent horrors the mother acknowledges responsibility and guilt).

"But guilt? Personal guilt?" she muses. "No more useful or impressive than adult nappy rash, and nearly as unsightly, and ought to be kept as private, ought guilt, as any other useless unimpressive unsightly inflammation. Not suitable for public exchange."

To divert herself from these unpleasant thoughts, the Homebody turns to her outdated guidebook. She reads with fascination and zest about great, virile men in long-forgotten wars, about the hill tribes of the Kabul Valley in the times before Christ, about the Great Bactrian Confusion, whatever that was. (The mere words, falling off her limber tongue, excite her.)

Her boring life revolves around her safe kitchen and her comfy living-room table with its frilly shaded lamp. And then by chance, as she searches for funny hats to enliven a party she will give (and dreads) for her husband's dull friends—where the revelers are to celebrate some incomprehensible minor technical achievement—she has a chance encounter with an Afghan merchant who sells her 10 exotic hats. As he prepares her bill, she notices that three fingers of his hand have been evenly sliced off.

Back home, she spins an elaborate fantasy of how, beyond morbid fascination, she might have reacted. Magically, she acquires the facility to speak fluent Pashtu and musters up unthinkable courage to ask what happened to his fingers. His imaginary answer gives us one of the great moments of the Homebody's monologue. But the lines have resonance largely because of what we witnessed in our newspapers and on television last fall, as one warlord after another switched loyalties and told outrageous lies, and we gained the distinct impression that in this land where fundamental Islam was practiced, and where the Department for the Promotion of Virtue and Prevention of Vice held sway, no one believed in anything, much less the truth.

The Homebody's confrontation with the terrible emptiness of her life leads to her disappearance. The playwright has her act on her romance, even if it means going to an unimaginably awful place, where she can take on the burqua, submit to a husband as his second or third wife, devote herself, unthinking like a teenager in a madrassa, to committing the entire Koran to memory. She acts on her romance, and she sticks to it. She has rejected the values of her home, of her life, of her society, of the West. In her act is the whiff of metaphysical treason.

The extraordinary act of the Homebody prefigures a similar act this past fall by a real-life romantic, who no doubt is every bit as screwed up as Priscilla. That is the American Taliban, John Walker. He also rejected the pleasures of his California culture of hot tubs and mood music, converted to Islam, joined the Taliban, fought at Masar-i-Sharif, was captured ... and, perhaps most surprisingly, was uncontrite and unrepentant. He too sticks to his romance, however misguided and incomprehensible it may be to most of us. And the price of Walker's phantasmagoria has been a potential charge of treason.

The family agony of Milton and Priscilla in searching for the missing Homebody makes good theatre, especially Milton's descent into drugs under the tutelage of the dissipated diplomat-junkie, Quango. Quango reminded me of characters in the colonial novels of Graham Greene and Evelyn Waugh, and he is meant to represent the corruption of the colonial. Afghanistan, he claims, has broken his heart, as well as blown his mind to bits. "It's like a disease, this place," he tells Milton. If Milton does not really care whether he finds his estranged wife, Priscilla's search for her mother is real and powerful.

Indeed, family agony drives the entire second act, and it has about it the air of Greek tragedy. No doubt, a few years ago, when Kushner conceived of this play, he put his emphasis on the characterization of the family, never dreaming that the ambience around them could drive the play just as powerfully. In 1999, who really cared about the Taliban or the Pashtun?

The most original and telling characters of *Homebody/Kabul*, at least as the play is seen in the wake of Sept. 11, are two Afghan characters, the Taliban Mullah and the woman Mahala. Both the Mullah and Mahala would seem to be secondary roles, but they speak most pointedly to the situation America now faces in central Asia.

It is the monsters, of course, who always fascinate us. Who are these barbarians anyway who force women into cloth cages and deny them work, who chop off hands and arms for petty crime, who bake their victims in locked metal containers in the desert, who blow up 2,000-year-old statues, who have a special stadium for public executions? ... and who for all that, purport to be holy men?

The Mullah Al Aftar Durranni makes his brief appearances on stage count. As Act 2 opens, we see him as the impresario of what seems to be an outrageous lie: that the Homebody is not only dead, but she literally has been torn limb from limb by the "rough boys" of Kabul, who have caught her improperly dressed without a burqua and in possession of debauched Western music. Frank Sinatra corrupts. Frank Sinatra is to be feared and suppressed. With wonderful menace, the Mullah says, "Impious music, which is an affront to Islam, to dress like so and then the music, these are regrettable."

Presenting the unfeeling face of the religious fanatic, his manner is cold, official, patronizing. "Kabul is not a city for Western tourist women," he says. Indeed, it is no place for a Western woman of any sort, as we saw countless times on our televisions this past fall, as intrepid women reporters braved the humiliations, the hardships and the real dangers to get the inside story. "We do not want them. No thing may be made or unmade unless Allah wills it. He fills our hearts with griefs, to see if we shall be strong. You are kaafer, you do not understand, but this is Allah's way." With such a credo, we see how atrocity is possible, everywhere, by anyone, for any reason. It is sanctioned, and even sanctified by God, just to see if the holy warrior is strong. As counterpoint to the Homebody's early reveling in history, the Mullah says blandly: "In Kabul now there is no history. There is only God."

Toward the end of the second act, the Mullah reappears in a dramatic and violent scene, and in it he delivers the rationale for the Taliban regime. When I read it in the script, the speech seemed simplistic and ignorant. But when played on the stage, his apologia has power and poignancy ... and even a kind of truth to it.

"Afghanistan is Taliban and we shall save it," the Mullah says in his stylized patois. "No one else shall, no one else care. England betray us. United States betray us, bomb us, starve us to ... distract [the world from the] adulterous debauch Clinton and his young whore. This is good for woman? U.S. and Russia destroy us as destroy Vietnam, Palestine, Chechnya, Bosnia.... As U.N. deny Taliban to be recognize. All plot against Islam. Iran plot against Islam. For four thousand years, no one shall save Afghan people. No one else but Allah may save it. We are servants of Allah."

In other words, the excuse for collective religious terror boils down to cruel order. The alternative, going back no doubt to the Great Bactrian Confusion, is chaos and exploitation.

My differing responses to the script and the performance suggest one way that the theatre trumps television and newsprint in making us understand. All fall, the newspapers and news-magazines had been confounded by Arab wrath. Why do they hate us so? The question echoed from the building tops.

What the theatre can display, better than any other medium, is passion. This includes the passion of the Arab religious fanatic and the passion of his most immediate victims. That passion is something the West desperately needs to understand ... in its own best interest. For this struggle has not been about ideas or religious tenets. In Arab psychology, everything is mixed together in an emotional stew: the oppression of history, the hatred of Israel and all European invaders going back to the 11th century, the ire against Israel's supporters, the envy of American wealth, self-loathing at the inability to master science and technology, the contempt for weak leadership of the

Arab world itself, horror at the disparity between the princes and the paupers, and the sheer grinding poverty and backwardness of the entire region. All that is left is passion and religion ... and in its worst despairing form, martyrdom.

It is from the mouth of the character Mahala in *Homebody/Kabul* that the counter-argument to the Taliban is forcefully delivered. She is a fascinating theatrical invention: the intelligent, bitter librarian, forced away from work, watching her library closed, losing her mind from disuse and her wits from the oppression both of her society and her household, the spurned wife of the doctor who has driven her from her house and (she is convinced) replaced her summarily with this docile, sentimental Westerner, the Homebody. Mahala is the most sympathetic of victims.

At Milton and Priscilla, the English travelers, she flies into a rage about the Taliban. They are occupiers, drug dealers, child murderers, torturers, Pashtun from the camps of Khandahar and Jalalabad who oppress all non-Pashtun. And then she turns her wrath on her Afghan translator. "And you call yourselves men. You suffer? We suffer more. You permit this? These criminals and savages to enslave and oppress your women? ... I say women are braver than you men of Kabul."

Her rant is riveting, and as she turns her wrath on them all, Kushner can even squeeze a laugh from the scene.

"Usually she is cheerier," her Afghan companion whispers.

And when another witness suggests that she may be going mad, Priscilla interjects, "She isn't mad, she's fucking furious. It isn't at all the same."

For this audience in the East Village of New York, the city that is the ultimate Western victim of Aghanistan-bred terror, the tension is highest when Mahala turns on America for its role in the horror of Afghanistan. In the wake of Sept. 11, these thoughts are seldom expressed—especially since, as victims, we Americans like to think we occupy the high moral ground. Unlike the Homebody, Mahala has no qualms about assigning guilt. In the face of Taliban atrocity, where is America? she asks. And then the charges fly. Afghanistan was used as an instrument to topple the Soviet Union and end the Cold War, and then the instrument was discarded. The CIA funded the Taliban secretly through Pakistan, exploiting her land as a buffer for Iran, against whom the U.S. was still trying to settle a 20-year-old score. Always the frontline surrogate. Always someone else's tool. In the editorial pages and news magazines, these are familiar charges. And yet from the mouth of the female victim, they carry greater weight.

Of the Taliban, Mahala says, "They'll turn on their masters sooner or later."

And so they did, and for their complicity in the horrendous crime of Sept. 11, they have been destroyed as a result. But the conditions that led to their rise remain. The gangster bin Laden is mentioned only once in *Homebody/Kabul*; George Bush, the World Trade Center, the Pentagon, al Qaeda, Tora Bora, not at all. We see no American flags fluttering on this stage, hear no macho one-liners from a Wild West American president. This is a play for those who are interested in the root causes that preceded Sept. 11, for those who can see through the fog of patriotism to the finer distinctions, who are finally ready to ask how on earth do we get out of this godforsaken place, who can bear to contemplate the thought that we have participated to some extent in our own tragedy.

The most shocking line of the play is left to Mahala.

"You love the Taliban so much.... Well, don't worry, they're coming to New York! Americans!"

FRAMJI MINWALLA

Tony Kushner's Homebody/Kabul: *Staging History in a Post-Colonial World*

Nations, like narratives, lose their origins in the myths of time and only fully realize their horizons in the mind's eye. Such an image of the nation—or narration—might seem impossibly romantic and excessively metaphorical, but it is from those traditions of political thought and literary language that the nation emerges as a powerful historical idea in the west.

—Homi Bhabha, Nation and Narration

To be a migrant is, perhaps, to be the only species of human being free of the shackles of nationalism (to say nothing of its ugly sister, patriotism).... The effect of mass migrations has been the creation of radically new types of human being: people who root themselves in ideas rather than places, in memories as much as in material things; people who have been obliged to define themselves—because they are so defined by others—by their otherness; people in whose deepest selves strange fusions occur, unprecedented unions between what they were and where they find themselves. The migrant suspects reality: having experienced several ways of being, he understands their illusory nature. To see things plainly, you have to cross a frontier.

—Salman Rushdie, "The Location of Brazil"

From *Theater* 33, no. 1 (2003). © 2003 by Yale School of Drama/Yale Repertory Theatre.

A few minutes into the astonishing hour-long monologue that begins Tony Kushner's new play, *Homebody/Kabul*,[1] the Homebody, a middle-aged, middle-class English housewife with a voracious appetite for uncommon words and dusty books, hesitates, looks directly at us, smiles ruefully, searches the antiquarian shelves of her mind for exactly the right way to make her apology, and then declares:

> I speak ... I can't help myself. Elliptically. Discursively. I've read too many books, and that's not boasting, for I haven't read *many* books, but I've read too many, exceeding I think my capacity for syncresis—is that a word?—straying rather into synchisis, which is a word. So my diction, my syntax, well, it's so *irritating*, I apologize, I do, it's very hard, I know. To listen. I blame it on the books, how else to explain it? My parents don't speak like this; no one I know does; no one does. It's an *alien influence*, and my borders have only ever been broached by books. Sad to say. Only ever been broached by books. Except once, briefly. Which is I suppose the tale I'm telling, or rather, trying to tell.[2]

Syncresis is not a word, but it resembles *syncrisis* (a rhetorical figure comparing diverse objects or subjects) and *syncretic* (the reconciliation of opposing beliefs or practices). It is a portmanteau that articulates a paradox. Synchisis, on the other hand, denotes, according to the *OED*, "a confused arrangement of words in a sentence, obscuring the meaning." What then might it mean for the mind to stray from *syncresis* to *synchisis*, from paradox to confusion? How does this affect the telling of stories? Is there an aesthetic and political consequence to making a character speak in a manner that rejects easy access to meaning, and to making a narrative that defies coherence, that maneuvers circuitously through multiple histories in order to arrive at its own irresolution?

The monologue relates two histories: one confessional, private, intimate (the life of the Homebody and her encounter with an Afghani storekeeper), the other violent, sociopolitical, public (a short history of Afghanistan). Both shift from the linear to the tangential to the barely comprehensible and back again as if to anatomize the exhausted overflowing of a contemporary mind tangled, for want of a better diagnosis, by the "posts"—the post-modern, the post-colonial, the post-structural (though perhaps not the post-national, post-feminist, or post-human). The Homebody suffers a pathological inability to get to the point, or more accurately, an inability to get to the point except by way of many, many other points. Her affliction derives as much from the dilemma she formulates partway through the monologue—the impossible demand to live ethically in a world where "the private is gone," where "all must be touched," yet "all touch corrupts" (11)—as it does from the paralysis she feels when confronting a world outside books, a world where the singular, the universal, the transhistorical are all deeply troubled categories, and where meaning and being have been deliberately unsettled.

How radically different in shape, tone, and style, then, are the two tales she gives us. The short history, mostly read from *An Historical Guide to Kabul* (published in 1965 and thus phenomenally outdated), proceeds chronologically and disinterestedly from origins to the present, in the grand tradition of such positivist narratives: "Our story begins at the very dawn of history, circa 3,000 B.C." (9). Firm facts follow each other, building an irrefutable architecture of dates, places, armies, births, deaths, and the perpetual transfer of peoples from one location to another, all happening in or passing through the valleys of the Hindu Kush mountains. Here follows a typical passage:

> In the middle of the second century BC, during the Greco-Bactrian Confusion, a Chinese tribe, the Hsuing-Nu, attacked a rival tribe, the Yueh-Chih, and drove them from their homes to what is now southern Afghanistan: Then the Hsuing-Nu, displaced from their new homes by another Chinese tribe, also migrated to Afghanistan and once again displaced the Yueh-Chih, who emigrated to the Kabul Valley. As the first century BC dawns, the valley, populated by Indo-Greeks, Mauryas, and Macedonians, is now surrounded by the restless nomadic kingdoms of the Yueh-Chih. By 48 BC the Chinese tribes are united under the banner of their largest clan, the Kushans.... From the city of Kapisa, the Kushan court came to rival the Caesars in Rome. Buddhism, Hinduism, Grecian and Persian deities are gathered into the valleys of the Hindu Kush where a remarkable cross-fertilization takes place. (16)

This series of dislocations, one tribe replacing another in an endless drama of conquest, is recorded in a mode that can only be called Orientalist. Using a distinctly nineteenth-century rhetoric to assert the accuracy of its accounting, the writer of the guidebook, Nancy Hatch Dupree, represents the East for the West, translating a strange terrain in familiar language to make it legible for the curious traveler embarking on a voyage to Kabul. Absent from this history, of course, are references to why these dislocations occurred; the social, cultural, and political contexts in which displacers and displaced endured; or any sense of the ordinary lives of the Macedonians, Yueh-Chih, or Kushans. The object of such narratives—to describe the world-historical movements of races and ethnic groups arriving at their manifest destinies—situates the calculus of colonization as an essential feature of the region. The Soviets, the Taliban, the United States—none of this is new; only the names have changed.

The end of the excerpt, however, dwells on a curiously unrepeated moment in this dismal history of conquest and occupation—"a remarkable cross-fertilization takes place." Remarkable because it never happens again? Remarkable because it figures a potential to make community out of difference? The guidebook doesn't say, and the Homebody, also remarkably, doesn't comment. This odd historical pause in which a community based in difference becomes achievable should be measured against the traditional narrative of colonization, a narrative in which mightier invaders, blind to the possibility of "cross-fertilization" because the plots they imagine refuse such "syncresis," erase the cultures of previous settlers, replacing them with their own *singular* ways of being and knowing. This region we now call Afghanistan serves as a palimpsest, endlessly revised by armies, religions, and empire builders who write their own history—and future—in Afghanistan's spilled entrails. The guidebook covers over these spilled entrails with its own definitive language. It is, after all, a guidebook, meant to lure the unwary tourist into the history—or is it mystery?—of the East.

The illusory comfort provided by the history's objective rhetoric— event leading inevitably to event in a steadfast march toward the moment from which the Homebody looks back—clashes against the second story, an anecdotal stream of private despair spun off from passages in the guidebook. The skeleton of this second story shapes the Homebody's trip to a London, shop to buy exotic hats for a party in honor of her overachieving husband. This outing serves as the impetus for a proliferating sequence of meditations on her marriage, her daughter, her chronic depression, her inability to speak plainly, and her fascination with the ancient, the foreign, the magical—with, as she says, "not the source but all that was dropped by the wayside on the way to the source" (9).

The Homebody inhabits the margins of imperial discourse, participating in the conventional structures of recognition and reversal only as an indiscreet observer. But unlike her ancestral sisters, Victorian women who traversed the colonial map keeping journals, making sketches, writing memoirs, conversing with native inhabitants their husbands rarely noticed, the Homebody speaks directly against what Sara Suleri Goodyear calls the feminine picturesque: "The picturesque becomes synonymous with a desire to transfix a dynamic cultural confrontation into a still life, converting a pictorial imperative into a gesture of self-protection that allows the colonial gaze a license to convert its ability not to see into studiously visual representations."[3]

The mode of the picturesque, like that of the memoir, is anecdotal, ahistorical, informal, confidential. In performance, such a confessional mode invites an audience into a secret compact with its narrator, making us sharers in the Homebody's post-colonial allegory of self-recognition as she conjugates her way to the heart of her own darkness. But the picturesque also attempts to contain what might otherwise spill into colonial terror. It strives to explain the enigma of the Other. The Homebody sketches using a language that tumbles over itself as it tries, and fails, to turn the world into a "still life."

The reason she so loves the guidebook is its ability to do exactly this. But her mind cannot, or will not, conform to such straightforward chronicling. Her mode of sketching consistently splashes paint beyond the borders she assembles. Her interest, she notes, is not the subject that sits before her but the landscape around it, all those drips and drops that escape the frame of her narrative. In this, she is not unlike her maker. Kushner describes this peculiar affliction as "an intoxication with language and its dangers, with the urge to specify, elaborate, and clarify, trying to pin down meaning. In the process, of course, words and meanings proliferate, thoughts become clearer and far more cloudy, both at once."[4] The elusiveness of language itself—and the effect of this elusiveness on the way it begets character, place, and time—becomes one of the central subjects the play explores.

Early in the Homebody's sketching we learn that she's tried before to get inside the mind of the Other. She swallows her husband's antidepressants so she can "know what he's feeling" (13). That this psychotropic experiment misfires is hardly surprising. Her husband, a computer programmer, negotiates in numbers—as he says later in the play, in "ones and zeroes, digitally reducing the unmediated slovenly complexities which exist ... in space by making of complicated nuanced things their simple non-nuanced identicals" (124). The Homebody, however, is "incapable ... of ... telling this simple tale without supersaturating [her] narrative with maddeningly infuriating or more probably irritating synchitic exegesis" (14). Where her husband's approach to living emerges as the colonial impulse to reference and classify, the Homebody resists domestication through a breathtaking linguistic promiscuity. The moral of this anecdote of the substituted pills—the radical failure of the picturesque in its effort to know—suggests the double-edged sword of a certain kind of post-colonial resistance that simultaneously disables the authority of fixed categories and the psyche of the articulating subject.[5]

The plot of her wandering narrative—buying exotic hats to give her party some "fizz," to "catalyze" a "transformation" among her guests so that they will, when wearing these hats, seem "surprising to themselves"—attempts to recuperate a real, as opposed to reported, engagement with the East, yet ultimately refuses to imitate the action she instigates. The hats as emblems of the picturesque fail to remain just hats. They become objects with their own diasporic history, attaining a generic refugee status embedded in the politics of global capitalism:

> Looking at the hat we imagine not bygone days of magic belief but the suffering behind the craft.... But whether the product of starveling-manned sweatshop or remote not-on-the-grid village, poor yet still resisting the onslaught of modernity ...; whether removed from the maker by the middleman to the merchant by filch or swindle or gunpoint or even murder; whether, for that matter, even Afghan in origin; and not Pakistani; or Peruvian; if not in point of fact made in London by children, aunts, and elderly uncles in the third floor flat above the shop ...: the hats are beautiful.... and sad. As dislocations are. And marvelous, as dislocations are. Always bloody. (17–18)

The proliferating history spills off the edges of her aesthetic palette, submerging the picturesque in an ocean of blood. To aestheticize, for the Homebody at least, means to turn a vital object into a commodity, to make the Other safe. But the logic of such encounters rarely delivers safe conclusions, which perhaps is the larger point the monologue performs. The allegory of the hats slips from the aesthetic into the real, where the "suffering behind the craft" alludes to the dark quilting of imperial control barely hidden by the dazzling surface that embroiders colonialism as a civilizing project.

The Homebody has, at this point in her tale, carefully removed one hat at a time from a shopping bag and placed each on the table next to her.[6] In both productions I saw, this activity elicited scattered "oohs" from the audience, revealing how embedded and automatic Orientalist responses are when predominantly Western audiences confront such exotica. The disjunctive spectacle of these vagrant hats neatly arrayed on a very English side table echoes again the way these two worlds scrape against each other. The sight is striking, almost beautiful. The hats, for a moment, transform the gray limbo of the English parlor. Stacked in a pyramid, ten hats "made of tough brilliant dyed wools and scraps of geometrically arabesqued carpet into which sequins and diamantines and carbuncles and glassene beading [have] been sewn," shimmer in the half-light (14–16). They are "marvelous" and "sad" precisely because of their dislocation. But as objective correlatives, emblems of the picturesque, they immediately focus our attention on how their "magic" has "shriveled into the safe container of the aesthetic" (17). The hats register as ornament, adornment. When the Homebody puts one on it looks almost silly perched there, an entirely botched attempt at reverse transculturation. But it remains on her head through the rest of her monologue, and its inflections complicate and multiply.

Kushner drives both these narratives—the history and the testimonial—toward a climax that dismantles the many fictions post-colonial subjects erect to brace the disintegrating certainties of imperial logic. The linear history—providing both context and opposition for the Homebody's fateful (and perhaps fatal) encounter with the Afghan merchant—culminates in a confrontation with its own limitations, unraveling even as it tries to harness Afghanistan's pedigree to the actualities of imperial rule. The shop on a deliberately unnamed London street is a repository of an exilic memory materialized in its exhaustive catalogue of accumulated objects. It allegorically reproduces the post-colonial world on a map we can all understand, yet at the same time undermines the succinct logic of dates, places, and names provided by the guidebook:

> The hats were in a barrel which could be seen through the window; puppets hung from the ceiling, carved freestanding figurines, demiurges, attributes, symbols, carved abstractions representing metaphysical principles critical to the governance of perfect cosmologies now lost to all or almost all human memory; amber beads big as your baby's fists, armor plates like pangolin scales strung on thick ropey catgut cordage meant to be worn by rather large rather ferocious men ...; hideous masks with great tusks and lolling tongues and more eyes than are usual ... and revolving wire racks filled with postcards depicting the severed heads of The Queen and Tony Blair ...; Glaswegian *A to Zed Guides* and newspapers in Arabic, in Urdu, in Pushtu, videotapes

of rock balladeers from Benares.... As if a many-camelled caravan, having roamed across the entire post-colonial not-yet-developed world, crossing the borders of the rainforested kingdoms of Kwashiorkor and Rickets and Untreated Gum Disease and High Infant Mortality Rates, gathering with desperate indiscriminateness—is that the word?—on the mudpitted unpaved trade route its bits and boodle, had finally beached its great heavy no longer portable self in a narrow coal-scuttle of a shop on _____ (*gesture*), *here*, here, caravanseraied here, in the developed, and overdeveloped, and over-overdeveloped paved wasted now deliquescent post–First World post-modern city of London; all the camels having flopped and toppled and fallen here and died of exhaustion, of shock, of the heartache of refugees, the goods simply piled high upon their dromedary bones, just where they came to rest, and set up shop atop the carcasses, and so on. (19–20)

This extraordinary inventory of Third World/First World flotsam, this deeply unsettling articulation of the hopelessness embodied in those camels who collapse willy-nilly not just because they've arrived at the acquisitive end of the trade route but also from their sheer inability to move one hoof further, this collection of exotic and mundane objects jostling for attention, this strange and estranging trail through debilitating diseases, bestow on this local habitation a deliberately hybrid identity, exposing the illusion of colonial separation between sovereign and subject. The post-colonial refugee, the Afghan, reverses the direction of conquest, returns to the source of his original humiliation, and establishes himself within the context of a global marketplace where capitalism assimilates the Other through a process of aestheticization and commodification. The realism of the Homebody's description devolves into an allegory of post-colonial despair through which the Other acquiesces to the demands of the metropolis in a way he never did when resisting from the margins.

The Homebody selects her hats, walks over to the cash register, and comes face-to-face for the first time in her narrative with a breathing, ethnic body. She hands her credit card—symbol of corporate power already marked as the object converting "that which was once Afghan ... into junk" (17)—to this smiling man and stumbles over his mutilated hand. Here beside the post-modern miscellany in this queer shop is a hand with three fingers chopped off "following the line of a perfect clean diagonal from middle—to ring—to little finger" (11). She holds up her own hand to describe it to us, and there, figured in the bending of three fingers, her thumb jutting out, are the contours of modern Afghanistan. The disbelief she registers, sending her eyes "to the roof of [her] skull and then off into the ether like a rapid vapor," comes as much from the hand itself as from its particular geographical location—"Here, in London, that poor ruined hand. Imagine" (21). There is little in the guidebook that prepares her for this violence. The deaths and displacements recounted there happened long ago; the guidebook was written before the Soviet invasion, the Taliban, Osama bin Laden, and U.S. missile strikes. Certainly such violence wasn't happening now, in 1998, in London, metropolitan center of her dull, civilized world. Her first sense-making impulse is to read the hand as a contemporary inscription of a mythic sign: "I have learnt since through research that Kabul ... was founded ... by none other than Cain himself. Biblical Cain. Who is said to be buried in Kabul" (21). This conflation, misreading the disfigurement as a mythic assignment of moral transgression, becomes the first in a series of attempts to discover who this man is and what happened to him.

The Homebody shifts her gaze so she doesn't have to see the hand and yet keeps returning her "mind's eye" to the image of her MasterCard pinched between its thumb and remaining finger. The ambivalence of her response ruptures the way she has previously constructed her image of the East. The guidebook, it seems, has utterly misled her. The trauma of this narrative displacement frees her imagination, and she discovers, while signing her credit card slip, that she can speak perfect Pushtu. She asks the merchant, in his own language, to relate the history of his hand. He responds, or rather, she responds in his voice:

> I was with the Mujahideen, and the Russians did this. I was with the Mujahideen, and an enemy faction of Mujahideen did this. I was with the Russians, I was known to have assisted the Russians, I did informer's work for Babrak Karmal, my name is in the files if they haven't been destroyed, the names I gave are in the files, there are no more files, I stole bread for my starving family, I stole bread *from* a starving family, I profaned, betrayed, according to some stricture I erred and they chopped off the fingers of my hand. (23)

The play constructs the merchant as an embodiment of Afghanistan, and the sliced hand transmutes into a symbolic marker representing all those imperial incursions and slicings of territory that the guidebook catalogues but never fleshes out. More crucially, however, this heaping of motive upon motive fractures the singular structure of cause and effect previously given to us. The complicitous incarnation of the beleaguered nation in the butchered hand delivers a history of collaboration, guilt, betrayal, recrimination, resistance, heresy, theft, shame, and need.

The ventriloquizing continues:

> *Look, look at my country, look at my Kabul, my city, what is left of my city? The streets are as bare as the mountains now, the buildings are as ragged as mountains and as bare and empty of life, there is no life here only fear, we do not live in the buildings now, we live in terror in the cellars in the caves in the mountains, only God can save us now, only order can save us now, only God's law harsh and strictly administered can save us now, only The Department for the Promotion of Virtue and the Prevention of Vice can save us now, only terror can save us from ruin, only never-ending war, save us from terror and never-ending war, save my wife they are stoning my wife, they are chasing her with sticks, save my wife save my daughter from punishment by God, save us from God, from war, from exile, from oil exploration, from no oil exploration, from the West, from the children with rifles, carrying stones, only children with rifles, carrying stones, can save us now.* You will never understand. It is hard, it was hard work to get into the UK. I am happy here in the UK I am terrified I will be made to leave the UK I cannot wait to leave the UK I despise the UK I voted for John Major. I voted for Tony Blair. I did not, I cannot vote, I do not believe in voting, the people who ruined my hand were right to do so, they were wrong to do so, my hand is most certainly ruined, *you will never understand*, why are you buying so many hats? (23–24)

The shape of this speech, shifting from the hand to Afghanistan to England, mirrors the journey the post-colonial subject takes and even suggests the reasons for this journey: the imperial destruction of home and family, its aftermath figured in the Afghan civil war, and the contradictions that make living there impossible—contradictions that reemerge in the newly adopted country. The reason such immigration occurs has everything to do with coercive economic and political policies, from within and without, that recolonize the already devastated infrastructures of poor nations.

The motives and psychology the Homebody confers on the Afghan merchant, however, echo her own. As the preceding section of the monologue shows, this is how *her* mind works—"elliptically," "discursively," "straying" from "syncresis" to "synchisis." Her empathy for the wounded hand, the hand without a home, becomes a projection of her own homeless, wounded psyche. She transfers her own dislocation onto his, positions herself as a fellow traveler in this post-colonial terrain. This is her moment of recognition, her anagnorisis, where the movement from ignorance to knowledge—about Afghanistan, about the physical effects of war, about herself—begins the tectonic shift in her thinking that leads directly to her own improbable journey.

Yet this projection of her fears, needs, and desires, spoken through his context, navigates the most literal boundaries of Orientalism. Inventing the Eastern subject in the image of the West has become an embodied habit. The Homebody wouldn't know how to see him in any other way. To interpret this merchant as the lacerated personification of his city, his borders redrawn by swords and scimitars, his living administered by the blessed marriage of creed and state—none of this is particularly inaccurate. But the fact of him standing in front of her, smiling, performing his labors—this she cannot yet acknowledge. Her description of his face, "broken by webs of lines inscribed by hardships, siroccos and strife, battle scars .... [a] life *unimaginably* more difficult than my own" (23; emphasis mine), simultaneously engraves yet more meanings onto his skin and constructs him as unimaginable.

After the World Trade Center bombing in 1993, *Sixty Minutes* ended a special report on terror with a shot of a vaguely brown man, his back to the camera, walking out of a terminal at JFK airport. The caption inscribed over his receding body read: "Who are you? Are you good? Are you bad?"[7] This inability to fix identity—the U.S. media, as recent coverage has shown, can't answer these questions because all brown people look the same—leads directly to that moral indecipherability underlying colonial anxiety. The official history written on the brown body—the history of the guidebook—stuffs the post-colonial subject with moral significance in order to contain the ambivalent terror it evokes. The Homebody's characteristic solution is to saturate this unnervingly *present* body with as many meanings as she can formulate, transforming the merchant into an Afghan Everyman, the archetypal post-colonial refugee.

Kushner deliberately breaks this ventriloquizing with a brief pause, then shifts the Homebody's narrative to a short aside on thinking, doing, and guilt.

> We mostly remain suspended in the Rhetorical Colloidal Forever
> that agglutinates between Might and Do.... What has this century
> taught the civilized if not contempt for those who merely

contemplate; the lockup and the lethal injection for those who Do. Awful times, as I have said, our individual degrees of culpability for said awfulness being entirely bound-up in our corresponding degrees of action, malevolent or not, or in our corresponding degrees of inertia, which can be taken as a form of malevolent action.... We shall most of us be adjudged guilty when we are summoned before the Judgment Seat. But guilt? Personal guilt? (*Wringing hands*) Oh, oh ... no more morally useful or impressive than adult nappy rash, and nearly as unsightly, and ought to be kept private, ought guilt, as any other useless unimpressive unsightly inflammation. (24)

The implicit suggestion here is that the Homebody blames and then admonishes herself for feeling guilty about the disfigured hand. Her borders now broached by more than just books, she finds her contemplative life profoundly embarrassing and deeply complicit in the violence she sees in front of her. She argues against the easy remedy—publicly displaying guilt "for the garnering of sympathy and the harvesting of admiration" (25). The Homebody's sarcastic imitation of Lady Macbeth scrubbing away the blood spot is as much an indictment of herself as it is a jeer at people who suffer over the pain of others but do nothing to alleviate that pain. The antithesis of this self-aggrandizing behavior—actually taking action—sticks against her earlier insight: "All must be touched. All touch corrupts" (11). The impossible choice this dialectic, presents cuts, perhaps, to Kushner's central concern. Neither *just* thinking nor *just* doing provides an adequate solution to the problems of the world. It is this opposition that the rest of the monologue attempts to work out.

To this end, Kushner reverses the expected narrative trajectory of colonial terror. Unlike Adela Quested in Forster's *A Passage to India*, whose trip to the Malabar Caves in search of the "real" India ends in the fantastic accusation that Dr. Aziz has raped her, the Homebody attempts to heal lacerations in the post-colonial psyche through sexual intimacy. Accompanying the merchant, she now sets out on an imaginary journey through ravaged Kabul, pushing her monologue past colonial romance to the seductions of magical realism. As they walk, hand in half-hand, he points out historic monuments and sites described in the guidebook—places not mentioned in that narrative find no realization here—culminating in a moment of lovemaking under a chinar tree: "We kiss, his breath is very bitter, he places his hand inside me, it seems to me his whole hand inside me, and it seems to me a whole hand" (26).

This remarkable image of "cross-fertilization," not to mention the shocking intimacy of such penetration, forces a visceral confrontation with colonial taboos. The imperial fantasy that the colored man will exact retribution on the white female body is fashioned here as a restorative act. The image of the battered hand inside her regenerative vagina, set against the idyllic, almost pastoral, topography—under a chinar tree, flocks of pigeons flying overhead—further reverses the stale trope that feminizes the East and then figures imperial conquest as rape. Equally crucial, this sequence defies the apocalyptic closures of most magical realist tales.

Yet Kushner immediately brings this attempt to heal back to the fact of the hand. It is still there, still hacked, passing the carrier bag full of hats across the counter. The failure of this post-colonial mode, magical realism, to enforce what it imagines, to make the healing real, scuttles any narrative bridging between East and West, Other and Self, replaying in a different key the end of Forster's *Passage*. "Half-kissing," Cyril Fielding, a British civil servant, asks Aziz, the novel's native protagonist, whether they can remain friends. Forster's omniscient narrator frames a reply: "The horses didn't want it—they swerved apart; the earth didn't want it, sending up rocks through which riders must pass single file; the temples, the tanks, the jail, the palace, the birds, the carrion, the Guest House that came into view ...: they didn't want it, they said in their hundred voices, 'No, not yet,' and the sky said, 'No, not there.'"[8]

In Forster's conclusion, the very geography imposes itself between the possibility of friendship, just as the transaction itself, buying the hats, does in Kushner's play. The Homebody hurries home, "a chill wind blow[ing] up [her] bones" (26), but the encounter has left its mark. She has literally internalized the Other. She now picks up the guidebook with a new awareness of its implicit derangement: "Its sorrowing supercessional displacement by all that has since occurred. So lost; and also so familiar" (27). She sees her own complicity in its pages, her own safety at home measured against the cost of that hand. The meeting results in her own un-homing. Kushner deliberately refuses to sustain an imperial distinction between Self and Other. And thus the Homebody's interpellation as a post-colonial subject, a refugee, a migrant, is complete. Kushner shifts the Homebody's narrative into the third person as she observes and judges her self from the space of the Other:

> Where stands the Homebody, safe in her kitchen, on her culpable shore, suffering uselessly watching others perishing in the sea, wringing her plump little maternal hands, oh, oh. Never *joining*

the drowning. Her feet, neither rooted nor moving. The ocean is deep and cold and erasing. But how dreadful, really unpardonable, to remain dry.... She does not drown, she ... succumbs. To Luxury.

The touch which does not understand is the touch which corrupts, the touch which does not understand that which it touches is the touch which corrupts that which it touches, and which corrupts itself.

And so yes, when unexpectedly a curtain I'd not noticed before is parted by a ruined hand, which then beckons, I find myself improbably considering.... (27–28)

The act of telling the two stories has changed her utterly. She has assimilated both narrative modes and can now use the objective rhetoric of the history to take apart her own psyche, just as she earlier bestowed on the Afghan merchant distinctive, subjective idiosyncrasies. We hear her revising her thinking even as she speaks. Where before the narrative heaped item upon item, anecdote upon anecdote, synonym upon synonym in an endless litany of inclusion—as if to leave some part out would send her into paroxysms of guilt—now she edits her mind toward precision. "The touch which does not understand that which it touches" finds its parallel in "the sentence which does not understand that which it defines," and the circle is now complete. The Homebody began the monologue safe in her living room, reading from the guidebook. She ends on the threshold of Afghanistan, hailed by the hand that parts the curtain, ready to plunge into a cold, deep sea. The fantastic expedition she conjures in the shop may or may not have been realized in her actual journey to Afghanistan. Kushner deliberately refuses to resolve this question, for it is exactly this ambiguity of motive that the Homebody articulates in the monologue—to understand so she can touch without corrupting, to heal the breach in her own psyche, to make amends for Britain's imperial past.

The monologue concludes with a final jarring juxtaposition—Frank Sinatra crooning "It's Nice to Go Trav'ling" set against a seventeenth-century Persian poem on Kabul. The Sinatra song, the Homebody tells us, played in the background at the party she gave for her husband while she related the story about the shopkeeper to a few guests. The hats, apparently, were a stupendous success. They were too small, she tells us, and so slipped off people's heads, generating great "amusement." The kitschiness of the Sinatra song reflects perfectly the ludicrous image of these English exchanging hats as they dance:

It's very nice to just wander
The camel route to Iraq,
It's oh so nice to just wander
But it's so much nicer, yes it's oh so nice
To wander back.

The hats, like the camel route to Iraq, become cute novelties that provide touristic *frisson* but no complicated engagement.

The poem is composed by an entirely different kind of traveler, one awake to the transformative force of place. Sa'ib-I-Tabrizi passed through Kabul on his way to Agra. "Moved only as one may be moved through an encounter with the beautiful and strange" (29), he declares he will never be the same again. His lyrical celebration, a genre completely separate from both the positivist historiography and the personal anecdote (though perhaps closer to the latter), articulates dearly the shift in the Homebody's assimilation of the Other:

Oh the beautiful city of Kabul wears a rugged mountain skirt.
And the rose is jealous of its lash-like thorns.
The dust of Kabul's blowing soil smarts lightly in my eyes,
But I love her, for knowledge and love both come from her dust.
I sing bright praises to her colorful tulips,
The beauty of her trees makes me blush.
Every street in Kabul fascinates the eye.
In the bazaars, Egypt's caravans pass by.
No one can count the beauteous moons on her rooftops.
And hundreds of lovely suns hide behind her walls.
Her morning laugh is as gay as flowers,
Her dark nights shine like beautiful hair.
Her tuneful nightingales sing with flame in their throats,
Their fiery songs fall like burning leaves.
I sing to the gardens of Kabul;
Even paradise is jealous of their greenery. (30)

Yet even in the very moment of its recitation, this *ghazal* of praise turns into a eulogy. The Kabul Tabrizi passed through is not the Kabul we have just heard about, nor does it resemble the Kabul Kushner presents in the next two acts. The poem marks the complex process through which encounter, especially post-colonial encounter, resolves into a story waiting to be told. The exhortation is that we take the same leap—daring, foolish, to our death—and that we, like the Homebody, refuse to remain dry.

Kushner ends the monologue by refusing all three narrative strategies the Homebody employs—the positivist chronology, the personal memoir, the magical fantasy. The theatrical form of the monologue, however, suggests a different mode—storytelling. Because of its local specificity, storytelling reproduces history not as a given truth, but as a conditional way of representing the past to the present—conditional, and thus, in Brecht's sense, alterable. Further, it marks the meanings we extract from history as strange fictions always mediated by our present location. Using direct address to upset the naturalizing impulse of both positivist historiography and realist performance, Kushner calls attention, here, to the artificiality of all narrative. History becomes fluid, ours to self-consciously fracture and mend.

The monologue's delicious language, its frantic shifts of tone, its grand overreaching, should place in relief our own confrontations with the Other. The monologue refracts post-colonial identity in ways that refuse easy oppositions between past and present, East and West, margin and center, subject and sovereign, colony and nation. The inner life of the Homebody now registers multiply—queerly—replacing the rhetorical "not/but" with a promiscuous "and ... and ... and" that attempts to retrieve a complex and contradictory sameness. "Not," as S.P. Mohanty writes, "the ambiguous imperial-humanist myth of our shared human attributes which are supposed to distinguish us from animals, but, more significantly, the imbrication of our various pasts and presents, the ineluctable relationships of shared and contested meanings, values, material resources "[9]

This is not to say something simplistic like "we are all post-colonial," or to allow rhetorical tropes to overwhelm the material conditions within which such confrontations are wrought. To turn the violence of power into a convenient metaphor ultimately would fail to apprehend how bodies fight and are crippled, live and die. It is rather to suggest that the at times melodramatic, at times farcical convergences of those profoundly artificial domains, East and West, deserve better denouements than those currently being enacted in places as different and as similar as Argentina, Australia, Afghanistan, and Algeria. And to assert that telling these discrete stories without erasing the suffocating cruelties of imperial, colonial, and neocolonial domination, as Kushner's bitter yet hopeful play does, is an imperative we cannot refuse.

NOTES

For crucial editorial suggestions I thank Sara Suleri Goodyear, Sheila Hale, Erika Munk,

Marilyn Kleinberg Neimark, Erika Rundle, Alisa Solomon, Annabelle Winograd, and Evan Zelermyer.

1. My essay discusses only the first act of *Homebody/Kabul*. It is unfair, I think, to criticize the *Kabul* half of this play because, as a work in progress, it, like Afghanistan, will have undergone great change before this is published.

2. Tony Kushner, *Homebody/Kabul* (New York: Theatre Communications Group, 2002), 12–13.

3. Sara Suleri, *The Rhetoric of English India* (Chicago: University of Chicago Press, 1992), 76.

4. Interview with Tony Kushner, April 2001, New York, N.Y.

5. To suggest that the Homebody's way of thinking and speaking is post-colonial, and to set it against the seemingly more productive language and behavior of her husband, does not necessarily construct "post-colonial" as a merely reactive condition. To fix post-coloniality in this way would bleach it of both the theoretical and material force it confers. For an excellent critique of the debate surrounding the use and abuse of "post-colonial," see Stephen Slemon's "The Scramble for Post-Colonialism." Slemon writes, "'Post-colonialism'... de-scribes a remarkably heterogeneous set of subject positions, professional fields, and critical enterprises. It has been used as a way of ordering a critique of totalizing forms of Western historicism; as a portmanteau word for a retooled notion of 'class' ...; as the name for a condition of nativist longing in post-independence national groupings; as a cultural marker of non-residency for a Third World intellectual cadre; as the inevitable underside of a fractured and ambivalent discourse of colonialist power; as an oppositional form of 'reading practice'; and ... as the name for a category of literary activity which sprang from a new... political energy going on within what used to be called 'Commonwealth' literary studies" (Slemon, "Scramble," in *De-Scribing the Empire*, ed. Chris Tiffin and Alan Lawson [London: Routledge, 1994], 16–17). No wonder, given this proliferation of meanings, that "post-colonialism" remains a contested category. In its most literal sense, "post-colonial" refers to all that follows first contact. *Post-colonial*, as I use it throughout this essay, refracts the continuing material and psychic repercussions of this encounter. Where colonial language consistently positions an imperial (usually white) Self against an exploited yellow, brown, black, or red Other, post-colonial "writing back" complicates this easy distinction by repositioning the Other inside the Self. Bodies are now seen as mutually contaminated. And in the contradictions produced by this unhappy coupling lie the possibility of intervention and change.

6. In Oskar Eustis's production at the Trinity Repertory Theater, the actor playing the Homebody went into the audience and placed hats delicately on the heads of audience members.

7. My thanks to Una Chaudhuri for drawing my attention to this.

8. E.M. Forster, *A Passage to India* (New York: Harcourt Brace Jovanovich, 1924), 316.

9. S.P. Mohanty, qtd. in Suleri, *Rhetoric*, 14–15.

Chronology

1956	Born on July 16 in Manhattan, second of three children of William and Sylvia (Deutscher) Kushner, both classically trained musicians. Family moves to Lake Charles, Louisiana, shortly after his birth.
1978	Graduates from Columbia University with a Bachelor of Arts degree in English.
1979–85	Works as a switchboard operator at the United Nations Plaza Hotel in New York City.
1984	Receives Master of Fine Arts degree in directing from New York University.
1985–86	*Yes, Yes, No, No*, a children's play, produced in 1985 in St. Louis, Missouri. In 1986, produced *In Great Eliza's Golden Time*, a children's play, and *The Age of Assassins*. Serves as assistant director of the St. Louis Repertory Theatre.
1987–88	Is the artistic director of the New York Theatre Workshop. *Stella*, a play adapted from that of Goethe, and *Hydriotaphia, or The Death of Dr. Browne* produced in New York City in 1987. *A Bright Room Called Day* produced in San Francisco in 1987. *The Illusion*, adapted from Corneille's play *L'illusion comique*, produced in New York City in 1988.
1989	Director of literary services at the Theatre Communications Group in New York City. Becomes guest artist at New York University Graduate Theatre Program, Yale University, and Princeton University.

1990–91	In 1991, *Widows*, written with Ariel Dorfman and adapted from a book by Dorfman, is produced in Los Angeles. Also in 1991, produces *Angels in America: A Gay Fantasia on National Themes, Part One: Millennium Approaches*.
1990–92	Playwright-in-residence at the Juilliard School of Drama. In 1992, *Angels in America: A Gay Fantasia on National Themes, Part Two: Perestroika*, produced in California.
1993	Wins Pulitzer Prize for drama, Antoinette Perry (Tony) Award for best play, and New York Drama Critics Circle Award for Best New Play for *Millennium Approaches*, part one of *Angels in America*.
1994	Receives American Academy of Arts and Letters Award and Antoinette Perry Award for best play for *Perestroika*, part two of *Angels in America*. *The Good Person of Szechuan*, adapted from the original play by Brecht, produced. *Slavs! Thinking About the Longstanding Problems of Virtue and Happiness* produced.
1995	*A Dybbuk, or Between Two Worlds*, adapted from a translation of the original play by S. Ansky, produced.
1996	Becomes permanent faculty member of New York University's Tisch School.
1998	*Henry Box Brown, or the Mirror of Slavery* produced, as well as *Terminating, or Lass Meine Schmerzen Nicht Verloren Sein, or Ambivalence*.
1999	*Homebody/Kabul* produced.
2003	*Angels in America*, directed by Mike Nichols, appears on HBO television. *Caroline, or Change* , a libretto, produced.

Contributors

HAROLD BLOOM is Sterling Professor of the Humanities at Yale University. He is the author of over 20 books, including *Shelley's Mythmaking* (1959), *The Visionary Company* (1961), *Blake's Apocalypse* (1963), *Yeats* (1970), *A Map of Misreading* (1975), *Kabbalah and Criticism* (1975), *Agon: Toward a Theory of Revisionism* (1982), *The American Religion* (1992), *The Western Canon* (1994), and *Omens of Millennium: The Gnosis of Angels, Dreams, and Resurrection* (1996). *The Anxiety of Influence* (1973) sets forth Professor Bloom's provocative theory of the literary relationships between the great writers and their predecessors. His most recent books include *Shakespeare: The Invention of the Human* (1998), a 1998 National Book Award finalist, *How to Read and Why* (2000), *Genius: A Mosaic of One Hundred Exemplary Creative Minds* (2002), *Hamlet: Poem Unlimited* (2003), and *Where Shall Wisdom be Found* (2004). In 1999, Professor Bloom received the prestigious American Academy of Arts and Letters Gold Medal for Criticism, and in 2002 he received the Catalonia International Prize.

MARK STEYN has been the host of BBC ratio's "Postcard from Gotham." He is the author of *Broadway Babies Say Goodnight: Musicals Then and Now*.

DAVID SAVRAN has been Professor of English at Brown University. He is the author or editor of several books, including *Communists, Cowboys, and Queers: The Politics of Masculinity in the Work of Arthur Miller and Tennessee Williams*.

CHARLES McNULTY teaches in the theater department at Brooklyn College. He has written on theater for the *Village Voice*.

JANELLE REINELT teaches at the University of California at Irvine. She has published *After Brecht: British Epic Theater* and is the editor or joint editor of other titles as well.

ALLEN J. FRANTZEN teaches English at Loyola College. He is the author of *Desire for Origins: New Language, Old English and Teaching the Tradition* and also is the editor or author of other titles.

JONATHAN FREEDMAN teaches English at the University of Michigan. He has edited *The Cambridge Companion to Henry James* and *Oscar Wilde: A Collection of Critical Essays*. He also has authored other titles.

BENILDE MONTGOMERY teaches at Dowling College. He has contributed to *Terrence McNally: A Casebook* and has published several other essays.

JAMES FISHER is Professor of Theater at Wabash College. He has published numerous works, including *Theatre of Yesterday and Tomorrow*. He staged the Indiana premiere of *Angels in America Part One: Millennium Approaches*.

JAMES RESTON, JR. is the author of several books, including *Sherman's March and Vietnam*. He has also written plays.

FRAMJI MINWALLA teaches English at George Washington University. He co-edited *The Queerest Art: Essays on Lesbian and Gay Theater*.

Bibliography

Andreach, Robert J. *Creating the Self in the Contemporary American Theatre.* Carbondale and Edwardsville: Southern Illinois University Press, 1998.

Austin, Michael. "Theology for the Approaching Millennium: *Angels in America*, Activism, and the American Religion. *Dialogue* 30, no. 1 (Spring 1997): 25–44.

Baker, Rob. *The Art of AIDS. From Stigma to Conscience. Music—Drama—Dance—Movies—Media.* New York: Continuum, 1994.

Bechtel, Roger. "'A Kind of Painful Progress': The Benjaminian Dialectics of *Angels in America.*" *Journal of Dramatic Theory and Criticism* 16, no. 1 (Fall 2001): 99–121.

Bennett, Susan. "Only in Alberta? *Angels in America* and Canada." *Theatre Research in Canada* 17, no. 2 (Fall 1996): 160–74.

Bilderback, Walter. "The Square Root of Queer." *American Theatre* (April 1998): 45–47.

Biship, Trevor. "How to Dramatize the Unimaginable: Anne Nelson's *TheGuys* and Tony Kushner's *Homebody/Kabul* as America's First Theatrical Responses to September 11, 2001." *Theatron* (Fall 2003): 19–35.

Bottoms, Stephen J. "Re-Staging Roy: Citizen Cohn and the Search for Xanadu." *Theatre Journal* 48, no. 2 (May 1996): 157–84.

Brask, Per, ed. *Essay on Kushner's Angels.* Winnipeg: Blizzard Publishing, 1995.

Broder, Michael. "Tony Kushner." In *The Gay & Lesbian Literary Companion*, 303–307. Detroit, Washington, D.C., and London: Visible Ink Press, 1995.

Chum, John M. *Acting Gay: Male Homosexuality in Modern Drama*. New York: Columbia University Press, 1994.

Cohen, Peter F. *Love and Anger: Essays on AIDS, Activism, and Politics*. New York: Haworth, 1998.

―――. "Strange Bedfellows: Writing Love and Politics in *Angels in America* and *The Normal Heart*." *Journal of Medical Humanities* 19, nos. 2/3 (1998): 197–219.

Colleran, Jeanne and Jenny S. Spencer. *Staging Resistance. Essays on Political Theater*. Ann Arbor: University of Michigan Press, 1998.

Dellamora, Richard. "Tony Kushner and the 'Not Yet' of Gay Existence." *Journal of American Drama and Theatre* 9, no. 3 (Fall 1997): 73–101.

Elam, Harry J. Jr. "'Only in America': Contemporary American Theater and the Power of Performance." In *Voices of Power: Co-Operation and Conflict in English Language and Literatures*, edited by Marc Maufort and Jean-Pierre van Noppen, 151–63. Liège, Belgium: L3-Liège Language and Literature for Belgian Association of Anglists in Higher Education, 1997.

Elkin-Squitieri, Michelle. "'The Great Work Begins': Apocalyptic and Millenarian Vision in *Angels in America*." *Anglophonia* 3 (1998): 203–12.

Fink, Joel G. "Performance Review: *A Dybbuk, or Between Two Worlds*." *Theatre Journal* 48, no. 4 (December 1996): 516–17.

Fisher, James. "'The Angels of Fructification': Tennessee Williams, Tony Kushner, and Images of Homosexuality on the American Stage." *Mississippi Quarterly* 49, no. 1 (Winter 1995–96): 13–32.

―――. "Between Two Worlds: Ansky's *The Dybbuk* and Kushner's *A Dybbuk*." *Soviet and East European Performance* 18, no. 2 (Summer 1998): 20–32.

―――. "On the Front Lines of a Skirmish in the Culture Wars: *Angels in America* Goes to College." *On-Stage Studies* 21 (1998): 6–30.

―――. "'Troubling the Waters': Visions of the Apocalypse in Wilder's *The Skin of Our Teeth* and Kushner's *Angels in America*." In *Thornton Wilder: New Essays*, edited by Martin Blank, Dalma Hunyadi Brunauer, and David Garrett Izzo, 391–407. West Cornwall, CT: Locust Hill, 1999.

Kiefer, Daniel. "*Angels in America* and the Failure of Revelation." *American Drama* 4, no. 1 (Fall 1994): 21–38.

Klein, Dennis A. "*Angels in America* as Jewish-American Drama." *Modern Jewish Studies* 12, no. 4 (2001): 34–43.

Lee, Haiyoung. "Two, Not One, in *Angels in America*." *Journal of Modern British and American Drama* 17, no. 1 (April 2004): 153–75.

Lochrie, Karma. "Apocalyptic Imaginings." *Modern Philology* 92 (1995): 351–59.

Lowenthal, Michael. "On Art, *Angels*, and 'Mostmodern Facism.'" *Harvard Gay and Lesbian Review* 2, no. 2 (Spring 1995): 10–12.

Marowitz, Charles. *Alarums & Excursions: Our Theatres in the 90s*. New York and London: Applause Books, 1996.

McCabe, Terry. "'Angels' in Our Midst." *Chronicle of Higher Education* 50, no. 15 (December 5, 2003): B17–B19.

Meisner, Natalie. "Messing with the Idyllic: The Performance of Femininity in Kushner's *Angels in America*." *Yale Journal of Criticism* 16, no. 1 (Spring 2003): 177–89.

Norden, Edward. "From Schnitzler to Kushner." *Commentary* 99, no. 1 (January 1995): 51–58.

Ogden, Daryl. "Cold War Science and the Body Politic: An Immuno/Virological Approach to *Angels in America*." *Literature and Medicine* 19, no. 2 (Fall 2000): pp. 241–61.

Plooster, Nancy. "Toxic Bodies and the Performance of Mourning in American AIDS Drama." *JAISA: The Journal of the Association for the Interdisciplinary Study of the Arts* 1, no. 2 (Spring 1996): 103–10.

Posnock, Ross. "Roy Cohn in America." *Raritan* 13, no. 3 (Winter 1994): 64–77.

Quinn, John R. "Corpus Juris Tertium: Redemptive Jurisprudence in *Angels in America*." *Theatre Journal* 48, no. 1 (March 1996): 79–90.

Rogoff, Gordon. "*Angels in America*, Devils in the Wings." *Theater* 24, no. 2 (1993): 21–29.

Savran, David. "The Haunted Houses of Modernity." In *Modern Drama: Defining the Field*, edited by Ric Knowles, Joanne Tompkins, W.B. Worthen, 117–27. Toronto: University of Toronto Press, 2003.

———. "Queering the Nation." In *Performing America: Cultural Nationalism in American Theater*, edited by Jeffrey D. Mason and J. Ellen Gainor, 210–29. Ann Arbor, MI: University of Michigan Press, 1999.

———. "Tony Kushner." In *Speaking on Stage: Interviews with Contemporary American Playwrights*, edited by Philip C. Kolin and Colby H. Kullman, 291–313. Tuscaloosa: University of Alabama Press, 1996.

Smith, Iris. "Authors in America: Tony Kushner, Arthur Miller, and Anna Deveare Smith." *The Centennial Review* 40, no. 1 (Winter 1997): 125–42.

Smith, Matthew Wilson. "*Angels in America*: A Progressive Apocalypse." *Theater* 29, no. 3 (1999): 153–65.

Sordi, Michele. "*Angels*, Critics, and the Rhetoric of AIDS in America." In *Reconceptualizing American Literary/Cultural Studies: Rhetoric, History, and Politics in the Humanities*, edited by William E. Cain, 186–96. New York: Garland, 1996.

Tuss, Alex J. "Resurrecting Masculine Spirituality in Tony Kushner's *Angels in America*." *Journal of Men's Studies* 5, no. 1 (August 1996): 49–63.

Vorlicky, Robert, ed. *Tony Kushner in Conversation*. Ann Arbor, MI: University of Michigan Press, 1998.

Weber, Myles. "Tony Kushner Talking." *New England Review* 21, no. 3 (2000): 215–19.

Wexler, Joyce. "Speaking out: Dialogue and the Literary Unconscious." *Style* 31, no. 1 (Spring 1997): 118–33.

Acknowledgments

"Communism Is Dead; Long Live the King!" by Mark Steyn. From *The New Criterion* 13, no. 6 (February 1995): pp. 49–53. © 1995 by The Foundation for Cultural Review, Inc. Reprinted by permission.

"Ambivalence, Utopia, and a Queer Sort of Materialism: How *Angels in America* Reconstructs the Nation" by David Savran. From *Theatre Journal* 47, no. 2 (May 1995): pp. 207–227. © 1995 by The Johns Hopkins University Press. Reprinted by permission of The Johns Hopkins University Press.

"*Angels in America*: Tony Kushner's Theses on the Philosophy of History" by Charles McNulty. From *Modern Drama* 39, no. 1 (Spring 1996): pp. 84–96. © 1996 by the University of Toronto. Reprinted by permission.

"Notes on *Angels in America* as American Epic Theater" by Janelle Reinelt. From *Approaching the Millennium: Essays on* Angels in America, Deborah R. Geis and Steven F. Kruger, ed.: pp. 234–244. © 1997 by the University of Michigan. Reprinted by permission.

"Alla, Angli, and *Angels in America*" by Allen J. Frantzen. From *Before the Closet: Same-Sex Love from* Beowulf *to* Angels in America: pp. 264–292. © 1998 by the University of Chicago Press. Reprinted by permission.

"Angels, Monsters, and Jews: Intersections of Queer and Jewish Identity in Kushner's *Angels in America*" by Jonathan Freedman. From *PMLA* 113, no. 1 (January 1998): pp. 90–102. © 1998 by The Modern Language Association of America. Reprinted by permission of the Modern Language Association of America.

"*Angels in America* as Medieval Mystery" by Benilde Montgomery. From *Modern Drama* 41, no. 4 (Winter 1998): pp. 596–606. © 1998 by the University of Toronto. Reprinted by permission.

"The Progress of Death in the Land of Pure Delight: *Hydriotaphia, or The Death of Dr. Browne*" by James Fisher. From *The Theater of Tony Kushner: Living Past Hope*: pp. 38–53. © 2001 by Routledge. Reprinted by permission.

"A Prophet in His Time: Premonition and Reality in Tony Kushner's *Homebody/Kabul*" by James Reston, Jr. From *American Theatre* 19, no. 3 (March 2002): pp. 28–53. © 2002 Theatre Communications Group. Reprinted by permission.

"Tony Kushner's *Homebody/Kabul*: Staging History in a Post-Colonial World" by Framji Minwalla. From *Theater* 33, no. 1 (2003): pp. 29–43. © 2003 by Yale School of Drama/Yale Repertory Theatre. Reprinted by permission.

Index